# Where the Law Ends

*the text of this book is printed
on 100% recycled paper*

*Books by Christopher D. Stone*

WHERE THE LAW ENDS

SHOULD TREES HAVE STANDING?

LAW, LANGUAGE, AND ETHICS (with W. R. Bishin)

# Where the Law Ends

## The Social Control of Corporate Behavior

**CHRISTOPHER D. STONE**

HARPER COLOPHON BOOKS
Harper & Row, Publishers
New York, Hagerstown, San Francisco, London

*For my mother, Esther Mary Stone*

# Contents

# Acknowledgments

The project from which this book was born was financed by a grant from the National Science Foundation, for whose support I would like to express my appreciation. In particular, I am grateful to Dr. Frederick W. Huszagh, former director of the Foundation's Law and Social Science Program, both for his encouragement and for his contributions to the planning of the project.

Under the grant, which extended from June 1972 through August 1974, six "cases" were selected that illustrated some of the problems corporations posed for the society: two variants on financial collapse (the Penn Central and Equity Funding cases); two variants on product defects (the production of potentially blinding MER/29 by Richardson-Merrell and the production by B. F. Goodrich of defective brakes for the A-7D); an episode of financial fraud (Equity Funding); and two variants on corporate influence on the political processes (one involving the long-standing lobby battles between the railroad and trucking industries, the other involving ITT). For each "case," a team of law school students made up data booklets reflecting a wide range of information that might bear upon why the problem had arisen—not only a narration of the critical incidents, but organizational charts, personnel data, industry statistics, corporation financial information, and the like. The requisite materials were pulled together by a team of University of Southern California law students, Larry Bass, Richard Becker, Paul De Koster, and Tom Levyn.

The booklets having been prepared, a group of social scientists were selected to examine the cases. These included a systems analyst, Stanley C. Abraham; Dr. James M. Burns, a specialist in complex organizations; Dr. Richard J. Kaplan, an experimental psychologist who deals with management information systems; Dr.

Jon P. Miller, an industrial sociologist; and Dr. Joel Shor, a psychoanalyst. These consultants, working independently of one another, were asked to write an analysis of the problems the cases presented from their particular standpoints: Why did they think the problem had arisen? What were the key failures within the organization?—The way in which roles were defined? The distribution of authority?—The information that was passing upward to top officers?—The pressures created by the organization's criteria for reward and advancement? How would they go about ameliorating the situation or preventing its recurrence? If they were, in effect, writing the law, what measures would they propose?

As these analyses came in, case by case, attempts were made to identify exactly where the law's assumptions about corporate behavior were most significantly at odds with those of the various social sciences. Tentative hypotheses were formulated and reformulated about what changes ought to be made in the law as it affects corporate actors. In this stage of the work I had the benefit of a number of law student researchers. I ought particularly to single out the contributions of Larry Bass and Richard Becker, as well as Ed Arnett, Richard S. Arnold, Sharyn M. Burks, Larry Gamble, John V. Hager, Larry Henson, Hank Heuer, Charles Horn, Greg Jones, Chris Layne, Christopher C. Murray, Mike Melton, Craig Sears, and Paul Smith.

I should like to thank, too, Cindy Hollister, who served as executive secretary to our project during the grant period, and give thanks to Shirley Gold and Linda Manning, who have taken the production in hand since then.

Finally, I would be remiss not to express my continuing debt to the entire staff of the U.S.C.'s Asa V. Call Law Library. From the beginning of this project, three years ago, they have suffered my requests with unflagging good spirits and competence.

Los Angeles
March 15, 1975

# Introduction

The uproar over the oil companies' role in the energy crisis is only the most recent assault on the part corporations are playing in our national dramas. For at least a century, and increasingly in the past five to ten years, there has grown up a whole body of literature that blames business corporations for a broadening range of the society's ills. Once it was crusading journalists and Grangers who railed against the "trusts" and "robber barons" for gouging farmers and corrupting politicians. Now the charges have expanded to include corporate entanglements in international relations, pollution, consumer safety, and "the quality of life"; and the list of would-be reformers has grown to include corporate executives who fashionably join the chorus for increased "corporate responsibility." "How much crime in the streets," a *Fortune* editor recently wondered, "is connected with the widespread judgment that the business economy itself is a gigantic rip-off?"

From one point of view, it is not hard to defend corporations against many of the charges that are currently being leveled against them. There are many other aspects of our society and physical environment to each of which we could as persuasively trace a large block of our current predicaments: the increase in population, the depletion of energy reserves and other natural resources, the acceleration of human aspirations and expectations, the increasing technological complexity of the means of production and distribution.

Yet, whether or not we feel that corporations are to blame for our present dilemmas, there is at least one terribly practical and appropriate sense in which we do well to consider them increasingly "responsible." For aside from governments and governmental agencies, more and more it is corporations that are effectively the *actors* in our society. It is increasingly they—and, indeed, an increasingly small number of them—who are our most evident producers, distributors, land managers, taxpayers, polluters, investors, investments, service providers, and now even, in the form of "agricorporations," farmers. Corporations have long since become, for better or for worse, the most effective "private" forces to do both widespread good and widespread harm. For this reason, to solve society's problems is, in no small measure, to come to grips with the corporation problem.

But what is "the corporation problem," and how is it to be dealt with?

People have been exposing the growth of corporate influence for decades (there is a series of articles decrying "the drift of things"—"the corporate principle is daily extending . . . what is to be the outcome of this?"—in the 1887 *Harper's*). Yet both the corporate influence and the dissatisfaction it provokes continue unabated. As for the continued corporate growth and influence, the explanation is fairly clear: the nature of our technology and our needs is such that the preeminence of large-scale corporate organizations in some form or other is inevitable. But the reasons why we cannot control them more to our satisfaction are not at all so clear—and merit a thorough inquiry.

To explain why corporations are a continuing social problem, it will not do merely to parade out the statistical tables and graphs reflecting the increases in corporate concentration, the growth in sales and assets of the top firms, and so on. What is lacking in all such perennial exposés is that while they can tell us a lot about corporations, they do not tell us about them in the light we need. Nothing in society is a continuing problem because of *itself*, per se; something becomes and remains a problem because of shortcomings in the institutional arrangements we rely on to deal with it. Thus, to come to grips with the "corporation problem" demands a simultaneous inquiry in two directions: Exactly what is it about corporations, and exactly what is it about the institutions we have available to control them, that so often seems to leave the one so frustratingly outside the grasp of the other?

The fact is, our society has given surprisingly little attention to this question. Traditionally when social commentators look at the law, their concern has been with how the system operates to control individual human beings. Thus, while we have a human-focused body of legal criticism and reform that goes back to Locke, Beccaria, Bentham, and Mill, and includes, in the present, the Gluecks, Menninger, Lord Devlin, and Erich Fromm, none of these people, nor anyone else, had given comparable systematic thought to whether the law's approach makes sense vis-à-vis corporations, labor unions, foundations, and the like—the "atoms" of contemporary social action.

This is not because a body of literature on group and institutional behavior is lacking. As early as Le Bon's *The Crowd*, in the sociological studies of Simmel and Durkheim, in Weber's analyses of bureaucratic decision-making, in Freud's *Ego and Group Psychology*, there were already suggestions that even mobs—much less formal, continuing institutions—were distinct phenomena with distinct ways of behaving. More recently, the possibilities latent in these early works have been developed by organizational theorists, group psychologists, and various other social and political scientists curious about institutional behavior. But there has been almost no attempt to bring to bear on the law the literature and insights they have produced. And this is especially unfortunate since it is quite likely not (whatever the fears) the individual cutpurse, stalking the streets, who is the society's most troublesome participant, but rather huge, institutional systems—the corporations in particular.

What is so fundamentally wrong about the measures we have adopted to control corporations? In the light of these short-comings, what can be done to improve existing measures? What sorts of new controls can be, and must be, designed?

# I

# Corporations
# and the Law Develop—
# But Not Apace

There is no simple answer to why existent legal mechanisms so often seem less than satisfactory when it comes to coping with business corporations. A full examination has to take into account a number of features of the moral and social environment in which corporations operate, ranging from corporate influence on the political processes, to the difficulties, in a highly technological society, of anticipating where dangers lie, to the reduced sense of responsibility for one's own acts that occurs when men are brought together into large institutional frameworks. Yet, it is not an oversimplification to claim that the problems we face in controlling corporations today have their roots in legal history; they are a legacy of the law's failure to search out and take into account special features of business corporations as actors that make the problem of controlling them a problem distinct from that of controlling human beings.

Briefly, the thesis of Part I is that at the time the law was in its formative stages, it was individual identifiable persons, operating outside of complex institutional frameworks, who trespassed, created nuisances, engaged in consumer frauds, killed, and maimed. The law responded with rules and concepts built upon contemporary notions about individuals—about what motivated, what steered, what was just toward *them*.

There were, it is true, "corporations" of various sorts during these formative years. Church corporations, municipalities, guilds, and universities, were all established forms by the twelfth century. The law, however, had very little occasion to consider whether the rules it was fashioning to control people might be inappropriate as applied to corporations. Some of the reasons were doctrinal—there existed doubts as to whether a corporation, a *persona ficta*, was conceptually capable of legal responsibility, as a result of which cases testing their liability would be few and far between. Others were practical—the social function of these early corporations was so limited, and their size and organizational structure so unprepossessing, that in those cases in which responsibility had to be lodged, it was usually not hard to reach into the organization and locate a meaningfully responsible individual, a "culprit," and apply the sanctions of the law to him.

Later, as corporations became diverse and ranging in their functions, and more complex in their organizational structure, more and more problems connected with corporations could no longer feasibly be dealt with by, in effect, ignoring them as entities and reaching inside to locate some specific, human malfeasors. Thus, over a period of years the compunctions about whether corporations might "themselves" be liable for various classes of wrongs were disregarded, one by one, until only a few vestiges remain.

But while the legal system was prepared to recognize corporations as actors it was not prepared to adjust to their presence by significant revisions of its human-oriented premises. Instead, corporations were generally assimilated into the preexisting general legal system by deeming them "persons," and allowing that once they have met certain formal requirements of "birth" (incorporation), wherever conceivable they should be treated indiscriminately like any other person.

This was the simplest way to deal with corporations. But not, as I shall show, the wisest or most effective.

# 1. The Corporation as Actor

In a way, the preoccupation with how the law affects human beings, and the relative disregard of its impact on organizations, is quite understandable. After all, the corporation *itself* (as lawyers are fond of reminding one another) is a *persona ficta*, a "legal fiction" with "no pants to kick or soul to damn."* What is meant is that while we can point to the corporation's steel and glass factory, or to its tangible chairman of the board, or to its offices in Rockefeller Plaza, there is no physical entity *the corporation* that we can point to—or that can, of itself, adulterate foods or pollute rivers. The corporation *itself*, it is said, "does no act, speaks no word, thinks no thoughts."[1] Viewed as a legal phenomenon, it acts only through its agents. From this it would seem to follow that when the law aims to control corporations, it should concern itself simply—and directly—with the corporation's constituent human beings.

But common sense can be misleading. And a corporation viewed as a legal phenomenon is not the same as a corporation viewed sociologically. Let me illustrate this by reference to a group the workings of which are familiar (and mysterious) to the lawyer and layman alike: a jury.

Imagine twelve jurors who are trying a prosecution for rape. There is a whole series of verdicts that they can return, not only "guilty" or "not guilty" of the rape charge, but combinations of "guilty" and "not guilty" on the series of what lawyers call lesser, included offenses, such as assault with intent to rape, aggravated assault, and simple assault.

* ". . . and, by God," this quote from one English jurist continues, "it ought to have both!" H. L. Mencken, *A New Dictionary of Quotations on Historical Principles from Ancient and Modern Sources* (New York: Knopf, 1942), p. 223.

Let us suppose that entering the jury room for their deliberations, three jurors, wholly believing the prosecution, are prepared to vote "guilty" on the rape charge. Two others, believing the defendant made the attack, but not believing that the rape was consummated, will vote "not guilty" on the rape charge, but "guilty" on the charge of assault with intent to rape. Three other jurors do not believe that the defendant ever intended rape, but do believe him "guilty" of aggravated assault. The remaining four jurors believe the prosecutrix (the victim) to have fabricated the entire story, and want to vote for a complete acquittal.

Now, notwithstanding how they started out, it is quite conceivable that the jurors (or as we would more ordinarily say, "the jury") will come back from their deliberations with a verdict of acquittal on all counts except the simple assault charge, and return a guilty verdict on that. Notice that this is a verdict that not any of the jurors originally wanted, and might not even be the verdict that any of them would ideally want now, if it were up to each of them individually.

How can we best explain this phenomenon? We could, of course, study as much information as might be available about each of the jurors as individuals. No one can doubt that such information, had it been available in advance, might have helped us to predict the final verdict. Nor can one doubt that the same information, used to screen potential jury members, could have exercised a strong influence on the outcome.

But another way to try to comprehend the jury's behavior would involve looking to characteristics not of the twelve individual jurors, but to institutional characteristics of "the jury itself." Some might object that to speak of the jury itself is metaphysical nonsense, if the term is meant to denote some entity transcending the twelve jurors. The jury, they might point out, is a "legal fiction," "its" existence depending upon an act of state—the swearing in of twelve citizens. But anyone who neglected the jury itself would fail to take into account a whole series of *formal constraints peculiar to the institution.* However the twelve jurors might have behaved as individuals outside the jury, now they find themselves fitted into an institutional framework in which:

1. Only a limited range of *appropriate judgmental categories* is available to them ("guilty," "not guilty," "rape," "aggravated assault");

2. There is a formal requirement on the *vote requisite for a decision* of "guilty" on any charge (traditionally unanimity);

3. There are certain *time constraints* under which they must operate;

4. The range of data available to them is limited by certain formal *information constraints* (the rules of hearsay, the fact that they cannot take the indictment with them into the jury room);

5. The *number of decision-makers* is fixed (twelve), as well as, to an extent *the physical setting* (they are to sit roughly in a circle about a table; they may be sequestered during deliberations);

6. There is a *formal role structure* (a foreman, deputy-foreman, alternates);

7. There is an authoritative *decisional framework*, laying down guidelines for analysis (whether special verdicts will be allowed);

8. There are *general qualifications for participation* in any of the roles (as dictated by formal legal qualifications for jury service, by the procedures for "challenge" on jury examination); and

9. There is a generalized sense of the *jury's social role* (consisting in a somewhat vague, but nonetheless shared or overlapping sense of the expectations of society as to what a jury is supposed to do).

In addition to these formal institutional variables, there are the *informal constraints* inherent in all group behavior. People in concert do things they would not do alone. For example, for each of the twelve jurors it is probably easier to vote the death penalty as a group than it would be if it were up to each of them separately. Along these lines, we would expect any sophisticated analysis of the jury's decision to point up significance in a series of phenomena that went on within, but were not predetermined by, the institutional framework: who served in the capacity of foreman, who spoke first, and so on.

Which of these possible ways of looking at the phenomenon— an analysis of the actors, an analysis of the institution itself, a "mixed" analysis of the individuals and the particular institutional framework in which they find themselves—is the most productive? In the abstract, without having identified our specific purposes, we cannot say, and for many purposes we would want to consider all three.

But let me suggest that if one's purposes were not merely to predict or influence the outcome of a particular trial, *but to institute a change in the performance and functions of juries as social institutions* (for example, to achieve either a higher or a lower rate of conviction, or to increase, in the society at large, a sense of fairness about trials, or to increase the speed of trials, or to minimize reversals on appeal), then the variables one would turn to would likely be the institutional variables, that is, what categories of evidence the jury would be allowed to receive, whether to compel it to make special verdicts (as opposed to allowing broad determinations of "guilty" or "not guilty"), whether to specify additional qualifications and powers for the job of foreman.

If such an institutional analysis (in a sense an analysis that considers "the institution itself" to be a significant actor) can advance our understanding of and increase our capacity to control the jury system, so much more would we expect it to be productive when our concern is with the corporation. For while a jury brings people together on an ad hoc basis for a rather limited time, and with rather limited aims, and in a rather flat hierarchical structure, the corporation brings together men, machines, and patterns of doing things into an enormous sociotechnical system that is far more complex, overwhelming, and powerful. Those who enter into one of these structures shed their uniqueness to become neither individuals, nor even men-in-groups, but fitted parts of elaborate subsystems—subsystems for the gathering and dissemination of information, subsystems of authority, subsystems of function—each of which is working with (and often at odds with) the other toward the realization of stated and unstated institutional goals and targets. The whole constellation, moreover, does not, like the jury, discharge its human members en masse when their limited task is through. The corporation, itself potentially immortal, continues with an inertia much its own as the individual human or mechanical "cells," whose lives in the corporations overlap, part and are replaced.

In this setting each man's own wants, ideas—even his perceptions and emotions—are swayed and directed by an institutional structure so pervasive that it might be construed as having a set of goals and constraints (if not a mind and purpose) of *its* own. This is not, of course, to say that the large business organization is just like an ordinary person, a "boss." But there is no reason to suppose that the motives of a corporation, the way it will respond and adapt to external threats, the way it will scan its environment for information, the way it will calculate and weigh its pleasures against its pains—in sum, its decisions and the way it arrives at them—will coincide with those of any one person within it, not even necessarily those of the president. Nor should we with any confidence presume to treat its decision processes as though the corporation were merely the aggregate sum of all the persons who are laboring within it.

What this suggests is that the law ought constantly to be searching out and taking into account the special institutional features of business corporations that make the problems of controlling them (and of controlling men-in-them) a problem distinct from that of controlling human beings in ordinary situations.

In what ways, exactly, this might best be done, we shall see. But first let us get a better sense of how much the law as it developed prepared for—and did not prepare for—the modern corporation.

# 2. "Corporate" and Individual Responsibility in Early Law

The law—modern law, in all events—never really sat down to consider the problems and possibilities of how best to deal with institutions. True, as Sir Henry Maine suggested, a sort of corporate (as opposed to individual) responsibility was at the very heart of primitive legal systems.* And as late as Anglo-Saxon times, blood feuds were still being instituted on the assumption that the clan, rather than the individual perpetrator, might be liable for a broad variety of offenses. As time went on, however, the legal system began, in several different ways, to cut off the individual from the group as the object of its attentions. And thus the interest in groups, and how to organize society through controlling them, never budded as it might have.

Some of this movement owes, obviously, to the changing intellectual climate as society moved toward the Enlightenment. Laws had to account for certain natural capacities and rights of the individual human being. The "natural capacities" that were to prevail included reason, dignity, will, perfectability, and freedom. The laws of man could no more overlook these facts of human nature than the laws of nature overlook the facts of planetary motion. It followed that law had to allow for each man's posses-

* Primitive law, Maine claimed, took "a view of *life*" (the italics are his) "wholly unlike any which appears in developed jurisprudence." Society was "not what it is assumed to be at present, a collection of *individuals*. In fact, and in view of the men who comprised it, it was *an* aggregation of families." The law "was so framed as to be adjusted" to this "system of small independent corporations." "Corporations *never die*, and accordingly primitive law considers the entities with which it deals, that is, the patriarchal or family groups, as perpetual and inextinguishable." Viewed from without, that is, by other groups, a crime committed by one group "is a corporate act, and extends its consequences to many more persons than have shared in the actual perpetration." *Ancient Law* (London: John Murray, 1930), p. 143.

sion of certain rights that he, as an individual, could raise against any secular ruler, and it also followed that he as an individual should be called to account, rather than the family, clan, or other institutional groups in which he might have participated.

But even before these individualist sentiments were crystallizing in social philosophy the law had set off in the same direction according to the dictates of its own inner, and perhaps less self-conscious, logic.

First, what we might call the *locus of punishment* tightened down on the individual and lost sight of the group. Part of this shift owed to an increasing reliance on penalties like hanging, torture, and mutilation;[1] it is one thing for a group to share and diffuse a fine—quite another to do so with something as personal as hanging. Then, too, the *standards of liability* changed. From "strict liability"—liability that made little distinction as to what was humanly just and possible—the law began to work in conceptions of "the average reasonable man," the "man of ordinary prudence and intelligence," the man who exercised "the foresight of which ordinary men are capable."

Finally, in no area was the focus on the individual more considered (nor to have a more continuing effect on the later problems with corporations) than where the nature and measure of punishments were concerned. It is probably fair to say that legal sanctions had always absorbed—not reflectively, perhaps—notions of what fears constrained, and what deserts were appropriate, for human wrongdoers. By the time the great rationalist reformers came to review the criminal law, they found all the elements that they were rebelling against: Its roots were commonsensical, theological, customary, superstitious, cruel—and unreconsidered in the light of human reason. To reform it, they began to articulate, more self-consciously and systematically than had been done theretofore, a theory of punishment. And their theory was built upon the utilitarian model of how the human being was supposed to think: the rational calculator of pleasures and pains, the paragon bargainer with the law.

Bentham, of course, is its most eminent advocate. "Nature has placed mankind under the governance of two sovereign masters, pain and pleasure. It is for them alone to point out what we ought to do, as well as what we shall do."[2] "The temptation [to commit crime] may be said to be strong, when the pleasure or advantage to be got from the crime is such as in the eyes of the offender must appear great in comparison of the trouble and danger that appear to him to accompany the enterprise";[3] from which it was but short arithmetic to the position that "the value of the punishment must not be less in any case than what is sufficient to outweigh that of the profit of the offense."[4]

In sum, from a time before the Conquest through the nineteenth century, the law—in its institutional arrangements and in its underlying theories—was paying increasing attention to the individual and less to the group. In this period when its rules and concepts were developing, they were developing around contemporary notions of what motivated, what steered, what was possible, just, and appropriate in the case of individual human beings. At its most reflective, it was a system built upon the notion that society's actors could be steered between right and wrong by threatening to add to units of what gave human beings pleasure, units of what gave them pain. Whether or not the law's conceptions of human beings was correct (and almost certainly it was superficial) will not be my major concern. What I shall be concerned with is rather that this model of law, a model built upon notions of human behavior and motivation, was almost as a body to be transferred, with a minimum of reconsideration, to corporations.

# 3. Corporations and the Law: The First Skirmishes

## The Earliest Corporations

There were, of course, corporations of various sorts even at these early stages of legal development when many of the rules of social conduct were being framed. These early corporations—perhaps we should call them "proto-corporations"—included ecclesiastical organizations of various sorts, municipalities, guilds, and universities. But the courts were little called upon to consider whether the human-oriented rules they were fashioning might be inappropriate or ineffective when dealing with this new breed of social actor.

The main reason is that the social function of these earliest recognizable corporations was not of a sort that would often bring them to the law's attention. Today's giant corporations produce, distribute, and market. But as originally conceived, the corporation was essentially a passive device to hold property, sometimes real estate and sometimes some special privileges. This can best be understood by considering the problem of church land. When some land was, in common understanding, "the church's," the question might yet remain for the law: Who owned it? If the current abbot owned it, then under the law it would pass, upon his death, to his heirs; if the abbot owned it, moreover, he would have the right to sell it.

Now, obviously, both of those outcomes were at odds with everyone's intentions. The land was not the abbot's to dispose of. But if the abbot (or some other tangible human being) did not own it, the question remained, who did? Who might "own" it in a way that satisfied the general understanding and desires?

The conceptual solution that resulted is not one that was struck overnight. Gradually and unsteadily, there grew up the notion that the land was owned by the abbot as (as we should say) a corporation—that is, in his "corporate" as opposed to personal capacity. Thus, when the abbot—the person—died, the land did not pass as his estate would, nor was there any question of his capacity to sell it in any manner during his lifetime. From here it was a short step to the notion not of a single ordinary human being owning the land in one of his dual roles, but of the land being owned by a separate, albeit intangible and perpetual entity —the church itself: a corporation.

The function of the other major corporations of the time was essentially the same: to hold property. And there, too, the facts of life were such that the separateness of the corporation from its members was "realized" by jurisprudential theory only later, and gradually, after the social circumstances had long required it. In the case of the towns and boroughs, the property to be held was a grant from the king giving franchised boroughs certain rights—most important the right to hold their own courts, exact their own customs, and enjoy freedom from toll. With merchant and trade guilds (the ancestors of the modern commercial corporation) the function was to hold in perpetuity a guild charter as individual merchants and craftsmen entered the calling and died. The charter granted the right to lay down rules for the organization of the trade—obviously with some monopoly overtones—and to hold court for the enforcement of its rules, the guild court having jurisdiction not only over its members but in some cases even over nonmembers.

What now about wrongs that these early corporations might have committed, wrongs of a sort that we could regard as ancestors to modern problems of consumerism and environmentalism? The short of it is that in this context, the various wrongs were all easily ascribed to, and gave rise to actions against, the *individual* townsman or guildsman—the individual toward whom the law in other respects was orienting.

Consider, for example, the person who was harmed by having purchased unclean meat. The butcher from whom he bought it was, let us suppose, the member of a trade guild. But he was not an *instrument* of the guild the way a modern employee is the instrument of his corporate employer. The butcher had, for example, personally purchased the animal in the first place; he had slaughtered it, salted or otherwise prepared it; he had personally negotiated for its sale. He had done so in facilities that he owned and controlled. If he had any employees or apprentices, their actions were under his supervision and authority in the finest detail. Thus, it would hardly have occurred to the purchaser of the meat that he seek redress against anyone other than the butcher.

Such a system, it can be said, made *almost* perfect sense in the circumstances. The cause for the qualification is this. One can imagine an ideal government that, even at this stage of commerce, saw that the corporation—the guild—was not wholly unconnected with such early commercial wrongs. Many guilds, after all, were deeply involved in the selection of apprentices, the skills that were being taught, the rules for inspection of products, and, through the guild courts, the strictness with which rule infractors were dealt. A government that recognized the possibilities latent in these connections might have traced specific social wrongs to specific features of the guilds. It could then have exercised continuing direct influence over these critical institutional features so as to stave off wrongdoing preventively, rather than just lend its court system to repair the harm afterward.

In all events, the government did not see or dwell upon these connections. The assumption at this stage was that, insofar as wrongs were done, individuals did them, and it was to individuals that the law was properly addressed. The doctrine that corporations could do no wrong, though nascent in the law, had rarely much practical significance anyway. A law calculated to deal with individual human beings as actors, rather than institutions, was not strongly at odds with the social facts, nor did it ordinarily work injustice.

*Regulated Companies: Budding Capitalism and*
*Incipient Managerialism*

The early regulated companies that began to spring up in the sixteenth century—the great trading companies—represented a step closer to the modern business corporation. But they were still, from one very important point of our analysis, closer to the guilds from which they grew. The way the trading worked, the "members" of the company did not, like the modern shareholders, place their capital in the hands of the company's agents, the agents (officers) to invest the money and run the business. On the contrary, membership in the company, like membership in a guild, simply gave the member a right to exercise the exclusive trading privileges held by the company. This the members did "on their own bottom," that is, in a ship of their own investment and under their own management (and/or that of agents of their own choosing). Sometimes a man would stake out the capital necessary for his own trade, and sometimes he would adventure jointly with other members. In either case, the function of the organization, like the function of the guild, was to hold the privileges of some particular trade (with the Czar for example), of establishing rules and regulations for commerce, of holding courts to adjudicate grievances among members, and of bringing suit to keep "interlopers" (nonmembers) from exercising the privileges reserved for the company. For us it is significant that under this arrangement almost all of the legal liabilities the operations would incur would give rise to actions against the members as individuals —or co-adventurers—under ordinary principles of law. The problem of the corporation itself as wrongdoer would still not ordinarily be significant.

In the early seventeenth century, however, a change took place, then subtle, but of considerable significance in retrospect. The system was getting less and less viable as the capital costs of adventures grew. Economies of scale in shipping were dictating larger ships, not within the financial capacities of one man, or even, ordinarily, several. The need to provide protection from pirates was dictating synchronized sailings of fleets, with armed escorts. Corporate enterprise—truly modern corporate enterprise —was about to burst forth. In 1612 the East India Company resolved that thereafter the trading should be *only by the corporation.*

Each member subscribed or "adventured" as much as he desired, or even declined to subscribe any amount at all, to a common fund to be placed in the hands of the governor and committees (directors) for management in behalf of such of the members as had participated in the subscription.[1]

In other words, the company, through its officers, was no longer merely laying down bylaws under which the members would engage among themselves, directly, as entrepreneurs. The members were now supplying capital to the management, and the management was directing the adventures, repaying the members —"shareholders" we could now more properly call them—in proportion to their investments.

Such an arrangement raises a whole new set of liability problems. Before, when the members were financing and, presumably, directing the voyages "on their own bottom" they were liable for wrongs committed by them or by their agents according to the then law of agency. But now that the suppliers of capital and the managers of the enterprise were separate persons, who would be responsible for wrongs—the officers of the company who managed its ordinary affairs, the members who had advanced the capital, or "the corporation," that is, the corporate treasury?

Insofar as legal doctrine was concerned, there lingered considerable doubts as to the conditions, if any, under which the corporation might be a "person" capable of committing wrongs in the eyes of the law. If it could be liable at all, was it only for acts specifically authorized by corporate deed or warrant? What if the directors or shareholders specifically authorized the wrongful act? or ratified it after the fact? or authorized the activity that resulted in the wrong? Could the corporation be liable for acts committed in the prosecution of some line of business that was outside the scope of its charter? Could the mindless corporation be liable for wrongs an element of which was a mental state of some sort—for example, malice or criminal intent? Could it be liable for crimes one of the punishments for which was imprisonment, the corporation not being imprisonable?

None of the answers was certain. But we can, I think, reconstruct what direction the various groups with an interest in the matter would have wanted the law to take.

To the officers it must have been obvious that corporations were becoming capable of involvement in a widening range of social injury, and that someone was going to have to pay. As long as the corporation was safe from suit, the effect would be to leave the pressure on them, as the corporation's most visible and wealthy agents. Thus, the more the management became a separate class from the investors, the more the managers were going to want to clarify the liability situation in favor of the corporation's being liable, rather than them.*

The investors would feel otherwise. Making the corporation liable would reduce the value of their shares. Worse, under existing law, if there was not enough in the corporate treasuries to pay the bill, an unsatisfied creditor could go after the shareholders personally to make up the difference. The shareholders would feel that since they were entrusting management with control over the company's day-to-day operations, the management should bear the liability, if anyone had to. If, however, the corporation were to be suable for wrongdoing, they would have favored a sort of compromise—limited liability. Since ancient times the liability of a person who invested in a shipping venture on the high seas was limited to the amount he had invested in the ship. If the corporation could be modeled after the ship in this regard (and there already were some early gestures in this direction), while any suit against the corporation would harm the in-

---

* As is discussed more fully in Chapter 6, if a judgment is won against the corporation, the effect on the salaries of the top management is likely to be minimal; if the company is well off, it will pay the judgment and continue the salaries unabated. Even supposing that the top management hold shares (or, as in modern times, options for the purchase of shares) they still do better to have the corporation sued. If they own, say, 5 percent of the shares, then the real impact on them of a $20,000 judgment is but $1,000, either indirectly through their proportionate share of what the corporation had to pay, or directly through their proportionate burden of any "leviation" that at this early stage might have been made on the shareholders for the unpaid balance that the corporation could not meet. In either case, it would have been in the interests of the management that under the law any trouble they got the corporation into would fall on it, rather than on them.[2]

vestors' interests, they could not lose any more than they had put into the company. In other words, the shareholders might settle for allowing a party injured by the corporation's acts to sue the corporation, but if the assets of the corporation were inadequate, to debar him from holding the shareholders personally liable for the unsatisfied balance.

Thus, at this point there were clearly growing tensions between the commercial environment and the hazy doctrines of corporate nonliability. The matter was going to have to be settled, and quickly. Some adjustments, some compromises, were in the offing.

## The Bubble Act Period

But then something untoward happened, something that confused, if not temporarily stultified, the development of corporation law for over a century.

By the early eighteenth century, unchartered joint-stock companies—a sort of hybrid of corporations and partnerships—had become a minor rage. A good deal of investment was lost in highly speculative undertakings. Then, in 1719, the greatest joint-stock calamity of them all: After a breathtaking rise in the price of its stock, the South Sea Company failed, or as it was commonly put, the South Sea bubble burst.

In the ensuing uproar, Parliament passed the South Sea Bubble Act of 1720. The intent was to eliminate the unchartered joint-stock companies, but the act, so hastily and poorly drafted that no one was quite certain what it meant, had "a paradoxical effect, stimulating the very type of enterprise it was supposed to suppress."[3] What happened was that as time went on without enforcement of the act, lawyers got bolder and bolder in inventing new legal forms to circumvent its vague contours, and set up nonchartered companies that were, in all but name, joint-stock companies established in such a way as to obviate having to apply to Parliament or the Crown for review. And when people did apply, on the up-and-up, for charters so as to become legitimate corporations, the distrust that the whole episode had engendered resulted in their being issued only suspiciously and sparingly.

Thus, at least in England, where much of the relevant law was being made (the Bubble Act never had much impact in America), the questions that seemed so on the verge of resolution were practically suspended in abeyance for want of testing.

No one, what is more, could anticipate in this period how significant corporations were going to become, and thus laying a considered legal foundation for them was out of the question. Adam Smith, in *Wealth of Nations*, holds the corporation, absent a monopoly privilege, "to have little promise except in limited fields of operations where all the operations are capable of being reduced to what is called 'routine,'" (giving as examples banking, cutting and operating canals, and insurance).[4] Blackstone, in his influential *Commentaries* published at the same time, dedicates only eight pages to corporations—and of that, little has to do with the business corporation. While he does recite, with a reference to Coke, that "a corporation cannot commit treason or felony or other crime in its corporate capacity,"[5] he does not even touch upon the problems of corporate civil liability because, apparently, corporate troublemaking was considered too insignificant for serious scholars to concern themselves with.

# 4. The Industrial Revolution—The Die Is Cast

This state of suspension in the law was to come to a jarring end. The Industrial Revolution, and perhaps improved transportation in particular, brought about previously unanticipated changes for corporations—changes in the function corporations played in society, in their size, incidence, and structure. And the law began, in every conceivable way, to accommodate to the social realities.

First, as to the changing function of corporations in the society. In earlier times the corporate privilege had been reserved for the few large-scale undertakings then in existence, some of the most eminent of which served almost as arms of government (the Bank of England, the East India Company, the Massachusetts Bay Company, the Virginia Company). Now, however, all sorts of traditionally private enterprises that had theretofore been operable on a sole proprietorship or partnership basis came to have the requirements for capital and for management flexibility that a corporation could best provide. Demands for charters increased with the demands for vast pools of centralized capital.

The pressure of these demands began to translate itself into the legal framework. To obtain a charter, early corporations had had to apply to the Crown (and, later, Parliament, or in the United States, a state house). This procedure of incorporation by special charter had at least one strong virtue. It gave the issuer of the charter a chance to consider each particular application on its merit, and to tailor the company-to-be's powers and privileges, and even its size and debt structure, to the limits appropriate to its particular undertaking. When, for example, Massachusetts granted the Maine Flour Mills a charter in 1818, it limited the total property the corporation might hold to $50,000, of which the land could not exceed $30,000 in value and had—all of it—to be in Kennebec County.[1]

Unfortunately, this system was simply not feasible in the face of the flood of applications for new charters. In addition, the special charter procedure was becoming increasingly unpopular, not merely because of its earlier association with monopoly favors, but because, especially in the United States, of its taint of legislative corruption. As a result, general incorporation laws gradually grew up to compete with the practice of applying for special charters. Under these laws, anyone who filled out the proper form, paid the fees, and met certain other requirements could operate as a corporation without applying specially to the legislature. By the end of the nineteenth century, the practice of general incorporation, begun in North Carolina in 1795, was not only a competing mode of incorporation, it had displaced special charters entirely.

The public, however, was not prepared to abandon all its traditional controls. Even the general incorporation laws, at their earliest period, provided that charters could be granted only on certain conditions designed to keep the proliferating corporations within certain confines. While charters could no longer be tailored on a case-by-case basis by special legislation, the purposes and powers of corporations of various classes were narrowly defined, indebtedness and capital limitations were subject to general limits, and various other restrictions were built into the system. In New York, authorized capital was at first a maximum of $100,000 for some businesses, $50,000 for others. In Massachusetts, the limit was at first $200,000 for some businesses, as little as $5,000 for others.[2]

But as the pace of industrialization picked up, even these limitations became unduly hindering. The "life" of the projected corporations was to be, if not perpetual, generally for twenty years at least. One year a $500,000 capital limit and a restriction to making cloth shirts might seem ample and reasonable, given the then existing requirements of the technology and the character of the market. But the way society was changing, in five to ten years, who knew what the corporation might want and need to be doing? Products produced in a small shop today (or un-dreamed of) would need corporate capital tomorrow.

In these circumstances those with capital began to seek out, as their state of incorporation, the state that least tied their hands. And the states, for their part, accommodated with a competition to outdo one another in leniency, a competition so keen it was to be dubbed "charter mongering." State legislatures began to allow anyone who came there to incorporate "for any lawful purpose." Capital limits were dropped. The insiders—the managers of the capital—were given increasing flexibility.*

Those who were concerned about this trend in the state legisla-tures still had the courts to look to. For a period, even though the statutes allowed a business to incorporate for "any lawful purpose," the corporation had to set forth *some* purpose in detail —that it intended to make paint, to operate a barge canal, to manufacture textiles. If a corporation exceeded its powers, trying to spread to other fields (like the modern conglomerate), the courts would say it was operating *ultra vires*, and the attorney general could deprive it of its franchise or charter, or a share-holder might enjoin the *ultra vires* activity. But the same "re-alities" that were operating on the legislatures became apparent to the courts. The courts began, in turn, to interpret the charter provisions more and more broadly—to say that some activity not expressly in the charter was "incidental" to the company's busi-ness and thus allowable. For example, one corporation originally

* The response the states made to these pressures might seem surprising: Why should anyone expect states to loosen up their restrictions on the corporations they let in? The answer lies partly in the anticipated state tax revenues that the "favored" state would realize and partly in the benefits to the local bar (which had, and has, a disproportionate hand in the drafting of the relevant legislation). But the most telling explanation is simply this: At an early stage, when corporate activity—both at the financing and marketing ends—was mostly intrastate, tough restrictions served to protect one's own citizens. But as the markets for capital and for the corporate product became more national, the protections that these statutes provided— such as they were—were largely protections for some other state's citizens. Further, the U.S. Supreme Court had made it clear that no state could keep out a "foreign" state's corporation seeking interstate business. In these circumstances the states with lenient restrictions would get the benefits of being the corporate homestead, without necessarily bearing a proportionate share of the possible burdens.

chartered to operate a railroad established a hotel and winter resort business in Florida; it was allowed to spread itself this way, as against the *ultra vires* claim, on the view that the hotel business provided traffic for its railroading operations.[3]

Thus, insofar as legislative and court control over the special ground rules for corporate functioning was concerned, the lid was off. Increasingly, the corporation could operate where it wanted to, grow to whatever size it wanted, manufacture any products, and provide any services it chose.

Not only were the social function and the legal framework of the corporation changing, but, led by the railroads, the structure of the organization as well. Before 1850 very few businesses required the services of a full-time administrator or had anything we would call an "administrative structure."[4] Even in mining, manufacturing, and transportation—where the "giant" businesses operated—the largest firms were directed by a general superintendent and a president or a treasurer.[5] The general superintendent supervised the labor force personally.

Obviously this situation could not last. In 1855 the general superintendent of the Erie noted that while a superintendent of a fifty-mile road can give the business his personal attention in every detail, "in the government of a road 500 miles in length, a very different state exists."[6] What was needed was special administrative personnel and administrative sophistication. He came up with one of the very first organizational charts ever printed, spelling out careful and detailed definition of lines of authority and communication.

By the 1860s and 1870s the Pennsylvania Railroad pioneered in even a more extensive structural definition:

. . . They spelled out the lines of communication and authority between the major and ancillary units within the transportation department and also between the transportation and the other major departments— the traffic and the accounting or financial departments. . . .

By the 1880s, the principle had been established that line officers at headquarters and in the local divisions gave the orders and made the decisions dealing with personnel, which included those of discipline, wages, hours, allocation of duties, hiring, and firing. Those executives at headquarters or in the divisions in the field who were concerned with the maintenance of way, motive power, or rolling stock —that is, the staff officials—communicated directly with personnel only on matters of standards and procedures. The line-and-staff concept was further extended to clarify the relations between the older transportation department and the newer traffic and financial departments. Again, the line officers—those directly involved with the railroad's primary function, transportation—dealt with people and the staff officers with things. Station agents, for example, received instructions on the obtaining and forwarding of freight from the traffic department, but the transportation department decided their pay and daily routine.[7]

What now about the wrongs that these burgeoning, complex creatures were increasingly involved in?

In short, the corporation could no longer be dealt with by, in effect, ignoring it as a wrongdoer. Increasingly, corporations were engaging in all the activities that individual persons had undertaken before—as well as some new ones. What is more, wrongs were occurring that it was increasingly difficult (expensive, unfeasible) to lay at the feet of any particular human wrongdoer: When a bridge collapsed, for example, *who* was at fault? More complicating still, even where the wrongful act could be traced to some particular tangible human, he was increasingly not, as in some of the early cases, a well-to-do (read, "suable") executive, but a railroad porter or a dock worker. When one looked behind this complex network of authority and communication, who— what particular individual—was his principal? The question was to become more exasperating and meaningless as the organization grew more complex.

What was simplest for the injured party was also, as I have indicated, the safest route for the management (and the simplest for the courts): to treat the corporation as the actor, making *it* liable for judgments and penalties. The shift of liability losses onto the corporation would have the effect of making investing (shareholding) a little more risky than before. But the problem could be, and was, ameliorated by giving the investors, as a sort of historical quid pro quo, limited liability.

Thus, over a period of years limited liability for the shareholders, once the exception, became the rule. And parallel with this development, the earlier "metaphysical" limitations on corporations being liable for various classes of wrongs were peeled back one by one.

The first steps were easy. A corporation itself might not be the subject of liability for all civil wrongs, but was at least liable where the wrongful act resulted from carrying out a writing under the corporation's common seal (1812).[8] It was liable for the trespasses of its agents acting within the scope of their authority (1842).[9] It was liable for acts of its agents, even if contrary to company instructions, if the agent was acting in the course of employment, in a manner "he thought best to suit the interest of his employers" (1862).[10] It could be liable for torts, an ingredient for which was malice, at least in the case where one of its agents acted from malice (1904).[11]

The reluctance to hold the corporation liable criminally was a little slower to yield. But by 1846 the English courts came to a position that was to prevail in both England and America, at least for a broad range of criminal offenses. The case involved a railroad company that had unlawfully destroyed a highway in the construction of its own bridge. Lord Denman reasoned that while the individuals who concurred in the vote to erect the bridge, and those who labored to put it up, might both be subject to criminal indictment,

the public knows nothing of the former; and the latter, if they can be identified, are commonly persons of the lowest rank, wholly incompetent to make any reparation for the injury. There can be no effectual means for deterring from an oppressive exercise of power for the purpose of gain, except the remedy by an indictment against those who truly commit it, that is, the corporation, acting by its majority.[12]

Even in so holding, however, Denman reiterated the view that corporations could not be guilty of treason, felony, perjury, or offenses against the person: "These plainly derive their character from the corrupted mind of the person committing them, and are violations of the social duties that belong to men and subjects."[13]

In the United States, the theoretical objections to a corporation's committing most sorts of crime were already somewhat discredited by 1909 when the U.S. Supreme Court held, "It is true that there are some crimes, which in their nature cannot be committed by corporations. But there is a large class of offenses ... wherein the crime consists in purposely doing the things prohibited by statute. In that class of crimes we see no good reason why corporations may not be held responsible for and charged with the knowledge and purposes of their agents, acting within the authority conferred upon them."[14] It is significant that the violation before the court, in that instance, a rebate in violation of the Interstate Commerce Act, was the sort of crime that a corporation is far more apt to commit than the old common-law crimes about which some doubts lingered, for example, larceny and manslaughter.

One of the latter crimes came before the highest court of New York later that same year. The Rochester Railway and Light Company had installed some fixtures in a Rochester residence "in such a grossly improper, unskillful, and negligent manner" that gas escaped and caused a death. The corporation was indicted for manslaughter. The court pointed out that the penal code defined homicide as "the killing of one human being by the act, procurement or omission of another." "This final word 'another,'" the court said, naturally meant "another 'person,'" not a corporation. The indictment was not allowed.[15]

At least where homicide is concerned, such reasoning has, as we shall see, some continued viability. It is, indeed, a rather extraordinary testimony to our legal processes that corporation lawyers should have been able, as early as 1878, to have corporations deemed "persons" under the Fourteenth Amendment to the Constitution,[16] and thereby accorded most of the benefits of due process, equal protection, and so on (designed to protect the freed slaves), while their being "persons" capable of suffering the burdens of a manslaughter statute should still be in doubt. But as a vestige of the past, the latter point is more ironic than significant. It is, in all events, hardly the worst legacy that these developments left us with.

# II

## The Historical Legacy

Only in a few ways did the law adjust to the corporation as a special sort of actor demanding the attention of specially adapted laws. These exceptions were almost entirely in areas such as shareholder-management relations, where the problems that arose were of a sort that only corporations could be involved in, and where, therefore, there was no preexisting rule into which each emerging situation could be fitted: How many directors needed a corporation to have? How were they to be elected and removed? On what grounds could dividends be compelled? How was a corporation to be dissolved? By the very nature of these problems, the law had to start relatively from scratch. And in seeking solutions, it often had the imagination to venture right inside the organization itself; that is, it laid down express requirements directly impacting the *organizational structure* and *decision process*: The directors could vest some of their power in a management committee, but certain decisions (the declaration of dividends, for example) were nondelegable; the corporate officers could make day-to-day decisions, like how many units to produce, but major organic changes (the sale of assets, or a merger) had to be submitted to shareholders for a two-thirds approval.

But it is important to remember that such meddlings with the corporation's internal operations were only the exception; even where they were introduced, they were basically conceived to protect and define in advance the interests—increasingly complex—of the investor, not those of the corporation's customer, its neighbor, or its fellow citizen. Insofar as the corporation was performing acts that, in theory, the ordinary mortal could perform—

polluting the environment, producing injurious goods, setting prices, committing crimes (in other words, insofar as it was dealing with the "outside world")—in those areas there already existed a body of law addressed to "persons," and the corporation was eased into this body of law in the simplest way possible: by ignoring, one by one, the earlier qualms about whether the corporation ("that invisible, intangible, and artificial being," Chief Justice John Marshall had called it)[1] could be a person, too. Through this device, whenever the law spoke, expressly or implicitly, in terms of, "no person shall . . . ," that rule was smoothly, if unreflectively, transferred to corporations.

As a result, many possible approaches to controlling corporations that would have taken special account of their special institutional natures were not developed as they might have been. Indeed, any distinctive treatment of this sort would have run counter to the way "the law" thinks. It is partly an Ockham's razor problem—the law seeks, wherever possible, as much simplicity and symmetry as it can—and partly a problem that, once the corporation was deemed a person, invidious distinctions among it and other "persons" would be frowned upon. One catches the flavor of this in *United States* v. *Kane*, arising out of an 1885 strike against a railroad. Judge (later Justice) David Brewer, in holding against the strikers, spun out some homely analogies to the simple employer-employee relationships that had prevailed in a fundamentally precorporate society, and added:

that which is true in these simple matters where there is a little piece of property, and a single owner and a single laborer, is just as true when there is a large property, a large number of employes, and a corporation is the owner. Rules of right and wrong, obligations of employer and obligations of employe, do not change because the property is in the one instance a little bit of real estate, and in the other a large railroad. . . .[2]

This is not to say that the law never saw that corporate growth was presenting problems that demanded distinct recognition. As corporate influence grew, new laws were needed and passed. Many of them—especially the most prominent federal legislation

(Interstate Commerce Act [1887], Sherman Anti-Trust Act [1890], Federal Trade Commission Act [1914])—can be viewed partly as attempts to fill the vacuum that had been left by the relaxation of the earlier charter restrictions on corporate assets and fields of operations. Some of these laws established agencies that lent (at least in theory) a measure of specialized expertise and continuing overview. But my fundamental point is not belied: The problems were seen only as those of "big business," without the added insight that remedying them might call for different measures than remedying problems caused by big persons—that is, human beings who just happened to be especially large and powerful. Even the federal agencies are not exceptions, for their ultimate enforcement powers, like the various statutes that emerged when a legislative tussle ended with the antibusiness forces more or less on top,[3] never swayed from confronting the corporation, fundamentally, with two basic strategies, strategies that had been developed around assumptions about ordinary persons.

The first strategy, the prevalent counterorganizational strategy, is simply to confront the corporation, as we confront the man in the street, with a negative profit contingency (a civil judgment, a criminal fine) should the organization wander outside the law— a threat, in other words, to the corporation's pocketbook.

The second fundamental strategy, invoked, for reasons that will appear, only in more limited instances, is to threaten certain "key" persons within the company with monetary losses or even imprisonment if they command or allow a particularly egregious corporate course of conduct.

Is it likely that either sort of sanction is adequate to keep the corporation in line?

# 5. What Do We Want the Law to Accomplish?

The first question that must be asked about measures to control corporations is not merely, "Do they work?," but, rather, "What does 'work' mean?" What is it we want our strategies for controlling corporations to accomplish?

The answer is that the law has different aims, not inconsistent, but which receive different emphases in different areas of conduct.

One goal is fundamentally *distributive*. When losses occur in society, the law aims to distribute them fairly and reasonably. If smoke from a company's coking operation is unjustifiably reducing the value of neighborhood homes, injuring the health of the occupants, then the law, if it is working well, should arrange for the company to pay the neighbors damages. Similarly, if a car does not perform as adequately as the purchaser was given fair reason to believe it would, the law, as an ideal, aims to place the unanticipated repair bills on the company's doorstep, rather than on the purchaser's.

But while making a corporation pay damages to persons it has injured is an important goal of the law, it is, in one sense, a secondary goal. A person who has received a cash settlement for the loss of his vision or his limbs has not really been, as the law is fond of saying, "made whole." (Who, in a free market exchange, would really be willing to "sell" his vision?)

Thus, what we should expect of the law, as a more primary goal, is that it reduce (within certain cost constraints discussed below) the incidence of harmful behavior in the first place. This is what we might call its *reductive goal*.

Now, this reductive goal itself has different aspirations in different areas of conduct. On the one hand, there is behavior so disfavored—murder, for example—that we want to eliminate it entirely, without giving the actor an option of maintaining or decreasing the level of harmful conduct, depending on his willingness and ability to pay the damages. I will call this conduct "absolutely disfavored conduct."

On the other hand, there is behavior that the law disfavors, but feels it cannot absolutely eliminate without risking social losses that could, in some cases, exceed the gains. This I will call "qualifiedly disfavored conduct."

Price-fixing, unlawful per se under the Sherman Act, is an example of corporate conduct that is absolutely disfavored. Price-fixing is so inherently objectionable, and we are so confident that it can be eliminated without any risk of offsetting losses, that antitrust laws aim to reduce it to zero—to abolish it entirely. We refuse, for example, to entertain a defendant's plea of "reasonableness" or "good intentions." More significantly, the threat we pose to the price-fixer is not merely that he shall pay the damages others can prove. To stamp the practice out, we threaten the corporation with triple damages plus criminal fines.

Most of the problems corporations get involved in, however, arise from activities that are not so unambiguously harmful and/or immoral as price-fixing. Pollution causes damages, but some degree of pollution seems to be a necessary adjunct of refining oil and coking iron; we know, therefore, that if we aim to make pollution unqualifiedly disfavored, we risk bringing certain useful activities to a halt, perhaps costing us more than we gain. Similarly, industrial accidents constitute one of the most shamefully underacknowledged problems in our society, and much more needs to be done to reduce them. But even so, we have to recognize that the steps necessary to reduce industrial accidents to zero would close down our factories.

Thus, whether, and to what extent, the harms represented by this second class of problems should be eliminated depends upon assessment of a number of factors. One would ideally want to know, for example, the damage that the harmful activity is causing, the value to society of the things the associated activity is resulting in, and the cost (to the company, but also thereby to the society) of various measures that might be taken to reduce the harms. When we get into this area, therefore, the steps we might be prepared to take against unqualifiedly disfavored conduct are too blunt. What we do, instead, is approximate the damage the company is causing and confront the company with those damages: no more and no less. The idea is that the company will thereby have to take the damages—the social injuries—into account in its decisions, the way it has to take into account its labor and supplies. If the damages are so high that it cannot bear them and remain in business (or it has to move elsewhere), well and good. This we would take to confirm suspicions that, even considering its benefits, the activity was, in fact and on net, causing more harm than it was worth. But if the company can bear its damages and yet continue in production (perhaps at a reduced level, or subject to adjustments of a sort described below), this we might take as evidence that, although the behavior had bad aspects, an unqualified elimination of it would have made society suffer more than it gained.

These, then, are the three goals of the law against which its success might be judged. It should eliminate unqualifiedly disapproved conduct, bring qualifiedly disapproved conduct into line with the damage it is causing, and, where those injuries that have to be lived with are concerned, the law should distribute them in an equitable manner.

What I want to emphasize here is that, as regards reducing the disfavored conduct (of either sort) the law must be capable of bringing about certain systematic changes within the organization. If botulism bacilli are appearing in a company's soup, there is some reason for it, an institutional weakness that will not go away until there have been changes in the corporation's purchasing standards, its cooking procedures, its quality-control requirements; there must be internal shifts in the direction of improved information systems, improved role definitions, improved authority structures, improved technical programs, improved corporate allocations of human and other resources. These are changes that will not come about automatically simply because a court has ordered a company to write a check to the government, or to a widow.

Consider, for another example, the problem of preventing automobile accidents. The success of our attempts in this direction depends, too, on the creation of various sorts of desirable institutional arrangements and responses.

Start with information flow. An information system that optimized auto industry safety (putting aside costs for a moment) would likely be one in which the producing corporation gathered information with respect to tests and accidents not only from within its own plants, branches, and task forces, but also from the highway patrols of the various states, from the Department of Transportation, coroners' offices, hospitals, auto repair shops, and independent testing laboratories. Not only would this information system have to be designed to draw data from the right places, both inside and outside the corporation, but it would have to gather and transmit them in appropriate form for action, and deliver them to the "right" desks: those of the company's design engineers, its quality-control staff, its test drivers—perhaps to the board of directors. What is more, to minimize accidents, the organization must not only design and implement the information system—gathering the right data, in the right way, and channeling them to the right places—but it must make changes to bring about the ideal configuration of authority for the problem's amelioration. For example, if the accidents owe to an eminence, at the design stage of the car, of the sales and stylist-oriented task forces over the safety-oriented engineering personnel, then all the information in the world will not bring about the right car. And even if the information is there, *and* the authoritative organizational pattern is adequate (in theory), the required changes still have to attend upon the appropriate internal allocation of resources: an increased amount spent on research and development of a safety-oriented sort.

Of course, costs cannot be put aside, as the distinction between qualifiedly and unqualifiedly disfavored conduct recognizes. A perfect system for accident prevention would not be one that reduced accidents to zero if the costs of doing so were greater than the benefits. If some company, in the design and implementation of "improved" safety systems, wound up spending $10 million to allay damages of $100,000, many people would well doubt that the company was balancing social resources appropriately. And by the same token, if the law *forced* the corporation to institute those systems, on the figures the hypothetical assumes, the problem would be "overregulated."

Thus, putting aside for a moment the knotty problem of how willing we should be to balance the cost of death and maiming in monetary terms, the original question about whether the law is working, at least insofar as the reductive goals of the law are concerned, might be rephrased as follows.

1. Where the society has agreed (in whatever way) that some conduct is qualifiedly disfavored, is the law adequate to make the corporation institute the most effective internal organizational changes to the extent of the cost of, but at no more than the cost of, what doing so saves the society?

2. Where conduct is unqualifiedly disfavored, is the law getting the corporation to do whatever most effectively and economically brings the conduct to an immediate halt?

The answer, I am afraid, is that as long as the law remains within the framework of our existing major strategies, successes are going to be limited.

To understand why this is so, I will begin by examining first the legal strategies that are oriented toward the organization as an entity, and then those oriented toward "key" corporate individuals.

# 6. Measures Aimed at the Organization Itself

Before I examine how our present counterorganizational strategies do work, let me observe two things they do *not* involve.

The first has to do with the old legal saw about a corporation having no conscience or soul. When we look at the total social strategies that are available for keeping human beings in line, we see that the law is only a part of, a complement of, more pervasive forces. What prevents most of us from committing murder is not a calculation based upon the threat of what the law will do, but mechanisms—guilt, shame, anxiety, conscience, superego—internalized within us through the forces of family, school, church, and peer group. By virtue of these processes a certain amount of potential antisocial activity is repressed or sublimated before it is even thought of. And a certain amount, though emergent into consciousness, can be stayed by moral argument ("Don't you see, you ought not to do that?"). The law is only a last resort.

When we turn to controlling corporations, however, two problems emerge. When individuals are placed in an organizational structure, some of the ordinary internalized restraints seem to lose their hold. And if we decide to look beyond the individual employees and find an organizational "mind" to work with, a "corporate conscience" distinct from the consciences of particular individuals, it is not readily apparent where we would begin— much less what we would be talking about.

This does not mean that we cannot build into the institution itself mechanisms that play the function of guilt, shame, and a sense of responsibility, in human beings. One of the main purposes of this book is, indeed, to show both that this must be done and how it can be accomplished. Let us just observe at this point that our present strategies for dealing with corporations are not geared to achieve such a result. *Thus, ironically, present law has to carry, vis-à-vis giant corporations, more of the burden of social control than the law has to carry in dealing with ordinary human beings.*

Second, what makes our greater dependence on the law in the case of corporations worse yet is that some of the major sanctions that we can call on to control human beings are unavailable in the case of corporations. Most obviously inapplicable are imprisonment and the death penalty. (Forfeiture of corporate charter, while a theoretical analogue, is simply too draconian to be a realistic threat against all but the smallest corporation, and even then, the feasibility of a quick reorganization and rechartering render it a rather illusory "death").[1] What is more, there are other legal remedies applicable to humans (psychotherapy as a condition of probation, rehabilitative job training) for which there are no present counterparts when one deals with the corporation.

## The Basic Strategy: Does the Pocketbook Control?

At present, the basic counterorganizational strategy we are left with is fairly straightforward: Whether we are threatening the corporation with private civil actions, criminal prosecutions, or the new hybrid "civil penalties," we aim to control the corporation through threats to its profits. (Even where an injunction or a cease-and-desist order is issued, or where a corporation is prohibited by statute from shipping goods of a certain type, the corporation not being imprisonable, the implicit threat against it is still monetary.)

The underlying reasoning is pretty much the same "bad bargain" analysis that we have brought forward from theorists like Bentham, and have simply transferred from people to corporations without reflection. On this view, to stop a person from, say, stealing, "we are dealing with a simple matter of bookkeeping. The thief must be caught and so punished that pain brought by the penalty will just barely outweigh in the thief's mind the pleasure (profit) brought by the crime."[2] The punishment must "fit the crime" in the sense in which a good bookkeeper will recognize that, when the likely gains are balanced against the likely losses, the prohibited activity is a "bad bargain."

Sometimes—as when we are dealing with qualifiedly disfavored conduct—the bargain we tender is not even a "bad" one. Not being prepared to eliminate the activity at all costs, we use what might be called the "fair bargain" strategy. The fair bargain threatens the corporation not with such costs as will necessarily force the questioned activity to a halt, but at least with such costs as constitute the full measure of the damages it is causing—no more, no less. Suppose, for example, that a company's production results in pollution that costs the society $10,000 a day. If the law were to impose on the company a fine equivalent to, say, $15,000 a day, then an activity that is on the whole socially beneficial might be forced to close. And, on the contrary, if the damages are $10,000 a day but the threat of the law is only $5,000 a day (either because of the size of the fine, or because of the size of the fine discounted by the likelihood of getting caught and convicted) an activity that is on balance harmful is not being adequately discouraged. In the first case, the threat against the corporation—through fine or otherwise—should be reduced; in the second, the answer is to increase the amount of the fine (and/or frequency of enforcement), or increase the capacity of the legal system to gather civil damages together and lay them at the corporation's feet (as, for example, by facilitating class actions).

But (the argument continues) once these steps are taken, nothing further need be done. For supposing the corporation to be a "rational economic man" writ large, under those circumstances the corporation will respond by changing its internal institutional configurations "just the right amount." That is to say, if there are institutional variations (improved communication networks, preferable production processes, improved centralization of authority) that will reduce the socially harmful activity (the accidents, the faulty products, the pollution) then as the law raises the "pinch" on the corporation to the justified level, the corporation will, "of its own," undertake to devise and implement the improved systems to an extent that is in line with the social cost and value of the undertaking. By the same token, at the point where the corporation ceases effecting changes in response to the increased "pinch" of the law, that is a sure sign that changes beyond such point were not warranted on a social cost basis, that is, that the marginal value of the change did not equal its marginal cost.

It ought to be apparent that while the bad-bargain strategies and the fair-bargain strategies differ, they differ only in degree. Both approaches are based upon the notion that the most effective way to manipulate corporate behavior is through its pocketbook. Thus, to understand whether the law makes any sense, we have to consider whether the corporation is—as the American folk culture has it—a profit maximizer, pure and simple. If so, then our present strategies are exactly right, for on that reasoning, every time the law makes a feint at the corporation's profit centers, it will smoothly and reflectively institute just the proper amount of internal remedial changes.

But those who have examined the actual behavior of corporations have become increasingly skeptical that they behave the way the economics textbooks say they *ought* to behave. Indeed, when we turn from one corporation to the next, and as we watch a single corporation develop over time, we are likely to find— if the goal terminology is to be used at all—something that looks like a variety of goals, each associated not only with different corporate types but even with different stages of development of any single corporation. As with the human being, there is certainly a fundamental stage that is nearly entirely profit-oriented: The corporation, like the human being, seeks first of all survival. But once survival is secure, the corporation, especially the corporation that is in the hands of inside management, is more likely, as Simons, Galbraith, and others have suggested, to seek a *satisfactory* level of profits—that is, enough profits to stave off shareholder insurrections (that are increasingly hard to mount as shareholdings are dispersed among current shareholders). Corporations that can meet the first two stages, that is, can survive and maintain profits that are "satisfactory" in this defensive sense,

may advance to stages in which their behavior can best be understood by the posit of still higher level goals. The next stage might
be the satisfaction of employee (especially white-collar employee)
financial well-being, and then, at the next higher stage, goals such
as expansion, prestige, innovation, and the creation of an exciting
internal environment. There is evidence that companies that have
passed these stages show, at a higher stage of security, an increasing social orientation—for instance, sponsorship of cultural events
to an extent that cannot really be justified as profit-maximizing
"goodwill."*

There are thus considerable reasons to doubt that corporations
always, in every way, are perfectly attuned to their bank accounts.
In all events, how large the deviations from profit maximization
may be, it is not necessary for us to get involved in; for my immediate concern lies not in detailing the limits of profit maximization in general, but in the narrower subproblem that is critical
here: How responsive is the corporation's behavior to profit threats
that emanate from the law?

What I want to show is that even the corporation we might concede to be overwhelmingly a profit maximizer in *most* of its
calculations is apt to be far less sensitive to the intimidations
of the law.

## The Place of the Law on the Corporation's Horizon

The first factor that those who trust to the law's profit threats
regularly fail to take into account is that the law and its contingent liabilities constitute only a small range of the threats that

---

* One might also expect to find a single corporation manifesting different
goals in the carrying out of its different functions. For example, a company's
pricing policies might be profit-oriented even at a time when its hiring
policies were prestige-oriented; that is, by paying more than the marginal
value to hire some well-known, sought-after executive, the company might
be sacrificing financial calculations in the interests of securing prestige among
its peers. A corporation might be quite profit-oriented in the planning of,
say, foreign investments (usually a board of directors' function), while in
its research and development (more likely in the hands of technicians who
exercise some independence from financial centers), we might find the
corporation to be pursuing technically defined goals with relative independence of profit constraints.

the corporation faces in dealing with the outside world. Corporate managers have to be alert to the uncertainties in acquiring and losing personnel, dealing with suppliers, anticipating the "moves" of competitors, opening new markets, developing improved methods of production, securing new sources of capital, and so forth. Thus, there are any number of areas from which profits may be enhanced or threatened, each of which competes with the law for the interests of the corporation. And of these, the law is not likely to occupy the foreground of the businessman's attention.

There are several reasons which, taken together, account for this.

1. Even the highest-level legal threat imaginable is apt to be far less of an item than other things that concern his business. Ford lost an estimated $250 million on the Edsel;[3] sales of the Mustang, in the first twenty-seven months alone, may have netted Ford $350 million.[4] When considered against those figures, a $7 million fine for EPA violations is significant, but no more so than a lot of things management has to worry about, and indeed far less so than many others.

2. To the executive and his business community peer group, having profits cut into by a lawsuit simply does not involve the same loss of face as losses attributable to other causes. Businessmen interviewed regularly indicated that the production of a car that would not sell, or a significant loss in market shares, reflected failures to do the sorts of things that businessmen were supposed to do. But being sued by the antitrust division, for example, while "a mess," was "understandable." This did not mean they approved such behavior; "but it could happen to anyone." The same sort of response was elicited when businessmen were questioned about product liability suits. Lawsuits against a pharmaceutical house were likened to being struck by lightning—that is, as unavoidable as an act of God, and something that (as with lightning) one just tries to take out insurance against. This attitude is carried right into the corporation's financial reports. Losses through major lawsuits are to be explained in the footnotes, as "nonrecurring losses." One doesn't gauge the business

or its management on them *really*. There is striking testimony of this attitude in the books being used in our business schools. The students are exposed to sophisticated (and supersophisticated) analyses of how to apply systems analysis, game theory, and management psychology to corporate decisions involving, it would seem, almost every variable and constraint one can imagine —except the law.

3. Business's concern for the law often seems undermined by a claimed uncertainty as to what the law means for the corporation to do (as in prohibiting "false and misleading advertising" or making sales "below cost"). I believe, personally, that businessmen tend to overstate such uncertainties, for other matters affecting the corporation that are equally uncertain are not so readily put aside. The real difference is more likely this: To the businessman, there are uncertainties as to the meaning of the law in a broader sense, too, that is, "What is the meaning of all this?," "Why, when we are having lunch with a competitor, shouldn't we be able to talk about problems of common interest—like costs and prices?" Businessmen are aware that the law sometimes seems to "whipsaw" them between apparently inconsistent policies, as, for example, when it requires in some of the antitrust laws that competition be free and open, and yet demands, in others, that prices be relatively withdrawn from free-market forces (e.g., by the Robinson-Patman Act). Some businessmen are simply exasperated, too, by the feeling that, as Dickens put it, "If the law supposes *that* . . . the law is a ass,—a idiot." Several interviewed gave instances where the policy of the law was acceptable or even laudable, but the materials demanded by governmental agencies in furtherance of it were not only burdensome to gather, but irrelevant to determining whether the law's policies were being carried out. The net result of the failure of the law to be comprehensible and credible in terms of the business community's ethos, where it exists, undermines fidelity to the law, and even an interest in it.

4. Even when the law is "meaningful" in both the narrow and the larger senses described above, there yet may remain large uncertainties as to how to implement the law (How does one

reduce pollution to the required level?). There may be uncertainties as to whether violations of the law will ever be detected. (Fidelity to the law is not apt to be encouraged by the feeling among businessmen, extraordinarily widespread according to a *Harvard Business Review* survey, that "the other fellow" is regularly cheating.)[5] There are uncertainties as to *when* violations will be detected (an especially significant consideration in light of the different time horizons for various individuals and groups within the organization—X trusts that by the time the violation is, if ever, discovered, he will have gotten his promotion). Too, even if the violation is ever detected, and the corporation is sued, who knows what (or when) the ultimate settlement will be—perhaps a heavy penalty, but perhaps also a slap-on-the-wrist fine or consent decree.

Controlling corporations through law becomes not only, as behaviorists would say, a misplaced faith on "negative reinforcement" (trying to teach people through punishing undesired acts rather than by rewarding good ones) but it is also the worst sort of negative reinforcement, one administered almost randomly (or so it seems) by a nonrespected source. People don't learn that way, and there is no reason to suppose corporations do, either.

5. Then, too, any analysis of corporate compliance with the law has to take into account the place of the corporation lawyer in the organization. If we are counting on the law to impinge the corporation effectively, the organization must listen to, even seek out, its lawyers. Ideally they would have to be called in at a stage where some particular decision was still open, not after it has been made—with directions to "get this thing done in some way that will get it past the courts." More than this, for the law to be really effective, lawyers would ideally have to conduct "legal audits" throughout the corporation, interviewing personnel candidly, and checking sensitive files for possibilities of law violations before litigation is required. To so function, however, the lawyer needs a large measure of collegial trust, respect—and access to files. There is reason to doubt that the average corporate legal officer has it in amounts he needs.

One reason for the failure is that while most of the corporate organism seems to be moving, in fairly good synchronization, in one direction, the lawyer is regarded by his co-workers as the "no" man. At the least, as one troubled corporate lawyer told me, he is seen as the man who "holds things up—for no apparent [to his co-workers] good reason." Furthermore, so long as the total losses that may be suffered through lawsuits (over and above insurance) are small relative to the threats imposed by competitors, the vice-president of sales is going to be left closer to the president's ear than the lawyer. (Besides, the vice-president for sales is more likely to "talk the president's talk.") Some corporate counsel have suggested that the divisional lawyers (those outside the central corporate headquarters, working in the field) are particularly "frozen out" of information vital to their functioning, even lied to, because their co-workers regard them as potential "informers" to corporate headquarters. As one Westinghouse officer testified to a Senate committee, in the aftermath of the electrical equipment industry price-fixing case, there was an unwritten rule "not to tell the lawyers anything."[6] And, of course, the people down below—the "workers"—are even further alienated from the lawyers than that.

6. There is a certain amount of economically nonrational behavior, especially in the calculation of legal threats, that stems from deeply rooted features of the organization itself. As corporations become more complex, they tend to subdivide into various departments according to geographical divisions (manufacturing areas and distribution territories), functionally defined groups (finance, sales, advertising, legal), and so on. The central organization cannot leave each of these groups at large to realize "profit" as it sees best. Rather, the farther and farther down the operational ladder one moves, the more the "profit goal" has to be translated into subgoals—targets and objectives for the shop, the department, the plant, the division, the subsidiary. It is these subgoals that define the task environment of the people actually engaged in production at such a plant, not some abstract "corporate profit."

The significance of such a diversity of goals was fascinatingly testified to by a quality-control man with one of the major automobile manufacturers. His job was to visit local assembly plants and verify that the company's own quality standards were being complied with. Periodically, he and his staff would uncover any number of quality defects, some of which might ultimately result in warranty pay-outs, or even civil liability against the corporation. It was quite possible that, on a rational profit-maximizing calculation by the company as a whole, it would often have been in the interest of "the corporation" to stop the production line and remedy the potentially harmful defects. But any attempts by him to interfere (and, remember, he was a co-worker, rather than a government inspector) were met with strong resistance, and even subversion and chicanery, by every hierarchy of the plant. The *plant's* targets and objectives call for producing ten thousand or whatever number of units by such-and-such a date. It is these "immediate" goals and objectives that determine the horizons and interests of the workers there; it is their fulfillment of them that will determine their progress up the corporate ladder. The potential for future lawsuits—that is, the possibility that the comptroller of the corporation will someday have to write some plaintiff a check from corporate headquarters (perhaps five or six years thereafter, given the delays of litigation) is not merely a distant event to the life of the producing plant: *It is not even a part of its reality.*

Let me elaborate on what is meant by saying that the legal contingencies are not a part of the subsystem's reality, and also indicate why attempts to make the law a part of that reality are likely to run into factors that are not easily overcome even by serious "rational" economic threats. Note that if those at the top of the corporation are going to get those at lower levels to abide by the standards of the law, the top must both know that improper conditions exist and be able and willing to make the lower levels remedy the conditions that are putting the organization in legal jeopardy. On both counts—both on the prior knowledge and on the follow-up—the counterorganizational strategies, by themselves, are not likely to bring about systematic innovations that can overcome the organizational inertia.

First, as to getting to the higher-ups information adequate to appreciate the legal jeopardy their company is in, there is a natural tendency for "bad news" of any sort not to rise to the top in an organization. A screening process takes place, such that if a company has been touting a new drug, and the drug begins "experiencing difficulties" in the lab, lab employees and their supervisors just "know" that information about this is to be passed upward, if at all, only in the vaguest terms. If an automobile company has retooled and is geared to produce 500,000 units of some car, a test driver or his supervisor knows that information suggesting that the car turns over too easily is not going to be welcomed "upstairs." Worse still, certain sorts of wrongdoing of a more serious sort—for example, price-fixing or other criminal activity—is not just screened out casually; it becomes the job of someone, perhaps the general counsel, to intercept any such information that could "taint" his president or board chairman, divulging his suspicions only in private, if at all. In this way, the law not only fails to bring about the necessary internal flow of information, it may systematically operate to keep information of wrongdoing away from the very people who might best do something about it.

The law has a similarly hard row to hoe in trying to realize the second requirement. The law is based on an implicit assumption that when the court visits a monetary loss on the corporation from, say, the production of a faulty unit, the group responsible for the production of the unit will be made to "feel" what it has done in some way (as by decreased budget, personnel shifts, "calling down" supervisors, changes in quality-control procedures or mechanical layouts, stiffer design specifications). The prevailing practice in corporations today, however, does not include internal auditing procedures to provide such negative feedback to the subunit that was responsible. What is more, the organizational resistance to making such changes is not readily swayed by "rational" monetary threats. For one thing, the determination of what particular group *was* responsible is not easy even for the corporation (much less outsiders) to establish. When a corporate act goes wrong, the natural inclination of each functional group that had a hand in it is to put the blame on someone else. When a faulty automobile is produced, for example, the design engineers are apt to blame accidents on the drivers or the assembly people; the assembly people fault quality control; quality control lays it all at the feet of the design engineers, and so on. So finally nobody does anything. This situation is associated with the problem noted earlier. Each profit center and each functional group is inclined to describe "success" and "failure" in its own terms, and these terms are not likely to include, for a technical or engineer-oriented group, some adverse judgment rendered by a nontechnically trained judge and a lay jury—all at the orchestration of shyster lawyers.

## The Lack of Congruence Between Individual and Corporate Calculations

A second group of reasons to doubt the efficacy of the law's profit threats has to do with the fact that the calculations that will maximize the profit of "the corporation" do not coincide with the calculations that encourage and constrain the key personnel, who have the most influence over corporate policies. Threats to the corporate treasury don't necessarily intimidate them.

Indeed, this want of congruence is the very idea behind two of the most basic attributes of corporate existence: limited liability and bankruptcy. We have arranged things so that the people who call the shots do not have to bear the full risks.

Take, for example, a small corporation involved in shipping dynamite. The shareholders of such a company, who are typically also the managers, do not *want* their dynamite-laden truck to blow up. But if it does, they know that those injured cannot, except in rare cases, sue them as individuals to recover their full damages if the amount left in the corporation's bank account is inadequate to make full compensation (which it will be if the explosion has, say, leveled downtown Portland). What this means is that in deciding how much money to spend on safety devices, and whether or not to allow trucks to drive through major cities, the calculations are skewed toward higher risks than suggested by the "rational economic corporation/free-market" model that is dreamily put forth in the textbooks. If no accident results, the shareholders will reap the profits of skimping on safety measures. If a truck blows up, the underlying human interests will be shielded from fully bearing the harm that they have caused. And then, there is nothing to prevent the same men from setting up a new dynamite shipping corporation the next day; all it takes is the imagination to think up a new name, and some $50 in filing fees.

It is true that the giant corporations cannot be quite as protean in their dissolutions and re-formations as the small, close corporation. Indeed, only in a few fiascos like the Penn Central case will actual bankruptcy be a real issue. But when we turn to these more visible and influential giants a no less serious problem arises —the separation of shareholder from management interests. Suppose, for example, the corporation to be subject to an implied legal threat that if "it" produces a dangerous drug, "it" will suffer a damage judgment. To the corporate officers this threat means what? Their economic return is primarily through their salaries, not dividends, or the book value of stock. When a settlement check is drawn on the corporate treasury, the loss has an effect on management that is largely indirect. Of course, in theory, if there is a shareholder group powerful enough to remove management, even a salaried management will have to be closely concerned. But far more often in major American corporations the shareholdings are divided among so many different people that shareholders are relatively incapable of concerted action to toss out management. The result is that the salaries of top management, as well as their positions, are relatively buffered from the financial ups and downs of the corporation from whatever cause —and certainly seem to be independent of the most major damage awards the law has ever meted out. In 1972, for example, Ford Motor Company got caught (because one of its computers finked) in probably the largest violation of the Environmental Protection Act to date—ultimately resulting in $7 million in fines and penalties, as well, undoubtedly, as untold losses occasioned through marketing delays pending investigation and compliance. Yet, according to Business Week's executive compensation survey, the second and third highest paid executives in the United States in that year were Ford Chairman Henry Ford II ($887,795, up 27.4 percent over 1971) and Ford President Lee Iacocca ($873,852, up 27.1 percent over 1971).[7] It went still higher in 1973.[8] Does anyone really believe that their pay will be cut, or in any way impacted by these events, in 1974 or 1975? I am not aware of any serious sustained shareholder movement to oust a major corporation's management in the wake of *any* lawsuit—antitrust, environment, or bad product.

Granted, to the extent the most influential managers of the corporation are not just salaried, but also holders of common shares, or of option plans to purchase shares, their personal calculations fall more in line with those of the shareholders. Even then, however, it does not follow that there is a "unity" of their interests and the interests of "the corporation" (referring to some mix of interest of common shareholders, creditors, employees, and bondholders). One would have to know more about their relative sources of income. Consider, for example, a high-level executive of a pharmaceutical house, who is also a shareholder, and is charged with developing and marketing a new "miracle" drug. Certainly, both as manager and shareholder he hopes that the drug will not turn out to be dangerous. But he has two sets of calculations that are not congruent. As employee, he may feel that his success in getting the drug to market before his competitor does could result in his being promoted from a $40,000-a-year slot to a $100,000-a-year slot; over ten years' time, that would be a gain to him of $600 thousand. If the drug proves dangerous, his risks on the "down side" are probably little more than having to remain in his present slot for a few years longer. The balance of possible gains on this magnitude are quite likely to overshadow a distant and contingent unrealized "loss" of, say, twenty-five cents a share on five thousand shares if the drug turns out to do widespread damage and the company is sued.

This problem would persist in some degree even if management's shareholdings were so significant that they approached asymptotically the interests of the other common shareholders. The point to keep in mind here is that if one dissects "the corporation" closely, one finds "its" interests to be the product of many vectors: the interests of the bondholders, trade creditors, shareholders, employees, and others. The interest of the holders of common shares typically lies on the side of taking greater risks than any of the others. For example, the holder of $1 million in 6 percent corporate bonds will make $60,000 per year, whether the company grosses $60,000 or $600 million. On the other hand, he can lose his entire investment if the company gets in very serious trouble. This makes the interests of the bondholders especially conservative—that is, inclined against high-risk endeavors. In other words, if the choice is whether to market a new drug that can make the corporation millions—but if it is defective cost it millions in damage suits—the bondholders are more apt than the common shareholders to prefer that the marketing be delayed pending further research. The shareholders, on the other hand, are not only typically venturing someone else's capital ("leveraging"), but they have a technical claim on everything that the corporation makes over and above what it owes its creditors. Again, this does not mean the common shareholders want the corporation to get involved in an enterprise that will lead to the corporation suffering legal losses. But to the common shareholders, the possibility of making a $10 million profit balanced against a fifty-fifty chance of getting caught up in a $100 million lawsuit, may look far more "worth the risks" than it does to others with an interest in the corporation. Thus, even assuming a top management that has, through its own ownership of stock or options to buy stock, a bias that is increasingly congruent with that of its common shareholders, there is no reason blithely to suppose that a threat reasonably calculated to make lawbreaking a poor bargain for "the corporation" will change management's calculations in the direction the society desires.

Then, too, we have thus far been going along with the textbook notion that the top executives, in *their* decisions, are "rational" economic calculators. This assumption is as simpleminded as its counterpart regarding the corporation as a whole. To the extent that the individual managers are concerned about carrying out technology to its "logical" and dramatic limits, or being associated with a prestigious, expanding, product-innovating company, the law's money threats are not only economically uncompelling, they aren't even striking at some of the critical motivations to begin with.

## A Bigger Stick?

Of course, there are ways to increase the risks of lawbreaking. Fines can be raised. Instead of holding the corporation liable for the damages it causes, we can hold it liable for double or treble the damages. We can provide more public funds for enforcement of corporation-aimed laws, thereby increasing the chances that offenders will get caught. Disapproved behavior, in other words, can be made a worse and worse bargain for the offender. In this way, if the ordinary corporation is not so purely profit-sensitive that it will make the desired changes in the face of threats geared to an economically rational profit calculator, why not just escalate to whatever level it takes to get through the corporate skin? They may not be economically "rational," but no one says they are economically crazy either.

There is some validity to this response. And I most certainly agree that fines against corporations for many criminal violations should be raised. This seems so obvious, and flows so clearly from what has been said, that it needs no elaboration. But it is by no means the panacea that one may suppose.

The first problem with upping the ante indefinitely is the evident political one—that legislatures are not inclined to come down hard on their corporate constituents. And even if we can get beyond the political resistance, there arises to haunt us a host of lingering doctrinal problems. That is to say, although the theoretical objections on proceeding against corporations have largely faded, the vestiges of those early concerns that persist to this day—sometimes in the form of doctrine and sometimes, more subtly, as a judicial attitude—have especially continuing viability just whenever we try to get tough. The incredible legacy of these developments is to leave the corporation in less fear of the law than an individual engaged in the same course of conduct.

As just one example of the lingering doctrinal protection that

corporations get, as recently as 1961 a corporation whose dynamite-laden truck exploded, killing a passerby, managed to have
a manslaughter indictment thrown out on the grounds that it
was not a "person."[9] A manslaughter indictment against the
People's Natural Gas Company was similarly quashed in Pennsylvania in 1954.[10] This particular absurdity is not universal, and
might indeed be a blessing in disguise if, by taking off the corporation a pressure that is in all events somewhat illusory (it
cannot go to prison and the fines for manslaughter are minimal),
it forced public authorities to push their investigation a little
farther and discover what "key" individuals were responsible,
bringing manslaughter indictments against them. But we shall
see that the latter rarely happens.

Another vestige that works to the corporation's advantage involves the conceptual basis on which liability is sometimes rested.
There is a certain amount of doctrine suggesting that to hold a
corporation liable, it is not enough to show that "the corporation"
(somehow) committed a wrong. The plaintiff must connect the
wrongful conduct and prove the wrongful act, and, when appropriate, wrongful mental states of some particular individual
employees.[11] This conception is understandable considering the
way in which the law developed. The theoretical objections to
corporate wrongdoing were generally "solved" by imputing to the
corporation the wrongs of a particular employee; in other words,
if a carriage driver, the agent, committed a tort in the course of
his employment, the wrong was imputed to his master, the principal. In time, people reasoned that even if the corporation had
no mind, and could not therefore *will* wrongdoing, it was nonetheless the employer (principal) of human beings who could will
wrongdoing, and the corporation could be liable on master-
servant principles without having to perform a metaphysical
inquiry into "its" mind. Resting liability on this basis makes sense,
and is easy to invoke in the small, technically straightforward corporation, where it is easy to discover who the particular wrongful
agent was. But as corporations grow more complex, trying to
bind them with rules that grew up around the traditional master-
servant situation leaves troublesome gaps in law enforcement.

Suppose, for example, the case of an electric utility company that maintains a nuclear power plant. We can readily imagine that there might be knowledge of physics, evidence of radiation leakage, information regarding temperature variations, data related to previous operation runs in this and other plants, which, *if gathered in the mind of one single person*, would make his continued operation of that plant, without a shutdown, wanton and reckless—that is, if an explosion resulted, strong civil and criminal liability could and would be brought to bear on him—and/or, by the process of imputation described above, on his corporate principal.

But let us suppose what is more likely to be the case in modern corporate America: that the information and acts are distributed among many different employees engaged in various functional groups within the corporation. The nuclear engineer can be charged with a bit of information, *a*, the architect knows *b*, the night watchman knows *c*, the research scientist task force knows *d*. Conceivably there will not be any single individual who has, in and of himself, such knowledge and intent as will support a charge against him individually. (Indeed, all the fragments of knowledge that, in the aggregate, would support an action might exist only in the "mind" of the company's computer.) Thus, where corporate liability is based upon imputing to the corporation the wrongs of its agents, the corporation is less subject to the law than would be a single individual doing the same thing.

Fortunately, the law has evolved in such a way that escape from liability on such grounds is of increasingly limited effect where ordinary damage recoveries, suited to qualifiedly disfavored conduct and the redistribution of losses, are concerned.[12] But when, in an effort to decrease the conduct further, we seek to superimpose on the actual damages a criminal fine or special civil penalties, the ancient concerns rise up very much a part of the law. The New York Penal Law, for example, holds corporations criminally liable only when

The conduct constituting the offense is engaged in, authorized, solicited, requested, commanded, or recklessly tolerated by the *board of directors* or by a *high managerial agent* acting within the scope of his employment and in behalf of the corporation.[13]

That is to say, the law goes even beyond demanding proof of wrongdoing of *any* corporate agent, and insists on a connection (proved by a preponderance of the evidence) with someone fairly high up in the corporate hierarchy. This may be harder to do than first seems. Directors and high-up officers of corporations (like higher-ups of other institutions of state) could not know of everything their organization was doing even if they tried—and often, preferring not to know, they arrange patterns of reporting so they cannot find out (or, at least, if they do find out, they find out only in such a way that it can never be proved).

This lingering influence of the early doctrines operates with a similar result when someone tries to assess corporations for punitive or exemplary damages. Here, too, the corporation emerges enjoying what we might call a "preferred position" as wrongdoer.

The problem arises this way. Often in the law, when an actor has harmed another not merely through his negligence, but through "willful or wanton," or "morally culpable" conduct, the courts in a civil action brought by the injured party go beyond an award of ordinary damages, designed to compensate the injured man for his injuries; the action being regarded as, in my terms, "unqualifiedly disfavored," they superimpose above that sum certain punitive or exemplary damages, the design of which is to fulfill some of the functions of a criminal suit—most significantly, to deter such conduct in the future. As other early qualms about corporate liability were reduced, those regarding punitive damages maintained themselves in several areas. Even today the state courts are quite divided on whether they still allow exemplary damages against corporations, and the federal rule limits such recoveries sharply, forcing the plaintiff to identify particular executives who participated in the wrongdoing.[14]

Granted, doctrinal considerations per se need not haunt us: Why not peel away these old legalistic qualms the way we did the others? The answer is that these lingering protections of the corporation are not likely to be abolished readily, for the sentiments that keep them alive reflect, in large measure, considerations that have a certain amount of appeal. The most sobering evidence of this is that even where the technical barriers to stiff measures against corporations have been removed, and the case against a corporate defendant is horrifying, the company may be let off light anyway. The recent Roginsky case is a particularly illuminating illustration of this.[15]

The facts, briefly, are these.[16] Richardson-Merrell is the pharmaceutical company that had distributed thalidomide in the United States, the drug that, when taken by expectant mothers, caused numerous stillborn and deformed children. In the 1950s it began to develop a drug called MER/29, which it believed had high promise of repressing cholesterol. While its top officers were enthusing about the drug, and preparing for a major marketing campaign, other parts of the organization were receiving bad news. In one laboratory test all the female rats on a high dosage died within six weeks. In a subsequent test, all rats on a somewhat lower dosage had to be destroyed halfway through the experiment. On autopsy, it was revealed that they had suffered abnormal blood changes. Corneal opacities were observed in other animals. Monkeys suffered blood changes and weight loss. But, as the California Court of Appeals later explained, a lower-level executive simply ordered the lab technician "to falsify a chart of this test by recording false body weights for the monkeys, by extending their records beyond dates after which the monkeys had been killed, and by adding data for an imaginary monkey that had never been in the test group at all." When the technician protested to her immediate superior, she was told: "He [the executive] is higher up. You do as he tells you and be quiet."

When the company finally filed a new drug application with the FDA, seeking permission to place MER/29 on the market, its application contained "many false statements," among them "that only four out of eight rats had died during a certain study, whereas in truth all had died"; and that "wholly fictitious body and organ weights and also blood tests were reported for dead rats as if they had continued to live and to take MER/29."

If this sounds incredible, it also turns out that in January 1960 Richardson-Merrell completed another study, in which nine out of ten rats developed eye opacities. The company reported to the FDA that eight out of twenty rats had developed mild inflammation of the eye. A month later the company completed a long-term test of the drug used in rats. Of thirty-six test rats in this group, twenty-five developed eye opacities. The results, like all the adverse results, were withheld from the FDA.

In April 1960 the FDA granted Richardson-Merrell's application to market MER/29. The drug was not on the market long before evidence of alarming symptoms began to come to Richardson-Merrell's attention. It was almost all intercepted at various levels of the corporation and not turned over to the FDA. Denials and whitewashing of the drug continued until, in May 1962, its dangers had become so generally evidenced that the FDA ordered it withdrawn. In that two-year marketing period, however, 400,000 people had taken it. In the first year alone it added $7 million to Richardson-Merrell's gross sales.

Approximately five hundred of those who had taken the drug developed cataracts. One of these was a man named Roginsky, who had begun dosages in February 1961. By June he noticed scaling, rashes, and falling hair, which he reported to his doctor. Despite treatment, the conditions became aggravated. Around the end of the year, he noted disturbing eye symptoms, which became cataracts. Subsequently, in a suit against Richardson-Merrell, the jury awarded Roginsky compensatory damages of $17,500 and punitive damages of $100,000. In California, in the parallel litigation quoted from above, $500,000 punitive damages were allowed a victim of the drug on the grounds that there was evidence from which the jury could infer that

responsible corporate officials, at least up to the level of vice-president, had knowledge of the true test results of MER/29 when used in animals, and that some, or all, joined in a policy of nondisclosure of this information to the Food and Drug Administration and the medical profession.

But on appeal of Roginsky's case to the U. S. Court of Appeals for the Second Circuit, Judge Henry Friendly, while agreeing that Richardson-Merrell's liability had been proven, observed that the possibilities of multiple punitive awards "on the part of hundreds of plaintiffs are staggering," and added that if insurance wasn't available to keep the company whole,

A sufficiently egregious error as to one product can end the business life of a concern that has wrought much good in the past and might otherwise have continued to do so in the future, with many innocent stockholders suffering extinction of their investments for a single management sin.[17]

Thus, although punitive damages might technically have been allowable under the law, the implications "in a case like the present" were deemed too serious.

Wherever the reasoning represented by Judge Friendly's opinion prevails, the net result is that the most a "reckless" corporation stands to lose from civil suits is the sum of the injuries provable against it; the extra measure of the deterrence that exemplary damages afford against wanton and reckless human beings is not applied as consistently where the "egregious error" is that of a corporation. This loophole is even more significant than may at first appear, because to the corporation, the true impact of punitive damages makes them far more to be feared than ordinary damages. A company can obtain insurance to "level" the cost of settling ordinary damage claims, but cannot as a rule insure against liability from wanton negligence (or from crimes: in a criminal suit for making false statements to the FDA Richardson-Merrell pleaded no contest and was fined a paltry $80,000).[18] Similarly, ordinary damage settlements may be used to reduce taxes as "an ordinary cost of business," but punitive damage awards are not so easily passed back to the government.[19]

From one point of view, the situation seems ludicrous. But I am not very sanguine about the law changing very much in these regards. For the reservations such as Judge Friendly expresses reflect traditions that are deeply rooted in our society: There is something that seems fundamentally unfair (and unproductive) about taking action that seemingly falls upon the wrong people—the shareholders and consuming public—rather than whatever team of unseen bureaucrats really "did it."*

---

* Friendly, one of the nation's most respected jurists, took a similar position in the litigation that arose out of the *Texas Gulf Sulphur* affair. True, the corporation had issued a misleading press release, down-playing a fantastic copper find in Canada; and true, many investors, misled, had suffered. But the magnitude of possible recovery against the corporation was "frightening," and such judgments, if allowed, would be "payable in

I do not mean to suggest that the shift to bad-bargain strategy in selected areas is not possible, or even likely. But there is, I think something of a theorem we must recognize, that our *counter-organizational measures will always be skewed toward fair-bargain strategy and away from bad-bargain strategy*, more so in the case of the corporation than of the human being. That is, we will incline to make the punishment "fit the crime" in the sense of collecting damages, or depriving the corporation of its unjust enrichment—its ill-got gains—rather than to make it "fit the crime" in the more severe sense of making the action a dreaded risk in the future. Exceptions will occur only in a narrow band of the most highly visible, unqualifiedly disapproved conduct. And even where legislators make severe penalties possible, courts and administrative agencies, in invoking them (absent repeated violations, and sometimes even in the face of repeated violations), are going to be inclined to employ their discretion in such a fashion that even criminal fines will ordinarily be administered in the more lenient, "fair-bargain" spirit.

Thus, the overall picture is that our strategies aimed to control corporations by threatening their profits are a very limited way of bringing about the internal changes that are necessary if the policies behind the law are to be effectuated. Indeed, I would go so far as to suggest that those who deplore "the fact" that corporations are motivated solely by profit are not only wrong, but missing an important point. The problem the society is having with modern American corporations is probably not so much that they are profit-oriented as that they are in fact operating subject to a number of less easily identified nonprofit goals, as well. If they were profit-oriented pure and simple, then it would be much easier to control them than it is. We could just reform the law to assure that the social costs of their actions were brought to bear on them. As things are, however, bringing to bear on them the "costs" of their behavior, and even a lot more than the costs of their behavior, is no guarantee that they will respond as we should like.

---

the last analysis by innocent investors," the very people the Securities Acts were established to protect. *S.E.C.* v. *Texas Gulf Sulphur*, 401 F. 2d 833 (2d. Cir. 1968), concurring opinion.

# 7. Measures Aimed at "Key" Individuals

As long ago as 1910, Woodrow Wilson observed:

You cannot punish corporations. Fines fall upon the wrong persons; more heavily upon the innocent than upon the guilty; as much upon those who knew nothing whatever of the transactions for which the fine is imposed as upon those who originated and carried them through —upon the stockholders and the customers rather than upon the men who direct the policy of the business. If you dissolve the offending corporation, you throw great undertakings out of gear. You merely drive what you are seeking to check into other forms or temporarily disorganize some important business altogether, to the infinite loss of thousands of entirely innocent persons and to the great inconvenience of society as a whole. Law can never accomplish its objects in that way. It can never bring peace or command respect by such futilities.[1]

On first blush, the solution Wilson offered—"to give the law direct access again to the individual,—to every individual in all his functions" smacks of perfect good sense. But the anti-individual approach holds far less promise than one might first suppose, and may even, in some areas, do more harm than good.

The measures that we raise against the individual employee are of two sorts. First, he faces—in theory—the possibility of direct civil and criminal liability. The Sherman Anti-Trust Act, for example, is in its terms as applicable to individuals as it is to corporations. Theoretically, too, a person whose own part in the manufacture of a product is negligent could be liable equally with his corporate employer. Second, the highest-level management, the directors in particular, can be made liable for law violations in a slightly indirect way—by having to repay the corporation out of their own pockets for failure to steer it clear of serious losses. Suppose, for example, that the corporation has engaged in price-fixing; the government brings a criminal suit against it, imposing a fine of, say, $50,000; subsequently private civil actions are brought against the corporation, arising out of the same wrongful price-fixing, and to settle these the corporation is forced to pay out $1 million more. At this point, a shareholder can bring suit on behalf of the corporation against the directors (called a shareholder's derivative suit) not on the theory that they were directly engaged in the price-fixing, but on the theory that their failure to exercise due care and attention to corporate affairs allowed the wrongful activity to take place. If the suit were fully successful, the directors would have to reimburse the corporation for the $1,050,000 it had had to lay out.

But while both sorts of actions are possible in theory, realistically they are apt to have much less impact than one would suspect. As for the actions for direct wrongdoing, there is, to begin with, the problem noted earlier, that a good number of corporation-caused injuries are traceable most immediately to lower-level workers who are not ordinarily worth suing. Second, even where wrongs could be traced to a higher-echelon, more solvent officer, who cares? In almost all cases, inasmuch as the corporation, as his principal, will be liable too, the injured person will proceed against the corporation rather than go to the trouble of identifying the particular individual responsible and trying to collect against him. More than this, all lawyers know that if they sue an officer in his own name, he will fight like hell in a settlement proceeding; the money he is being asked to pay comes from his own pocket. But when he is settling on behalf of the corporation, he can and will be more pliable; the money he is settling with is the company's, not his own.

Essentially, then—putting the derivative actions aside for a moment—when we speak about putting legal pressure on corporate employees, we are considering the possibility only in a narrow range of actions, in suits brought by the government almost always criminal, or criminal-like (civil penalties), in nature.

This is quite significant, because while some of the most objectionable forms of wrongdoing are technically criminal—bribery of officials, price-fixing, manufacture and shipment of a highly dangerous product—a great many of the desiderata of corporate behavior are not worked into the criminal law, and probably could not be. For example, neither under present law nor under any imaginable future criminal law is some executive apt to go to jail for actions that lead to a defective product, that adversely affect life-style, employee dignity, or the environment—or for failure to develop a pollution-free engine. Thus, when we talk about regulating corporations through strategies aimed at key individuals, we are considering measures likely to be invoked (if at all) only for the most blatant sorts of acts—which are not necessarily those with the most adverse impact on society.

And even in this narrow range of possible cases that remains there arises, almost at once, a particularly frustrating fact. Ideally, one would want to apply legal pressure to people fairly high up in, if not at the very top of, the corporate hierarchy; for it is they who can most likely effect a change in corporate direction. But it is men exactly at these levels toward whom the threats of the law may be most hollow. There are several reasons for this.

First, there is the problem of the limited knowledge that those at the top have—and feasibly can be expected to gather. Some heads of giant concerns, like Andrea Olivetti, may be able to support a legend of knowing everything that is happening within their organization. But for the most part, men at the highest levels will be involved almost to the full extent of their day with major investment and financial decisions, personnel and budget matters, and long-range policy planning. Insofar as they are concerned with operations, they serve not as institutors or implementors of policy, but as reviewers, mediating claims and proposals that arise from lower corporate levels. Such a function does not acquaint them with day-to-day detail on pollution emission controls, product design data, and the like. For this reason, most management of high enough level to be visible to, and potential targets for the law are not likely to be familiar enough with wrongful corporate activities to be tainted with the mental states and actions that, combined, comprise the elements of various crimes. True, this varies considerably with the particular wrongful activity being considered. Certain white-collar crimes, especially those connected with financial manipulations, do take place not only under the direction of, but almost completely in the hands of, a discrete number of fairly high-up individuals. That is why financial manipulations result in occasional criminal conviction of top-echelon officers. Similarly, if the government were so minded, such matters as wrongful political contributions could result in criminal convictions, inasmuch as such acts can be traced to identifiable heads and identifiable hands—with due prosecutorial diligence. But consider the range of problems presented by corporations that are of particular interest to most people today, and that are, or feasibly might be made, criminal: the worst consumer and pollution abuses, for example. In an enormously complex organization, the responsibility for the acts that, say, brought to market a defective car or tainted meat are apt to be widely spread among many men—and machines. Note that this is true even when we are speaking of the ascription of "responsibility" in the ordinary, moral use of the term; to assign responsibility *legally* is all the harder, especially in criminal actions, where the burden of proof lies particularly favorable to the defendant.

Second, men at the top of the corporation are "protected" from incriminating evidence not only through the abstractness of their own affairs, but on account of the natural screening of "bad news" referred to earlier: everyone in the organization simply knows that the executives above a certain level "don't want to hear about" the fact that tests on a promising new drug are producing cataracts in laboratory animals, or that a brake is burning out in trial runs, or that next year's model automobile has a tendency to roll over. It is not that the underlings *lie* (a concept that is entirely inadequate to capture the nuances of misleading corporate communications) but that the underlings know that if some tests are not proving the drug, brakes, auto, to be satisfactory, new tests just sure as hell ought to be designed that prove they do work—or someone had better find some way to fix them.

Third, information does not get to the top for another reason—not because of the "natural" screening processes alone, but because the law itself often results in the systematic insulation of top-level officers from information of possible wrongdoing. There are a number of reasons for this. We saw earlier that the corporation's criminal and punitive damage liability may hinge upon whether or not some top-level officer ratified or even knew about the wrongful acts. Thus, a desire to protect the corporation would be reason enough systematically to screen the top executives from potentially incriminating information. But the stronger reason is that the top-level executive himself is afraid of legal trouble, and the organization banks on the unwritten hope that "what he doesn't know cannot hurt him." This, indeed, is certainly one of the most significantly counterproductive features of our present law. Ideally, we would want those with most power in the corporation to be most sensitive to areas of possible wrongdoing; but in fact, the law positively discourages this very awareness.

Let me illustrate this absurdity in the context of shareholder derivative actions, referred to earlier. Top officers and directors face the possibility of suit by the corporation itself (at the instance of a shareholder) if they have negligently allowed some law violation to take place. Theoretically, the threat of such actions should provide incentive for the directors to keep the corporation within the law. But what happens in practice is typified by the following. After the celebrated antitrust suits in the electrical equipment industry, a shareholder of Allis-Chalmers, one of the convicted companies, brought an action against the directors on the theory that their failure to exercise due care and attention to the corporate affairs had allowed the crimes to take place, and that they ought especially to have been on notice in the light of earlier antitrust troubles the company had gotten into some years before. In dismissing the claim the Delaware Supreme Court said:

The precise charge made against these director defendants is that, even though they had no knowledge of any suspicion of wrongdoing on the part of the company's employees, they still should have put into effect a system of watchfulness which would have brought such misconduct to their attention in ample time to have brought it to an end. . . . On the contrary, it appears that directors are entitled to rely on the honesty and integrity of their subordinates until something occurs to put them on suspicion that something is wrong. If such occurs and goes' unheeded, then liability of the directors might well follow, but *absent cause for suspicion there is no duty upon the directors to install and operate a corporate system of espionage to ferret out wrongdoing which they have no reason to suspect exists.*

The duties of the Allis-Chalmers Directors were fixed by the nature of the enterprise which employed in excess of 30,000 persons, and extended over a large geographical area. By force of necessity, the company's Directors could not know personally all the company's employees. The very magnitude of the enterprise required them to · confine their control to the broad policy decisions.[2]

Such reasoning has two negative ramifications. It both vitiates the possibility of derivative actions in this area (successful instances of holding directors liable for allowing law violations, although theoretically possible, virtually never occur) and also reinforces the practice of keeping the top management insulated from the very details the society might most want them to *have to hear*—and do something about.

Fourth, the higher one goes in the corporate hierarchy to find someone worth pressuring, the more he runs into a series of hurdles other than the technical standards of proof: considerations of "fairness," and jury and court attitudes toward corporate officers, for example. In cases of "white-collar" crime, the prosecution finds itself trying to convict church-going, well-dressed, well-spoken, community leaders—men not apt to be judged harshly, except in the most extreme cases where responsibility and bad faith are unmistakable (the salad oil swindle, the Billy Sol Estes matter, perhaps the present Equity Funding scandal). Even in the infrequent cases in which someone is convicted, our present social attitudes are apt to leave the offenders off light. The Richardson-Merrell case was unusual in that criminal charges against three of the employees were even brought at all; but typical in that, once guilt was established, instead of the five years in prison and $10,000 fine that the defendants could have received, they were placed on six months' probation. Prison sentences are rare, and reserved for the headline-grabbing wrongs only. Recently, in one of the largest—if not the largest—embezzlement case ever prosecuted by the federal government, one

Lamar B. Hill, former director and president of the First National Bank of Cartersville, Georgia, was sentenced to ten years for embezzling $4,611,473.35. This is an amount that comes, in the *Wall Street Journal's* calculations, to about $400 for every man, woman, and child in Cartersville. At the close of the article, Neil Maxwell, the *Journal* reporter who followed the proceedings observed:

One thing that showed up starkly at yesterday's sentencing session is the differing penalties for conventional crimes and the white collar variety Mr. Hill chose. Just before he got 10 years for massive embezzlement, three young men who had stolen $13,834 from the Tunnel Hill branch of the First National Bank of Balton, Ga., were sentenced. Though they took less than 1% of what Mr. Hill was accused of taking, they were sentenced to 16 years each—more than half again the sentence Mr. Hill got.[3]

Indeed, even the sentence is hardly the true measure of how much time each of these offenders will spend in prison. One is tempted to venture that when parole is being considered, Mr. Hill, called by the wife of the pastor of the local church "the best president that's ever been in the First National Bank," is likely to meet far more sympathetic consideration than the three bank robbers.

Fifth, even if some of the attitudes referred to above did change—that is, even if courts and juries were to take a more indignant view of misfeasance and nonfeasance by corporate officers—it is still not at all clear that the threat of the law would be effective.

For one thing, it would not mean that the individual "wrongdoers" were really going to bear the final brunt of the fines and judgment. The first way around the law is through indemnification: The company simply reimburses the officer (with the stockholders' money). General Motors, for example, indemnifies all its directors and officers "against any and all judgments, fines, amounts paid in settlements and reasonable expenses, including attorneys fees, incurred by him in connection with" any claim whatsoever.[4] True, indemnification is not available in the case of the criminal proceeding where the man convicted "had . . . reasonable cause to believe that his conduct was unlawful." But the Corporate By-Laws go on to provide an immediate hedge: the conviction "shall not in itself create a presumption" of bad faith, and if an "independent legal counsel" writes an opinion that the officers or director "acted in good faith for a purpose which he reasonably believed to be in the best interests of the corporation . . . and . . . had no reasonable cause to believe that his conduct was unlawful" he is entitled to indemnification as of right! What is more, even in those cases in which indemnification may be unavailable, how does one prevent a corporation from reimbursing a director or officer his $5,000 or $10,000 fine in other ways—by "bonuses" or delayed raises?

In fact, for a broad variety of wrongs top executives might get involved with, the corporation can take out directors' and officers' liability insurance on their behalf, the premiums to be paid for by the corporation. The new Delaware Corporation Code—the bellwether for other corporation codes across the country—specifically empowers corporations to purchase and maintain insurance against such liability for their executives "whether or not the corporation would have the power to indemnify [them] against such liability under the provisions" of the rest of the Delaware law.[5] The new law seems, in other words, an invitation to corporations to give executives insurance protection that goes even beyond the increasingly lax indemnification standards. If even criminal fines are going to be "passed on" by executives to someone else, then short of a radical increase in imprisonment of executives—not too realistic a threat as regards most sorts of corporate wrongdoing—the strategies aimed at key individuals are apt to be of only limited deterrence value.

And, indeed, though no one should underestimate the impact increased jailings *would* have on executives, let me just observe that by itself, even jailings would not guarantee significant changes in corporate direction. The very nature of a bureaucracy, as Weber so well demonstrated, is to make the *individual dispensable*. So long as the functioning of some particular office is not altered, and so long as there are not attendant changes in the design and structure of the balance of the organization, some wrongful acts would persist even after particular "responsible" individuals had been removed to prison—and another absorbed into his place in the system.

It is tempting to suppose that the difficulties of keeping corporations within desirable bounds through threats aimed at key individuals owes to unrealistic legal policies that could be eliminated by reform. One might, for example, suppose that if we did away with indemnification, and abolished directors' and officers' liability insurance, we would increase the effectiveness of the law. It has been suggested that some of the problems would disappear if we changed the elements of liability, allowing conviction of a corporate executive without having to prove his actual formulation, ratification, or awareness of the crime, so long as the evidence showed "that by the exercise of reasonable care [the defendant] could have discovered and prevented the crime."[6]

For my part, I am skeptical that reforms of such sort, even if they were feasible politically, would go very far toward shoring up the effectiveness of the antipersonnel strategies. The point is that the "shortcomings" of our present system owe not simply to legislators and judges being "soft" on corporate criminals (although that is part of it); much of the reason lies in a fundamental sense of fairness and practicality that runs throughout the law, and that dictates we be reluctant to hold liable someone who we cannot feel is really "to blame." This is an especially effective consideration when emerging forms of antitrust, environment, and securities liabilities could make directors of major corporations personally liable for literally millions of dollars in damages. As a result, even under existing liability rules, the stakes have just gotten too high for courts and juries to invoke the law to the fullest. From this point of view the Delaware Supreme Court in its decision in *Graham* v. *Allis-Chalmers* was not being merely promanagement when, having recited the enormity and complexity of Allis-Chalmers, it observed that "it is not practicable for the Board to consider in detail specific problems of the various divisions," that is, the prices being set by the power equipment division. Putting aside the gratuitous stuff about directors having "no duty . . . to install and operate a corporate system of espionage," the court was being practical and it was being—in a fundamental way—moral. If we are to design legal strategies that will be implemented and effective (and if we want men of any ability and sense to serve on boards) the law is going to have to be both those things.

Let me close this review of antipersonnel strategies with one final observation on a matter that, though intangible, pervades all the problems of this chapter. The law is only one force among many, one vector tugging on those who labor within an organization. Its success ultimately depends upon its consistency with and reinforcement from the other vectors—the organization's rules for advancement and reward, its customs, conventions, and morals. If the law is too much at odds with these other forces, its threats will make the employees more careful to cover their tracks before it makes them alter their institutionally supportive behavior.[7] This is a problem faced by the law not just when it competes for the allegiance of those in a corporation or in the White House. In any social grouping, it is doubtful how effective legal threats can be as an instrument of social change, especially when the behavior to be changed has "customary" support within the group, involves means condoned (or at least not strongly condemned) by the larger community, and does not result in injuries that the individual actors can clearly and vividly connect with their own behavior. Some of the necessary features are conspicuously lacking where much of corporate wrongdoing is concerned, a point that was noted by the sociologist E. A. Ross as early as the turn of the century. He saw a "new modern sin" being ushered in by corporations, sin that was not "superficially repulsive" and lacked "the familiar tokens of guilt."

The stealings and slayings that lurk in the complexities of our social relations are not deeds of the dive, the dark alley, the lonely road, and the midnight hour. They require no nocturnal prowling with muffled step and bated breath, no weapon or offer of violence. . . . The modern high-powered dealer of woe wears immaculate linen, carries a silk hat and a lighted cigar, sins with a serene soul, leagues or months from the evil he causes. . . .

. . . The hurt passes into that vague mass, the "public," and is there lost to view. Hence it does not take a Borgia to knead "chalk and alum and plaster" into the loaf, seeing one cannot know just who will eat that loaf, or what gripe it will give him. . . . The owner of rotten tenement houses, whose "pull" enables him to ignore the orders of the health department, foredooms babies, it is true, but for all that he is no Herod.

Often there are no victims. If the crazy hulk sent out for "just one more trip" meets with fair weather, all is well. If no fire breaks out in the theater, the sham "emergency exits" are blameless. The corrupt inspector who O.K.'s low-grade kerosene is chancing it, that is all. Many sins, in fact, simply augment the risk. Evil does not dog their footsteps with relentless and heart-shaking certainty. When the catastrophe does come, the sinner salves his conscience by blasphemously calling it an "accident" or an "act of God."[8]

In such circumstances, the law may be *there*, but it lacks the persuasiveness, reality, and immediacy of the other, competing aspects of the employee's environment. Consider, as a contemporary example, the scandal involving Equity Funding. Its life insurance subsidiary (Equity Funding Life Insurance Co.) had been reporting over $3 billion total life insurance in force, of which $2 billion worth (representing $25.4 million annual premiums) turned out to be bogus. The company's whole way of doing business had almost guaranteed that it would be continually cash-hungry. To get the cash it needed, Equity found itself making up nonexistent human beings, writing policies on them, and selling (ceding) the policies on the nonexistent persons to other companies. Without getting deeply involved in the mechanics of how all this was carried out, and how more than $20 million of assets "vanished," let me just observe that this is not a case of a fraud achieved by one or two insiders working secretly in a top-floor office. Keeping the auditors, stockholders, purchasers of "policies," and others in the dark required—and got—the cooperation of the entire organization. According to the *Wall Street Journal*, the scheme had "long been known around the company as 'the y business' or as 'department 99.' It was widely talked about in offices and corridors. 'It even became a joke, a game,' says one former official. 'People laughed and laughed about it.' "[9] To effectuate and conceal the scheme took "teams of employees [who] worked after hours forging policy files that the auditors had requested, and others posed as policy holders when the auditors tried to confirm the existence of business that was bogus." As the volume of bogus business increased dramatically, "it would have been physically impossible to dummy up enough [policy files] to cover all the fictitious policies. Nevertheless, [Equity] had managed to keep the auditors at bay with an in-house institution—the forgery party." When the auditors showed up asking for files to cross-check against the premium receipts, "that night a half dozen to a dozen employees would sit down to forge the missing ones so they could be ready the next day. 'It takes a long time, and you have to be careful about date stamps and other details,' says one participant, who says he did it once to find out what was going on. 'But I had fun being the doctor, giving the guy's blood pressure and all that.' "[10]

The point is that in this environment of fun, excitement, and do-as-you're-told corporate loyalty, the law's threats are simply no guarantee that people are going to comply. Indeed, what is worse, I have a strong suspicion—shared by others who have represented corporate clients in their tangled affairs—that being on the edges of the law can even lend a tingle of 007 intrigue to the life of middle-level corporate operatives. Surely, if corporations are to be kept honest, the law should be prepared to close in, wherever feasible, on key personnel. But more often than one might suppose, our threats will be hollow—and far less than the solutions required. What these more effective solutions are, I want to hold in abeyance for a moment until I have looked at the problem from a slightly different angle.

# III

## The Corporate Social Responsibility Debate

The problems that corporations pose for our society are subtle, complex, enormous. Yet the "solutions" that are offered so often seem vague, limp, and visionary. For years in this country the movement for corporate reform rallied around the notion of "shareholder democracy," as though to suppose that the common shareholders, if only they could be reinstated to their control over the management, would exorcise all the practices that had been lining their pocketbooks. From time to time we see a revival of the notion that "the corporation problem" would wither and die if only we had federal corporate charters and/or publicly elected representatives to boards of directors. None of these ideas is entirely vacuous, and all might be worth implementing, as I shall show. But no one who has taken the time really to think through the functions of corporate charters or of the board of directors can seriously suppose that either institution can be so shaped as to bring under control, even marginally, the vast majority of corporate problems that people are complaining about.*

---

* For example, while I have a good deal of sympathy with the aims of those who advocate federal charters, what is written in a corporation's charter plays a very limited role in regulating most corporate activity today; most of the regulations to which corporations are subject are imposed through law, and any corporation that could be made subject to federal charter requirements is right now constitutionally amenable to ordinary

It is tempting to be similarly skeptical, even cynical, about the proposal that is being most widely espoused today: the notion that we must develop a higher degree of "corporate responsibility" and "corporate conscience." Bad enough that the notion is fuzzy. Even worse, it is transparently this very fuzziness that accounts for its broad consensus of support. The public at large, frustrated by the apparent inability of the law to bring corporations under rein, awed by the magnitude of the problems, baffled by the mystique that surrounds the inner workings and influence of corporations, will grasp at any promising scheme that sounds plausible and straightforward. For them, "corporate responsibility" offers to go to the heart of the matter—to bring about a decent economic order, springing not from the threats (lame threats) of the laws and of consumer pressure, but from the better potential of informed human judgment. For the businessman, his sense of purpose flagging after decades of public criticism for doing "nothing more than making money," corporate responsibility holds the promise of a renewed sense of mission, of repaired public relations—and it sounds like a more gossamer prod than fines and increased governmental intervention. For the students at the business schools, where the movement seems to have particularly active if not widespread support, the idea promises assuagement of similar career misgivings and gives *them* a chance to feel part of the social reform ethos that for some time has been brewing elsewhere on the campuses, on and off. If we are to look only at the face of the movement, corporate responsibility has all the promise of Saint George stalking the dragon with a PR campaign. It is "needed," its "time has come," but it is not certain what it is.

Even so, the notion of corporate social responsibility should not be put aside too readily. It is vague, true, and certainly will not be of much significance unless and until someone can define its scope and purpose with enough precision that its *spirit* can be translated into tangible institutional reform.

---

federal legislation. The advocates of federal chartering have to show that whatever they would accomplish via federal charters could not be accomplished directly by tougher federal laws.

But this can, I think, be done. And oddly, the best place to begin may be with a close examination of the arguments that have been raised against corporate social responsibility. Why *shouldn't* corporations be responsible, where to be responsible entails doing all the things the various "pro" responsibility groups advocate, for example, putting corporate resources—questions of profitability aside—toward repairing the environment, ameliorating racial tensions, improving the arts, advancing technology? Why, in sum, shouldn't corporations see their role as something above and beyond making money?

The questions are not, as they may sound, rhetorical. Those who oppose corporate social responsibility have provided answers to them, some of which are quite sensible. But in the last analysis, the opponents of corporate responsibility have been no more adequate in defining and confronting the really critical issues than the supporters. And if the current proresponsibility literature asks too much, or the wrong things, the antiresponsibility advocates as clearly ask, and their arguments prove, too little.

By clarifying what it is that each side is rightly concerned about, and identifying the relative strengths and weaknesses of their respective positions, one not only emerges with a better idea of what the "corporate responsibility" debaters are (or might be) arguing about. One also begins to stake out the areas in which some dynamic (still vaguely defined as corporate responsibility) is appropriate. And once the areas have been located—once we have identified these *functions* that we need some sort of corporate responsibility to perform—we can proceed to propose more concrete and appropriate measures than have yet been put forward.

# 8. What Exactly Are the "Antis" Against?

To begin with, let us merely observe that there is no real consensus among the opponents of corporate responsibility as to what, exactly, they are against corporations doing. There seem to be as many as four views in circulation.

First, there are any number of references in the literature suggesting that the corporate managers should not do anything other than maximize company profits (or, as it is sometimes put, "the return on shareholders' investments"). But if we take this position literally, it invites the corporation to calculate the financial costs and benefits of obeying the law against the costs and benefits of breaking it (discounting the risks of getting caught). A coal mining corporation may be able to maximize its profits by ignoring safety and health rules—and then bribing inspectors, tampering with monitoring tests and equipment, shredding or refusing to produce documents. For some period of time (until one of its workers was struck with moral qualms) Jones & Laughlin's Cleveland steel plant was saving itself the cost of effluent treatment, and yet avoiding fine under the Rivers and Harbors Act, by systematically dumping its effluents into the Cuyahoga River in the dead of night.[1] I sincerely doubt that the most hard-boiled "antiresponsibility" man wants to support such activity; thus, most people who claim that the "sole obligation of the corporation" is maximizing profits probably—or hopefully—mean to say "maximizing profits within the constraints of (at least most) laws."

According to this modified thesis, rather than have corporation managers decide how to resolve competing social claims, they follow the dictates of the market within the constraints of the law. If the majority of the people believe the law inadequate to keep corporations within socially desirable bounds, the society can, through its democratic processes, make more satisfactory—

tougher if need be—regulations. Unless and until it does so, however, we are all better off if corporations steer themselves by profit, rather than by their managers' various and vague personal notions of what is best for the society. So stated, there is a great deal that can be said for this modified thesis. Why, the advocates of this position might ask, should we have to augment market forces and legal duties with some nebulous demand that corporations be "responsible" in some sense over and above obeying the laws?

The question is a good one because it forces us to identify more clearly exactly in what areas, and in what ways, trust in the law is misplaced—an inquiry it is important to return to.

In the meantime, let me just continue my survey of the "antis'" view by observing that some of the people most closely identified in the public mind with the "pure profit" thesis (above) actually claim to be adherents of a third view, one that sounds quite different—more conventionally moral, in fact. But what this view is, is not entirely clear.

In *Capitalism and Freedom*, Milton Friedman does not quite state that the corporate officers' sole obligation is to maximize long-range profits; he adds that they should do so while "abiding by the rules of the game,"[2] a phrase which, though vague, he was fond enough of to repeat eight years later in a celebrated piece on corporate responsibility in the *New York Times*,[3] and three years after *that* in an interview in *Playboy*[4]—still without much in the way of elaboration. What does he mean by "the rules of the game"? He suggests in *Capitalism and Freedom* that it involves engagement "in open and free competition, without deception and fraud." But what does that rule out? If he means nothing more than that corporations should avoid *actionable* fraud and deceit, then he is simply an adherent of what we have called the "modified thesis"—stay within the law. Could, however, "rules of the game" have referred to some broader obligations than these— in effect, a second modified thesis?

The answer has to be "perhaps." In his celebrated *New York Times* article Friedman suggests at the beginning that the "responsibility" of business is "to make as much money as possible while conforming to the basic rules of society, both those em-

bodied in the law *and those embodied in ethical customs.*"⁵
Which ethical standards, one wonders, would management be
allowed to factor in over and above the demands of the law? And
in what cases? Unfortunately, two columns after Friedman makes
this observation, when putting an actual case to illustrate his
views, he seems to backtrack; asking whether a corporation, in
order to improve the environment, should "make expenditures
on reducing pollution beyond the amount that is in the best
interest of the corporation *or that is required by law,*"⁶ Friedman
takes the negative view. He drops the "ethical customs" qualifications without any explanation.

It is a shame that Friedman, when he comes to analyzing a
real case, robs us of the chance to see what significance, if any,
he attaches to the notion of "rules . . . embodied in ethical customs." Many would be inclined to say that if corporate management was to conform not only to the rules embodied in law but
also "to those embodied in ethical customs," his hypothetical
corporations might well be obligated to stop polluting people—
perhaps on the basis of a principle as fundamental as "do unto
others as you would have them do unto you." Indeed, the moral
objection to continued pollution might hold even where "the
good" is defined with reference to the most narrow economic
criteria. Suppose, for example, that the corporation's plant was
emitting a pollutant that caused $200,000 damage annually to the
environment, but which the corporation could remedy by the construction of a pollution-abatement device that costs, amortized,
$50,000 annually. One can imagine jurisdictions in which the
addition of the device is not required by the law. In such a case,
it would not be in the best interest of the corporation, and it
would not be required by law, to add the device. Yet, the imposi-
tion on society of a $200,000 social cost which the corporation
could remedy by an outlay of $50,000 is the very sort of evil that
Friedman specializes in—a clear misallocation of resources. If the
management knew these facts, could one not argue that their
failure to install the device was a violation of one of those rules
"embodied in ethical custom"? Or suppose, for further example,
that the community had sought to remedy the weaknesses of
private civil actions by establishing a pollution control board.

Suppose further that the plant is producing a pollutant not yet detectable by the local board, or is of a sort the dangers of which are not known to the public generally, but are known, or strongly suspected, by the corporation's management. Under these circumstances, should the corporation install the device, even though not "in the best interest of the corporation or . . . required by law"? Would failure to do so be unethical? Would Friedman be willing to call such a failure a "deception" or a "fraud"? Or suppose that the corporation did not *know* the dangers inherent in its pollutants, but could (as we may well assume) make progress toward assessing the damages by setting up—at the cost of shareholder profits—a scientific task force? Would the corporation that failed to establish such a program be acting improperly under Friedman's formulations?

Part of the difficulty in understanding Friedman is that we do not know precisely what moral rules, of what level of generality, he or those who have voiced similar sentiments have in mind; nor do they seem to consider the qualification really significant enough to carry out its implications in detail. To do so on their behalf we would have to have the answer to a more fundamental question: What do they see as the justification for any corporate conscience at all? Where do even our most dedicated exponents of laissez-faire implicitly regard legal and market forces to be so inadequate as a means of achieving social good that self-imposed moral restraint may be called for? We shall have to formulate our own answers.

A fourth position that could be threshed out from the "anti" literature is based upon a distinction not between profit-maximizing and non-profit-maximizing activities, so much as between those activities that a company is well equipped to handle and those that it is not. These critics do not object to all non-profit-maximizing activity, but only to those acts that place the corporation in fields not related to, in F. A. Hayek's phrase, their "proper aim."[7] "Corporations," Ronald Coase observes, "should avoid involving themselves in activities which impede the carrying out of their main function and which they are in fact ill-equipped to perform."[8]

There is a certain solid good sense to this position. As

one businessman with reservations about the corporate social-responsibility movement has observed, "in the case of the railroad industry . . . which is in deep trouble, what society wants and has not received is an imaginative modern system of transportation supplying both passenger and freight service. . . ."[9] Similarly, what one wants from a steel company, at least in the first instance, is good grade steel at noninflationary prices. In this regard, too, it is interesting to consider some recent experiences of Atlantic Richfield Oil Company (ARCO). "Awakened" by riots, it undertook efforts to

retrieve "hard-core dropouts from society" in Philadelphia. Recruiting about 100 ex-convicts, former drug addicts and perennial welfare recipients [the company] spent about $1 million—$10,000 each—"to see whether there was some combination of education, aptitude training and work experience that might unlock the door that made social prisoners of these people." The results were nil; no dropouts were saved. Mr. Bradshaw [the company president] was nonetheless philosophical about it: "Is a social experiment ever a failure? We think we gained experience from this experiment which will enable us to make the next one more fruitful."[10]

Sad to say, while ARCO management was putting the company's funds toward this ill-fated mission to rescue dropouts, a natural gas seepage was developing in the vicinity of an ARCO drilling rig in the Santa Barbara channel. In June 1973 an oil slick had spread across several miles of water. This happened, almost certainly, without any legally provable fault of ARCO, or of anyone else.[11] But one is tempted to suggest that if ARCO is to get involved in some nonprofitable activity, not required by law, its money, expertise, personnel, and other resources would better have been put to surveying underwater geological conditions in the vicinity of its rigs—matters that it knows more about than the rest of us—than trying (with the best of intentions, let us suppose) to retrieve dropouts, which it doesn't.

Furthermore, even if one is attracted to this position, it is not always clear how it would be applied in a wide range of cases less stark than the example above. How is the "proper aim" or "main function" to be determined without begging the very question the "pros" are trying to debate? If one is to consult the corporation's charter, there might be some clue, but the charters of many major corporations are extremely open-textured, sometimes to the point of simply containing an "all purposes" clause ("The purpose of the Corporation is to engage in any lawful act or activity for which corporations may be organized under the General Corporations Law of Delaware"). And even if one tries to discover the corporation's "proper aim" by looking to what the corporation is doing in fact (making automobiles, banking) rather than to what it might do and still be operating *intra vires* its charter, few if any of the problems posed by the proresponsibility people can be squarely met. Consider, for example, the problem of whether an auto company ought to develop clean engines before the law (or market forces) requires it to do so: Would expenditures in this direction be within the "proper aim" of the company—an incident of auto manufacturing—or would it be outside the "proper aim," defined, perhaps, as making-money-through-auto-manufacturing? Or consider these examples: (1) a bank is confronted with the question of whether to make low-interest (or high-risk) loans to minority businesses; (2) a steel company is confronted with the question of whether to make its working conditions "humane" beyond the level the unions, through their negotiating power, can wrest from management. How would either of these cases be disposed of under the "proper aim" or "main purposes" test? Or consider the difficulties of invoking these tests when the position of the "pros" would be not to expand the corporation's activities but to contract them. A regulated utility is confronted with the question of whether it ought to engage in an advertising and lobbying campaign to influence legislation (the expenses for which it will build back into its rates). Is influencing the regulations to which it is subject a part of its "proper aim"?

The point of these examples is not to deny that there is a germ, even an important germ, of validity to this position. But if the "main purpose" of a corporation is to be the touchstone, how are the contours of "main purpose" to be established? If we really try to apply this test, it gives us as little direction as Friedman's.

# 9. Why Shouldn't Corporations Be Socially Responsible?

So far we have seen that the opposition to corporate social responsibility comprises at least four related though separable positions. But I have not yet challenged the fundamental assumption that underlies all four of them. Each assumes in its own degree that the managers of the corporation are to be steered almost wholly by profit, rather than by what they think proper for society on the whole. Why should this be so? So far as ordinary morals are concerned, we often expect human beings to act in a fashion that is calculated to benefit others, rather than themselves, and commend them for it. Why should the matter be different with corporations?

## The Promissory Argument

The most widespread but least persuasive arguments advanced by the "antiresponsibility" forces take the form of a moral claim based upon the corporation's supposed obligations to its shareholders. In its baldest and least tenable form, it is presented as though management's obligation rested upon the keeping of a promise—that the management of the corporation "promised" the shareholders that it would maximize the shareholders' profits. But this simply isn't so.

Consider for contrast the case where a widow left a large fortune goes to a broker, asking him to invest and manage her money so as to maximize her return. The broker, let us suppose, accepts the money and the conditions. In such a case, there would be no disagreement that the broker had made a promise to the widow, and if he invested her money in some venture that struck his fancy for any reason other than that it would increase her fortune, we would be inclined to advance a moral (as well, perhaps, as a legal) claim against him. Generally, at least, we believe in the keeping of promises; the broker, we should say, had violated a promissory obligation to the widow.

But that simple model is hardly the one that obtains between the management of major corporations and their shareholders. Few if any American shareholders ever put their money into a corporation upon the express promise of management that the company would be operated so as to maximize their returns. Indeed, few American shareholders ever put their money directly *into* a corporation at all. Most of the shares outstanding today were issued years ago and found their way to their current shareholders only circuitously. In almost all cases, the current shareholder gave his money to some prior shareholder, who, in turn, had gotten it from B, who, in turn, had gotten it from A, and so on back to the purchaser of the original issue, who, many years before, had bought the shares through an underwriting syndicate. In the course of these transactions, one of the basic elements that exists in the broker case is missing: The manager of the corporation, unlike the broker, was never even offered a chance to refuse the shareholder's "terms" (if they were that) to maximize the shareholder's profits.

There are two other observations to be made about the moral argument based on a supposed promise running from the management to the shareholders. First, even if we do infer from all the circumstances a "promise" running from the management to the shareholders, but not one, or not one of comparable weight running elsewhere (to the company's employees, customers, neighbors, etc.), we ought to keep in mind that as a moral matter (which is what we are discussing here) sometimes it is deemed morally justified to break promises (even to break the law) in the furtherance of other social interests of higher concern. Promises can advance moral arguments, by way of creating presumptions, but few of us believe that promises, per se, can end them. My promise to appear in class on time would not ordinarily justify me from refusing to give aid to a drowning man. In other words, even if management *had* made an express promise to its shareholders to "maximize your profits," (a) I am not persuaded that the ordinary person would interpret it to mean "maximize *in every way you can possibly get away with,* even if that means polluting the environment, ignoring or breaking the law"; and (b) I am not persuaded that, even if it were interpreted as so blanket a promise, most people would not suppose it ought—morally—to be broken in some cases.

Finally, even if, in the face of all these considerations, one still believes that there is an overriding, unbreakable, promise of some sort running from management to the shareholders, I do not think that it can be construed to be any stronger than one running to *existent* shareholders, arising from *their* expectations as measured by the price *they* paid. That is to say, there is nothing in the argument from promises that would wed us to a regime in which management was bound to maximize the income of shareholders. The argument might go so far as to support compensation for existent shareholders if the society chose to announce that henceforth management would have other specified obligations, thereby driving the price of shares to a lower adjustment level. All future shareholders would take with "warning" of, and a price that discounted for, the new "risks" of shareholding (i.e., the "risks" that management might put corporate resources to *pro bonum* ends).

## The Agency Argument

Related to the promissory argument but requiring less stretching of the facts is an argument from agency principles. Rather than trying to infer a promise by management to the shareholders, this argument is based on the idea that the shareholders designated the management their agents. This is the position advanced by Milton Friedman in his *New York Times* article. "The key point," he says, "is that . . . the manager is the agent of the individuals who own the corporation. . . ."[1]

Friedman, unfortunately, is wrong both as to the state of the law (the directors are *not* mere agents of the shareholders)[2] and on his assumption as to the facts of corporate life (surely it is closer to the truth that in major corporations the shareholders are *not*, in any meaningful sense, selecting the directors; management is more often using its control over the proxy machinery to designate who the directors shall be, rather than the other way around).

What Friedman's argument comes down to is that for some reason the directors ought morally to consider themselves more the agents for the shareholders than for the customers, creditors, the state, or the corporation's immediate neighbors. But why? And to what extent? Throwing in terms like "principal" and "agent" begs the fundamental questions.

What is more, the "agency" argument is not only morally inconclusive, it is embarrassingly at odds with the way in which supposed "agents" actually behave. If the managers truly considered themselves the agents of the shareholders, as agents they would be expected to show an interest in determining how their principals wanted them to act—and to act accordingly. In the controversy over Dow's production of napalm, for example, one would expect, on this model, that Dow's management would have been glad to have the napalm question put to the shareholders at a shareholders' meeting. In fact, like most major companies faced with shareholder requests to include "social action" measures on proxy statements, it fought the proposal tooth and claw.[3] It is a peculiar agency where the "agents" will go to such lengths (even spending tens of thousands of dollars of their "principals'" money in legal fees) to resist the determination of what their "principals" want.

## The Role Argument

An argument so closely related to the argument from promises and agency that it does not demand extensive additional remarks is a contention based upon supposed considerations of *role*. Sometimes in moral discourse, as well as in law, we assign obligations to people on the basis of their having assumed some role or status, independent of any specific verbal promise they made.

Such obligations are assumed to run from a captain to a seaman (and vice versa), from a doctor to a patient, or from a parent to a child. The antiresponsibility forces are on somewhat stronger grounds resting their position on this basis, because the model more nearly accords with the facts—that is, management never actually promised the shareholders that they would maximize the shareholders' investment, nor did the shareholders designate the directors their agents for this express purpose. The directors and top management are, as lawyers would say, fiduciaries. But what does this leave us? So far as the directors are fiduciaries of the shareholders in a legal sense, of course they are subject to the legal limits on fiduciaries—that is to say, they cannot engage in self-dealing, "waste" of corporate assets, and the like. But I do not understand any proresponsibility advocate to be demanding such corporate largesse as would expose the officers to legal liability; what we are talking about are expenditures on, for example, pollution control, above the amount the company is required to pay by law, but less than an amount so extravagant as to constitute a violation of these legal fiduciary duties. (Surely no court in America today would enjoin a corporation from spending more to reduce pollution than the law requires.) What is there about assuming the role of corporate officer that makes it immoral for a manager to involve a corporation in these expenditures? A father, one would think, would have stronger obligations to his children by virtue of his status than a corporate manager to the corporation's shareholders. Yet few would regard it as a compelling moral argument if a father were to distort facts about his child on a scholarship application form on the grounds that he had obligations to advance his child's career; nor would we consider it a strong moral argument if a father were to leave unsightly refuse piled on his lawn, spilling over into the street, on the plea that he had obligations to give every moment of his attention to his children, and was thus too busy to cart his refuse away.

Like the other supposed moral arguments, the one from role suffers from the problem that the strongest moral obligations one can discover have at most only prima facie force, and it is not apparent why those obligations should predominate over some contrary social obligations that could be advanced.

Then, too, when one begins comparing and weighing the various moral obligations, those running back to the shareholder seem fairly weak by comparison to the claims of others. For one thing, there is the consideration of alternatives. If the shareholder is dissatisfied with the direction the corporation is taking, he can sell out, and if he does so quickly enough, his losses may be slight. On the other hand, as Ted Jacobs observes, "those most vitally affected by corporate decisions—people who work in the plants, buy the products, and consume the effluents—cannot remove themselves from the structure with a phone call."[4]

## The "Polestar" Argument

It seems to me that the strongest moral argument corporate executives can advance for looking solely to profit is not one that is based on a supposed express, or even implied promise to the shareholder. Rather, it is one that says, if the managers act in such fashion as to maximize profits—if they act *as though* they had promised the shareholders they would do so—then it will be best for all of us. This argument might be called the polestar argument, for its appeal to the interests of the shareholders is not justified on supposed obligations to the shareholders per se, but as a means of charting a straight course toward what is best for the society as a whole.

Underlying the polestar argument are a number of assumptions—some express and some implied. There is, I suspect, an implicit positivism among its supporters—a feeling (whether its proponents own up to it or not) that moral judgments are peculiar, arbitrary, or vague—perhaps even "meaningless" in the philosophic sense of not being amenable to rational discussion. To those who take this position, profits (or sales, or price-earnings ratios) at least provide some solid, tangible standard by which participants in the organization can measure their successes and failures, with some efficiency, in the narrow sense, resulting for the entire group. Sometimes the polestar position is based upon a related view—not that the moral issues that underlie social choices are meaningless, but that resolving them calls for special expertise. "I don't know any investment adviser whom I would care to act in my behalf in any matter except turning a profit. . . . The value of these specialists . . . lies in their limitations; they ought not allow themselves to see so much of the world that they become distracted."[5] A slightly modified point emphasizes not that the executives lack moral or social expertise per se, but that they lack the social authority to make policy choices. Thus, Friedman objects that if a corporate director took "social purposes" into account, he would become "in effect a public employee, a civil servant. . . . On grounds of political principle, it is intolerable that such civil servants . . . should be selected as they are now."[6]

I do not want to get too deeply involved in each of these arguments. That the moral judgments underlying policy choices are vague, I do not doubt—although I am tempted to observe that when you get right down to it, a wide range of actions taken by businessmen every day, supposedly based on solid calculations of "profit," are probably as rooted in hunches and intuition as judgments of ethics. I do not disagree either that, ideally, we prefer those who have control over our lives to be politically accountable; although here, too, if we were to pursue the matter in detail we would want to inspect both the premise of this argument, that corporate managers are not *presently* custodians of discretionary power over us anyway, and also its logical implications. Friedman's point that "if they are to be civil servants, then they must be selected through a political process"[7] is not, as Friedman regards it, a *reductio ad absurdum*—not, at any rate, to Ralph Nader and others who want publicly elected directors.

The reason for not pursuing these counterarguments at length is that, whatever reservations one might have, we can agree that there is a germ of validity to what the "antis" are saying. But their essential failure is in not pursuing the alternatives. Certainly, *to the extent* that the forces of the market and the law can keep the corporation within desirable bounds, it may be better to trust them than to have corporate managers implementing their own vague and various notions of what is best for the rest of us. But are the "antis" blind to the fact that there are circumstances in which the law—and the forces of the market—are simply not competent to keep the corporation under control? The shortcomings of these traditional restraints on corporate conduct are critical to understand, not merely for the defects they point up in the "antis'" position. More important, identifying where the traditional forces are inadequate is the first step in the design of new and alternative measures of corporate control.

# 10. Why the Market Can't Do It

In my view, much of the literature today reflects too little appreciation that, whatever its limits, the "invisible" hand of the market is the most effective force we have to keep corporations operating within socially desirable bounds, especially when the various costs of our legal mechanisms are considered. Nonetheless, the case for the market (as well as the case against it) is easily and often overstated.

For one thing, even at its ideal best, the market is not a remedy for all the problems a society may have with its commercial actors, but plays a general allocative role, encouraging capital, labor, and other factors of production to flow to those industries and firms that can put them to the most beneficial social use. One's willingness to trust to the market to fulfill the resource allocation function, such as by leaving firms autonomous in their pricing policies, rises or falls depending upon how he responds to a series of questions. To what extent is one willing to accept dollar values as the measure of most beneficial social use? To what extent are giant modern corporations freeing themselves of the forces that restrained small producers historically, allowing them to administer prices and manipulate their own consumer demand? These questions have been discussed too fully and too well elsewhere to reiterate the matter anew. It is safe to say, however, that, although economists may differ as to the advisability of various *forms* of intervention with market dictates, or as to the various *sectors* at which intervention best takes place (banking, farming), few if any are satisfied that the market of itself can allocate resources adequately to fill social needs.

What is more, when one turns from the market as resource allocator to inspect its capacity to fulfill other societal desiderata, the case of the free-market man is even harder to support. One ought to be clear that those who have faith that profit orientation is an adequate guarantee of corporations realizing socially desirable consumer goals are implicitly assuming: (1) that the persons who are going to withdraw patronage know *the fact* that they are being "injured" (where injury refers to a whole range of possible grievances, from getting a worse deal than might be gotten elsewhere, to purchasing a product that is defective or below warranted standards, to getting something that produces actual physical injury); (2) that they know *where* to apply pressure of some sort; (3) that they are in a *position* to apply pressure of some sort; and (4) that their pressure will be *translated* into warranted changes in the institution's behavior. None of these assumptions is particularly well-founded.

As for the first, over a range of important cases the person who, under this model, should be shifting his patronage, does not even know that he is being "injured" (in the broad sense referred to above). For example, from our vantage point in the present, we can look back on history and appreciate some of the dangers of smoking on a cigarette consumer's health, or of coal dust on a worker's lungs. But the basis for these doubts was not adequately appreciated by the earlier consumer, who might have wanted to shift his patronage from, say, nonfilter to filter cigarettes, or to the worker who might have shifted his career from coal mining to something else. It hardly strains the imagination to believe that we today, as consumers, employees, investors, and so forth, are being subjected by corporations to all sorts of injuries that we will learn about only in time. But we are not able to translate these general misgivings into market preferences because we simply do not know enough about where dangers lie.

Second, that the individual knows *where* to apply pressure, is, in many instances also, too facile an assumption. Consider the case of the consumer disaffected by a certain product. If the free-market mechanism is working perfectly, he would be expected to withdraw his patronage from the management that produced that product, thereby "penalizing" those responsible for it and encouraging their rivals. But to do so, what exactly is he supposed to "boycott"? Consumers identify products by brand name, not usually by the producing company, of whose identity they are often ignorant. A dissatisfied Tide user who shifted from Tide to Dash, or to Duz—or to Bold, Oxydol, Cascade, Cheer, or Ivory Soap—would still, whether he knows it or not, be patronizing Procter & Gamble. Or suppose another sort of problem: Theoretically, people concerned over ITT's involvement with the federal government might withdraw patronage from ITT products and services. But to judge the effectiveness of this "remedy" the reader has only to ask himself if he can identify the stereo set, color TV, hotel, bread, plumbing fixture, book, or windshield wiper behind which ITT, at varying degrees of distance, stands. The consumer could, at a cost, undertake to find out what other products were produced by the company that had produced brand Z, or was engaged in the undesirable activity, but even this search could be unsatisfactory. The company he finds at the end of his chase may itself be part of a larger shell of corporations so complex that even the Congress sometimes has trouble determining what are the "real" interests behind a corporate name.

Even where the first two criteria are met—that is, the person being injured knows the fact that he is being injured and can discover against whom to apply pressure—he may still not be in a position in which he can apply pressure. This could come about for at least two major reasons.

First, the model presupposes the existence of some negotiating interface between the corporation and the person disaffected with it. Such a relationship is available for a worker who is a member of a union recognized by the corporation, and for a person who is directly a consumer of the corporation's products or services. But consider, for example, a person whose grievance is with an aluminum company that is showering his land with pollutants, or that is, in his estimate, exercising objectionable influences in Latin America. If, as is likely, he is not a direct purchaser of aluminum, what recourse does he have: to do a study of all the products he is contemplating buying that contain aluminum so as to determine the "parentage" of their aluminum components and know which of them to boycott? The problem is hardly an isolated one. We are living in a society in which a number of major companies—for example North American Aviation and General Dynamics—produce too few consumer products, even indirectly, such as submit them to classic market pressures. Furthermore, the problems of our society are increasingly of a sort in which those affected are third parties to the negotiation; even when a company sits down with its union to discuss pulling up roots from some small towns, the town itself may have almost no say.

Second, even if such a negotiating interface exists, the person dealing with the company may have no viable alternative source of supply or employment. The most obvious example is when the company with whose actions someone is concerned is a monopoly or near-monopoly. Many people in Southern California, for example, feel that some of the local utilities have been overly slow in hiring minority-group workers. But how does one who feels this way communicate his disaffection into market "language," there being no other source of electricity? And even where one is not confronted with a monopoly in the strict sense (such as a regulated utility), often as a practical matter the availability of desired products is in the hands of but one or two corporations. For example, there has been considerable concern recently over the low nutritional value of breakfast cereals, as well as some distaste expressed over the amount of rat hair and other extraneous matter that turn up in the boxes. But a disaffected consumer confronts a market in which 90 percent of the breakfast cereals are produced by four companies.

Finally, one ought to be chary, too, of the assumptions that even if economic pressure can be brought to bear on the "offending" corporation, the pressure will be smoothly translated into changes in the institution's behavior. The assumption rises and falls with one's belief that corporations are pure and simple profit maximizers, a position criticized in Chapter 6. A company whose customers are being "turned off" for one reason or another may well, just as the model suggests, turn their patronage elsewhere. But this does not assure that the management will know why it lost sales, or, discovering the reason, that it will remedy the problem in the most desirable way possible. There is a vivid example of this in a recent episode involving "snack packs," little cans of pudding with metal, tear-away lids, that had become a popular lunchbox item for school children. Unfortunately, not only were children cutting their fingers on the sharp, serrated edges, but they were regularly licking the custard from the snapped-off metal top, which Consumers Union found sharp enough to cut a chicken leg.[1] Reports began to filter in of cuts. The surest remedy for this would presumably have been to replace the metal snap-off top with a plastic or screw-on variant. "It is easier to change the design of the can," one third-grade teacher wrote Consumers Union, "than it is to change the natural tendencies of a child." Well—that's what the third-grade teacher thought. What she overlooked is that for the company to change its top called for it to change its way of doing things—its own "natural tendencies." Instead of changing its tops, the company undertook an advertising campaign, distributing posters that told kiddies, in essence, to be careful. It took who knows how many complaints before the company finally gave in and promised to start using a safety lid or withdraw the product. The episode is not atypical. What those who put all their faith in the market fail to account for is one of the most fundamental principles of organizational theory: All large organizations seek to seal off or "buffer" their technical core from disruptive environmental influences (like the market—or the law).[2] So far as possible their tendency is to fight rather than to switch.

# 11. Why the Law Can't Do It

Wherever the market is inadequate as a control, one can, of course, act to shore it up by law. Earlier, we saw this accounted for in the position that a corporation's social responsibilities are discharged if it follows the dictates of the market within the constraints of the law. Its fundamental idea is that laws, as the expression of popular sentiment, should be the source of guidance for corporate direction, not the personal preferences of each corporation's management. If the majority of the people believe the market and present laws inadequate to keep corporations within socially desirable bounds, the society can, through its democratic processes, make tougher laws. But unless and until such laws are made, this argument goes, it is best for all of us if the corporation managers guide themselves by profit.

As indicated earlier, however, even if one regards this position as persuasive generally, it does not really prove that corporate social responsibility is unnecessary; it merely invites the "pros" to identify more clearly just exactly where and in what ways reliance on the law is an inadequate method of keeping corporations within socially desirable bounds.

Now, we have seen in Part II that those who trust to the law to bind corporations have failed to take into account a whole host of reasons why the threat of legal sanction is apt to lack the desired effects when corporate behavior is its target—for example, limited liability, the lack of congruence between the incentives of top executives and the incentives of "the corporation," the organization's proclivity to buffer itself against external, especially legal, threats, and so on. But I am now suggesting that even if the corporation followed the law anyway, it would not be enough. The first set of reasons involves what I shall call the "time-lag problem"; the second concerns limitations connected with the making of law; the third concerns limitations connected with the mechanisms for implementing the law.

## The Time-lag Problem

Even if we put aside the defects in the impact of the sanctions, there still remains the problem that the law is primarily a reactive institution. Lawmakers have to appreciate and respond to problems that corporate engineers, chemists, and financiers were anticipating (or could have anticipated) long before—that the drugs their corporations are about to produce can alter consciousness or damage the gene pool of the human race, that they are on the verge of multinational expansion that will endow them with the power to trigger worldwide financial crises in generally unforeseen ways, and so on. Even if laws could be passed to deal effectively with these dangers, until they are passed a great deal of damage—some perhaps irreversible—can be done. Thus, there is something grotesque—and socially dangerous—in encouraging corporate managers to believe that, until the law tells them otherwise, they have no responsibilities beyond the law and their impulses (whether their impulses spring from the id or from the balance sheet). We do not encourage human beings to suppose so. And the dangers to society seem all the more acute where corporations are concerned.

## Limitations Connected with the Making of Law

To claim society's desires will be realized so long as the corporations "follow the edict of the populus" fails to take into account *the role of corporations in making the very law that we trust to bind them.* This is, incidentally, not an especially modern development or one peculiar to laws regulating corporations. The whole history of commercial law is one in which, by and large, the "legislation" has been little more than an acknowledgment of rules established by the commercial sector, unless there are the strongest and most evident reasons to the contrary. Thus, in many areas such as food, drug, and cosmetic regulation, and, more recently, with respect to the promulgation of safety rules by the Department of Transportation, the government effectively adopts the standards worked out with the industry. Such processes do not always bespeak, as is sometimes intimated, sinister sales of power. The real roots are more cumbersome, more bureaucratic, more "necessary," and therefore more difficult to remedy: The regulating body is considerably outstaffed and relatively uninformed; it knows that it has to "live with" the industry it is regulating; it does not want to set standards that it always will be having to fight to enforce.

A related problem arises when an overseeing agency is in fact staffed with industry personnel—a problem that reaches its extreme form when the law that establishes the agency expressly provides for industry representatives to sit on the board. By its very constitution, California's Dickie Act, for example, effectually seats representatives of polluters on the Water Pollution Control Board.[1] The milk laws put the producers on the board that determines the distribution and price levels of milk.[2] Now, I am not here arguing the concept of having industry representatives on some regulatory boards. There are good reasons (whether or not they should ultimately prevail) for doing so in some cases. What I am saying is just that insofar as the corporations are engaged in making the regulations to which they are supposedly subject, it is absurdly circular to argue that their social responsibilities are discharged so long as they are living within the constraints of the law.

The argument overlooks, too, the obvious fact that the laws corporations are "under" are being shaped indirectly through *corporate manipulation of public opinion*. The auto industry has begun right at the school level with its massive efforts to convince that pollution is not all that bad—and the worst offender is Mother Nature, anyway. In trying to persuade the public that there is an "energy crisis" the gas companies' trade association has taken out advertisements displaying deceptively truncated graphs.[3] The railroads' efforts to mobilize public sentiment against truckers—largely through secretly subsidized front organizations—is notorious.[4]

Of course, to set out one's positions on public matters is a right guaranteed by the First Amendment, and one which I do not think should be or could be specially curtailed in the instance of corporations. This is particularly true when one considers that corporations (and trade associations) are well situated to inform on a broad range of public issues. But a corporation's right to speak out should be no license for clandestine and distortive manipulations. The problem is especially acute because while a corporation can be sued for fraud and deception in the sale of goods, there are no effective legal constraints when it is "merely" bamboozling the public, not as their seller, but as their fellow citizen. What this means is that as corporations increasingly engage in opinion-framing activities, here, too, just obeying the law simply isn't enough.

The "anti" position implicitly assumes also that the lawmaking body is as informed on the relevant facts as -is the regulatee. Often this is more or less true. When a lawmaking body considers, for example, what the speed limit ought to be, it can obtain as well as the companies such relevant data as injuries at various speeds.

But when we attempt to legislate in more complex areas, we find an information gap. Even the specialized regulatory agencies, much less the Congress, cannot in their rule-making capacities keep technically abreast of the industry. Are employees who work around asbestos being subjected to high risks of cancer? What psychological and physical dangers lurk in various forms of manufacturing processes? What are the dangers to field workers, consumers, and the environment of various forms of pesticides? Congress and the various regulatory bodies can barely begin to answer these questions. The companies most closely associated with the problems may not know the answers either; but they certainly have the more ready access to the most probative information. It is their doctors who treat the employees' injuries; it is their chemists who live with and test the new compounds; it is their health records that gather absentee data. Granted, there are practical problems of getting corporations to gather and come forward with the relevant data, problems I shall consider in

Part IV. But at this juncture my point is only this: Here, too, it is a lame argument that working within traditional legal strategies we can keep corporations in line.

In many cases lawmaking is an unsatisfactory way to deal with social problems not because of a lack of "facts" in the senses referred to above, but because we, as a society, *lack consensus as to the values we want to advance.* For example, people do not want corporations to deplete natural resources "too fast," but desiring the luxuries that the resources can yield, differ on what "too fast" means. Then, too, we who live in the present do not know how to take into account the values that future generations might attach to the resources.[5] Problems of this sort exist everywhere we look. Consider a drug that can benefit 99 percent of people who suffer from some disease, but could seriously injure 1 percent: Should it be banned from the market? People value inexpensive power. They also value a clean environment. These factors point toward construction of nuclear generating stations. But such stations put a risk on life. The problem ushered in is not merely a "factual" one in the narrow sense—for example, what is the probability over any time horizon of an accident that will cause such and such a magnitude of disaster. It is more complex still. For even if we could agree upon these "facts," how can we agree upon and factor into our decision the various values involved—the value of human life, the value of a relatively clean environment, those "fragile" values so easily lost in the shuffle of a technological society with its computers geared for the consumption of hard, quantifiable facts?

A closely related difficulty involves our increasing *lack of confidence as to causes and effects.* Let me explain this by a contrast. Suppose A shoots B, intending to kill him, and B dies. We place A on trial for murder. Why A? No one who has reflected upon the matter would be so naïve as to suppose that A was the "sole cause" of B's death either in any valid scientific sense or from a broader social perspective. As the defense attorney might remind us, "A was a product of a broken family, an intolerable social environment," and so on. What is more, by focusing on A as the legally responsible entity, we are overlooking the effect that a judgment of guilt will have on those other than A. His family will also be hurt by meting out "justice" to A. If he was a productive worker, the whole society will suffer to some degree. Thus, when we select A as the focus of legal responsibility, we are making simplifying judgments both on the causality side—supposing him to be the sole cause—and on the effect side—overlooking the effects on others. The more one thinks about the matter, the more complex and uncertain we could be about it. Notwithstanding these doubts, though, most people today—even those who feel the law is not the only way to solve the social problem of violence—are still prepared to support a law that, in that last analysis, deals with murder by focusing on A.

There are today, however, a whole host of major social problems that remain so for the reason that we cannot accept the simplified judgments as to causality and effect that traditional legal solutions demand. Take, as example of a major contemporary social dilemma, the problem of "inner-city blight." What entities can we single out for responsibility, either pragmatically or morally? The slum dwellers? Slum landlords? City employers who take their operations to other states? How complex, uncertain, and even counterintuitive are the implications of any particular remedy that we may try. Worse, our uncertainties seem only to increase the more we develop methods and machinery to take into account the variety of factors we are increasingly capable of seeing are involved. A sort of legislative paralysis results—or worse, a legislative panic.*

---

* At this point the reader might well interject that if the society, through its institutions, cannot reach consensus on what values to take into account, and is left paralyzed in the face of cause-effect uncertainties, how can we expect corporations, which are not representative bodies, to know what to do? First, we should not ignore the fact the corporations right now are acting to promote some values over others, whether they be broadcasting companies or toy manufacturers. Aware of this, and aware of the limits of the law, we should prefer corporations to exercise informed, sensitive choices on matters of major concern, than that they just ignore their responsibilities altogether. Consider the problem of how stiff automobile bumpers ought to be. One might well prefer a system in which automobile manufacturers carefully thought in advance about whether to design bumpers *either* to advance the value of lower repair bills *or* to advance the value of driver safety (so far as those are inconsistent) than the alternative implicit in the "antiresponsibility" position—that they should overlook either problem and

Even in those instances when the relevant facts can be established, and the relevant values are matters of consent, we may be able to agree upon what to do only in the most general way, inadequately for translation into viable legal rules. As the earth gets more and more crowded, and life more complex, increasingly such problems arise. For example, while we can all agree that bad odors ought to be held to a tolerable level in residential or mixed residential areas, it is not easy to translate this decision into enforceable legal machinery. How does one spell out a rule so that those bound by it know how to orient their behavior? How can one "prove" that the rule has been violated?[6] This sort of problem is most critical where criminal-law standards are to be applied. Here the "fair warning" function of the law is strongly felt as a value in our society, and even constitutional objections can come into play where an unduly vague provision is tied to criminal penalties. But our reluctance holds true in civil areas as well. We are prepared to say that a man puts up an unsafe building at his own risk—meaning that if it collapses and injures people physically, the legal system will hold him liable. But if he puts up an ugly building, the resulting "injury" is left to lie outside the legal system. This, I think, is not merely because physical injuries are deemed more serious than aesthetic ones (although that is part of it) but because the physical harm is more quantifiable and objective than the aesthetic harm, and the legal system less inclined to get involved in sorting out competing claims.

The vagueness problem has even more serious ramifications than appear on first glance. For one thing, the administration of justice in this country depends upon most litigation being settled out of court, and the more vague a statute, the more in doubt an outcome, and thus the more likely we are to find our court dockets crowded with cases that neither side is prepared to

---

just design the bumpers solely from a fashion and marketing point of view. We could prefer it, too, to the alternative of a society that, losing its faith in the manufacturers, decides to legislate uniformity of standards in these gray areas, and winds up imposing on every purchaser of automobiles the same features irrespective of their personal needs and preferences.

concede. A related point is that when standards are vague, the persons against whom they are turned are apt to feel personally and arbitrarily selected out for persecution, victims of men, rather than of the laws. When people—or corporations—feel themselves to have had no fair warning, increased friction between industry and government is likely to result, a development that has numerous regrettable ramifications. (The vagueness of the antitrust laws, real and imagined, is a common point of complaint among businessmen and serves as a justification for the short shrift they would like to give laws and "government interference" generally.) What is more, if the language really is vague, the law is that much less likely to be an effective force in the face of competing, more definite constraints on the organization, such as the "need" to return profits, increase price-earnings ratios, and the like.

One can, of course, try to obviate the vagueness by seeking more and more precision in the law's language. But in doing so we risk making matters considerably worse. There is the possibility that once we have unleashed the regulators to make finer and finer regulations, the regulations become an end in themselves, a cumbersome, frustrating, and pointless web for those they entangle. Second, what all too often happens when legislatures try to turn vague value sentiments into tangible, measurable legal terms is that the rules they come up with have lost touch with the values they were originally designed to advance. There is a fascinating example of this in the area of water pollution. In their study of the attempt to reduce pollution in the Delaware River area, Bruce Ackerman and James Sawyer have shown that the regulators have emphasized dissolved oxygen content (D.O.) as a critical standard—the amount of D.O. in the water being taken as an inverse measure of how badly the water is polluted.[7] What Ackerman and Sawyer show, however, is that if one looks at the values that lie behind efforts to minimize water pollution— boating and swimming, potable water, support of fish life— actually over a broad range of D.O. content, D.O. is an inadequate measure of whether or not any of those values are being advanced. Thus, while D.O. has the attractiveness of being traditionally recognized among sanitary engineers (it is "hard" and computerizable), gearing laws to it makes limited sense, at best.

Finally, the very creation of a huge, cumbersome network of rules may make those subject to them abdicate their independent responsible judgment; the law's limits become a sort of "bright line" to the very limits of which the businessman feels no compunctions about treading.

Last, in this discussion of framing social desiderata into the language of the law, there is a consideration that springs from the distinction—an uneasy distinction, I shall have to grant—between two sorts of morality, a morality of duty and a morality of aspiration.[8] Duties, characterized by "thou shalt nots" and the specification of minimum standards of conduct ("thou shalt not steal"), seem to lend themselves to legal enforcement better than aspirations, characterized by "thou shalts" and exhortations to realize one's fullest potentials ("thou shalt do justice"). In other words, law seems most appropriate where it is used to enforce acceptable minimums, rather than to force from each person what he is fully capable of. To the extent this is true, it is significant, for many of the problems we are having with corporations seem to be of the "aspiration" sort. One may feel, for example, that corporations are not aspiring to develop enough new products, not investing enough in research and development, "sitting on" (not developing or licensing) their patents. These problems of corporate inaction or omission seem somehow harder for the law to "get at" than acts of commission—problems connected with corporate action that is substandard or does harm. One of the major corporate problems today can be viewed as of the "aspiration" class: that American automobile manufacturers are not doing all they might to develop cleaner engines, a problem not only for the environment, but—considering that the Japanese companies are apparently prepared to build satisfactory engines—a problem for the balance of payments and unemployment among U.S. auto workers as well.

The lawmaking problems the distinction suggests, however, are not as valid, or at least not as straightforwardly valid, as may appear on first blush. The fact is, the law can and does make people (and corporations) aspire—at least in a way. When it says "thou shalt not drive recklessly" or "thou shalt not ship in interstate commerce any automobiles that do not meet minimal EPA standards" there is an obvious sense in which it *is* making people aspire—to drive carefully, to produce relatively smog-free engines. Yet, there is a germ of truth to the distinction, too. Though we can raise standards, so long as they remain standards of general application, they are going to be compromises applicable to all equally—to those companies that can far exceed the minimal standards as well those that can barely meet them, without distinction. A man with the skills of a test driver does not have to drive any more carefully than the average reasonable man; a corporation with a sizable profit margin and low conversion costs need not exceed the quality standards that apply across the board to an entire industry.

I have to add that it is not inevitable that the laws take this form; in other words, there is nothing inherent in aspiration-type desiderata that leaves them unenforceable legally. We *could* pass laws that tailored liability to what could reasonably be expected of each particular company, the more competent companies having to face a higher standard than the less. It is hard to believe that juries do not slip some such considerations into their deliberations right now. (We already formalize taking into account particular *in*capacities, for instance, in specially exempting the insane from the liability that attaches to the average person.) Yet, while the law could, in this way, be made more stringently exhortative, there would be considerable difficulties of implementing and enforcing such a system. For one thing, to do so would put outsiders (including juries) to the task of judging how well any particular person or institution *could* perform—a harder job than deciding what is reasonable. To prove the latter, one can bring in witnesses with experience in society or industry generally; to prove the former is enormously complex, especially where the leading company is concerned, because no one in the industry would have achieved X either, and its feasibility would be largely a matter of conjecture—a conjecture dependent to large measure on employees and records of the defendant itself. Aspirations, too, are apt to be less definitely communicable than minimum standards, and to that extent less likely to be effectively acted upon by the organization; getting companies to implement specified legal minima is hard enough.

Such difficulties, combined with our likely reluctance to make excellence a legal liability, make it unlikely that the law—at least through our present strategies—can ever be a good mechanism for drawing out of a company the best of which it is capable.

### Limitations Connected with Implementing the Law

When we do push ahead even in the face of our doubts as to values, our uncertainty as to facts, and the myriad difficulties of fashioning our wants into legal language, further problems lie ahead. Each of them raises its own doubts as to the virtue of a society in which the outer bounds of a corporation's responsibility are established by the limits we can set down through law.

The fact is that a combination of factors, including the increased expectations of today's citizens and the increasingly technical nature of the society, have left our traditional legal mechanisms unsatisfactory to cope with the problems that currently concern people. Consider, for example, the law of torts, the ordinary rules for recovering damages against someone who has injured you. A model tort case is one in which Smith, who is walking across the street, is accidentally but negligently driven into by Jones. Smith falls, suffering internal injuries, and sues for damages. Now, I call this "a model" case because certain of its features make it so well suited to traditional legal recovery. Note that (a) Smith knows *the fact* that he has been injured; (b) Smith knows *who* has caused the injury; (c) one can assess, fairly well, the *nature and extent* of his injuries; and (d) the *technical inquiry* involved in analyzing causality is not too extensive—that is, simple laws of physics are involved, not beyond commonsense experience*

But contrast that model case—a case in which the tort laws

---

* The model also assumes (e), that if the legal damages can be lain at the feet of the responsible actor, he is likely to adapt by changing his behavior in the future; this is a tenet that, as we have already shown in Part II, is somewhat questionable where the responsible actor is a corporation.

may be fairly adequate to make restitution—with the sort of case that is increasingly of concern in the society today. The food we will eat tonight (grown, handled, packaged, distributed by various corporations) may contain chemicals that are killing us, or at least reducing our life expectancy considerably. But (a) we cannot know with certainty the fact that we are being injured by any particular product; (b) it is difficult determining who might be injuring us—that is, even if we know that our bodies are suffering from a buildup of mercury, we are faced with an awesome task of pinning responsibility on any particular source of mercury; (c) we would have a difficult time proving the extent of our injuries (the more so proving the extent attributable to any particular source); and (d) the nature of the evidence that would have to be evaluated by the court is far more complex and technical than that in the "model" case above—perhaps too technical realistically to trust to courts or even agencies to handle. Thus, it seems inevitable that a certain percentage of harmful, even seriously harmful activity is not going to be contained by trusting to traditional legal mechanisms.

Then, too, at some point the costs of enforcing the law are going to transcend the benefits, and the law may not, on balance, be worth the effort. We can, for example, prohibit employers from discriminating on the basis of sex, and if we are using the law merely as a means of declaring social policy, it may make good sense to do so. But if we were to undertake serious systematic enforcement, the policing and prosecution costs (absent a strong sense by the employer that the law is right) would be questionably high. Some of the costs of falling back on law are obvious: administering court systems and staffing administrative agencies. (The FDA's budget is now $200 million a year.)[9] But there are other sorts of less direct "costs" hidden in such a system. There are various sorts of costs that arise from the attendant government-industry friction. A network of rules and regulations, backed by threats of litigation, breeds distrust, destruction of documents, and an attitude that "I won't do anything more than I am absolutely required to do."

The counterproductiveness of law can be extreme. I have already referred to the manner in which threatening directors and officers with legal liability impedes an ideal flow of information within the corporation, keeping potentially "tainting" knowledge away from those with most authority to step in and remedy the wrongdoing. But the law's bad effects on information are more pervasive still. To develop a system of total health care delivery demands not only a proper flow of information *within* pharmaceutical houses, but between the pharmaceutical houses and hospitals, doctors' offices, and coroners' laboratories. Information that doctors and hospital administrators should be regularly developing is, however, a potential source of medical malpractice liability. Because of the law, it may be best not to gather it and keep it on hand.

There are other sorts of counterproductive costs of law. Keeping bad drugs off the market is a valuable goal. But the other side of the coin is a delay in getting nonharmful, valuable medicine to the market. A two-year administrative hassle in getting approval for a key drug can result in thousands of needless deaths. Sam Peltzman, the University of Chicago economist who has attempted a cost-benefit analysis of the FDA's drug overseeing, has estimated that the 1962 drug amendments cost consumers of drugs—over and above any benefits—a minimum of $250 to $500 million per year.[10]

Related to the problems of framing values into language that were referred to earlier are the problems of proof, which become more exacerbated the further we try to extend the law. In a complex society, issues of the joint-casualty type become enormous. Not long ago, a freeway bridge under construction collapsed in Los Angeles killing six workers. A safety engineer stated, "In the old days this [the factors that brought about the collapse] would have been a clear-cut violation. Six men can't lose their lives in an incident of this type without negligence. It was not an act of God. . . . It had to be manmade." Notwithstanding, criminal prosecution was not recommended, based on the fact the Division of Industrial Safety "can't pin down the single causative factor."[11] How does one locate (much less prove in a court of law) what, exactly, went wrong, and which of the countless companies involved—contractors, subcontractors, suppliers, suppliers' subcontractors—did it?

An additional set of problems can be traced to the unsuitability of legal forums to resolve complex issues. More and more, the major problems that are falling to the courts to decide are those that are being called "polycentric issues"—issues characterized not only by their technical complexity, but by their impact on large and diverse groups of people, far beyond the parties immediately represented in court.[12] In such cases, not only are the rules unclear, but the underlying values—which ordinarily serve as the polestar for applying unclear language—are obscure or inconclusive as well. It is questionable how adequately courts, with their traditional trial-type adversary hearing, presided over by lawyers, lend themselves to the proper adjudication of the more broadly ramified and technical of these polycentric problems. As Maurice Rosenberg has observed,

The typical court adjudication is "bipolar," commanding that plaintiff win or plaintiff lose, and if the former, how much. Cases that involve the issue of where needed nuclear reactors will be sited, or how large they need be, do not precisely fit that mold. . . . Standard proof-taking methods, designed to determine as a yes or no matter whether the defendants' car ran a red light two years ago, are basically inappropriate to issues of that type.[13]

Bruce Ackerman and James Sawyer make a related point in the context of water pollution cases.

A judge will typically seek to effectuate his policy by issuing orders to each defendant-polluter specifying the amount the discharger is to treat its waste. The fact may be, however, that the cheapest and surest way of attaining the judicially determined environmental standard will not require that each discharger treat its own waste on an individual basis but will instead involve the construction of regional treatment plants and substantial dams as well as other measures that treat waste *after* it has been discharged into the stream. Nevertheless, the judiciary would properly refuse to adopt any of these strategies requiring courts to assume an intimate role in the on-going management of the river system. Finally, assuming these considerable obstacles were somehow overcome, and a plausible pollution control program were initially articulated, the court would be incapable of sustaining the scientific inquiry *beyond the time of the original decision* so that policies could constantly be modified as experience accumulated.[14]

The question of how well regulatory agencies can repair the various weaknesses of traditional legal mechanisms is a significant one, too vast to be reviewed here thoroughly. But several points have to be mentioned. First, one ought to recognize that the mere establishment of regulatory agencies does not get around the most significant weaknesses of traditional legal strategies when they are applied to corporate problems. In the last analysis, agencies, too, have to fall back on court enforcement and thus on fines and civil penalties with all the infirmities I have emphasized. By and large, agencies differ from traditional legal approaches not because their sanctions and other motivating strategies are any more sophisticated for dealing with a corporate-dominated society, but rather because their fact-finding and perhaps rule-making procedures are more specialized. This difference is not insignificant. So far as our problems of controlling corporations stem from the fact that traditional congressional legislation is too inflexible, or that Congress is too underinformed to solve complex problems, then, of course, a strong case can be made for specialized agencies—in theory. Our first federal agency, the Interstate Commerce Commission, was presented to the public in just that light some ninety years ago. What, however, has happened since then?

The agencies almost all show evidence (the more so as they age) of protecting the industries they are supposed to regulate, rather than the public. The ICC, for example, probably opposes railroads lowering their transportation rates more often than it intervenes to stop their price hikes (on the grounds that price reductions would be "disruptive" to the transportation industry, that is, the trucks and barges).[15] The agencies do not as a whole seem capable of developing consistent policies; they are often ineffective, and, if rarely corrupt, more than occasionally subject to influence peddling. Some agencies, from whatever the cause, do go through phases of getting tough on their regulatees. But even these episodes do not guarantee that the public interest will be served. A strong case can be made that part of the energy crisis (such as it may be) owes to overregulation by the Federal Power Commission.[16] And, as I noted, there are quite responsible commentators who are concerned that the FDA, oversensitive to congressional lambasting should there be another thalidomide affair, but subject to no countervailing "rewards" for hastening a promising new drug to the market, has been overly cautious in a way as detrimental to the public as to the pharmaceutical houses.

Indeed, commentators do not disagree on whether our agencies are adequate so much as on how bad they are, and—what is perhaps most important—on how much their shortcomings are *inherent* and how much (in the medieval philosophical sense) *accidental*.[17] Those who maintain the latter position ascribe present weaknesses to particular staffing problems, to lack of budget, to failure of appropriate congressional overseeing, or to some other such features of present agencies that are, at least in theory, transient and remediable. So far as one believes this, he can still hold out hope for better agencies—perhaps through the establishment of superagencies.

Obviously, there is something to be said for the "accidentalists." Some of the defects of our present regulatory agency system can be cured, or at least ameliorated. Recurrent problems of jurisdiction (for example, does the FCC have control over cable TV?) can be cleared up. But we must be sensitive to how irreducible some of the more nagging problems appear after nearly a century of experience. Take, for example, the vagueness in the ground rules under which the agencies operate, which is both a symptom and a cause of many of the problems the agencies evidence. The Federal Communication Acts tell the FCC to do what is "desirable in the public interest."[18] The National Transportation Policy, enacted by Congress in 1940 as a guide to the ICC, instructs the agency

to provide for fair and impartial regulation of all modes of transportation . . . so administered as to recognize and preserve the inherent advantages of each; to promote safe, adequate, economical and efficient service and foster sound economic conditions in transportation and among the several carriers; to encourage the establishment and maintenance of reasonable charges for transportation services, without unjust discriminations, undue preferences or advantages, or unfair or destructive or competitive practices. . . .[19]

The vague generality of the agencies' ground rules produces, understandably, all sorts of difficulties. The FCC, trying to work out some tangible criteria as guidelines for the granting of licenses, has produced some that seem almost inconsistent—as in seeking to maximize both broadcast experience and diversification of ownership—with no evident overriding principles to arbitrate the conflicts. Often the looseness of the agencies' mandate results in their turning over to their staffs equally foggy assignments, such as when the Civil Aeronautics Board directed one hearing examiner (with a total staff of one secretary) to "review the local air service pattern in the area covered by [seven] states and develop a sound pattern of service to meet the needs of the entire area."[20] If such generalities were products of carelessness or lack of attention, they could be remedied. But a good deal of the vagueness is more deep-seated and even inherent in the nature of the relationship between Congress and the agencies. The very situations that gave rise to agencies are those where Congress could not lay down hard-and-fast rules; if it could have, it would have. What is more, some measure of congressional vagueness may be born of political necessity: To muster enough votes for passage, proposed bills may have to become more and more watered down and ambiguous, leaving it to the agency to figure out what Congress "meant." (Consider, for example, the National Labor Relation Act's provision that the NLRB should get both sides to "bargain in good faith," a proviso that could be read by the Senate's labor supporters as a victory for them, and yet at the same time appear toothless enough to garner the votes that were promanagement.) With the agencies' basic ground rules cast in terms as open-ended as "the public interest," it is almost inevitable that the regulatees will have a disproportionately strong hand in filling in content. "The public," whatever it is, is distant and disorganized, "its" interests unclear, while the regulatees are present, organized, and vigilant—and they know what they want.

Let me close by observing that in these and many criticisms

of the federal agencies, I often find myself in strong agreement with the so-called "antis." But, in my mind, they fail to draw from their skepticism the correct implication for the corporate social-responsibility debate. If the agencies—or the other public control mechanisms—*were* effective, then it would be proper to brush aside the calls for corporate social responsibility by calling on the law to keep corporations in line. But the weaknesses of the agencies are simply a further argument that trust in our traditional legal machinery as a means of keeping corporations in bounds is misplaced—and that therefore something more is needed.

# 12. What "Corporate Responsibility" Might Really Mean

Against this background, we are now ready to see how much more potential there is in the notion of corporate responsibility than its proponents have yet grasped. Why it has not been seen is that, oddly enough, despite all the talk about corporations "being responsible," no one has ever made an attempt to carry the idea through seriously. If people are going to adopt the terminology of "responsibility" (with its allied concepts of corporate conscience) to suggest new, improved ways of dealing with corporations, then they ought to go back and examine in detail what "being responsible" entails—in the ordinary case of the responsible human being. Only after we have considered what being responsible calls for in general does it make sense to develop the notion of a corporation being responsible.

To begin with, for want of any real model of responsibility, the proponents of corporate responsibility all too often seem to identify it with corporate giving to charity—a sort of questionable copout, both theoretically and practically.* But responsibility should not be confused with altruism. In the case of human beings

* What happens in practice is that the managers of the donor corporation —those in charge of its decisions—wind up being generous to their favorite charities with money that is, in a relatively good sense, somebody else's. If charities are to be supported, why shouldn't management declare extra dividends and let the shareholders—whichever of them so choose—give to the charities of *their* choice? Or if there are social services that are not being adequately performed in the society, and if corporations have excess unexpended earnings at the end of the year, why not raise corporate taxes rather than put ourselves at the mercy of corporate largesse? If we took the latter route, excess monies would be drawn into and disbursed through governmental channels, where they would be subject to the democratic processes of a general electorate, rather than doled out at the whim of non-representative corporate managers.

it is to meet far more complex and subtle needs that responsibility is developed and nurtured.

We know that it is futile to hope that all socially undesirable behavior can be anticipated by legal rule-makers. We know that attempts to enforce all social desiderata by law would be more costly than it would be worth. We fear, too, that such attempts would unsatisfactorily enlarge the role of government while severely diminishing personal freedom. There are thus certain virtues, both to the individuals and to the society at large, of encouraging people to act in socially appropriate ways because they believe it the "right thing" to do, rather than because (and thus, perhaps only to the extent that) they are ordered to do so. Trusting to responsible behavior through some measure of self-control is often a preferable solution to some of the most difficult and perhaps otherwise insoluble problems of social organization.

Why these observations are important is that when we look back now on the unsatisfactoriness of present measures for controlling corporations, we can identify the very sorts of problems that have led to the nurturing of responsibility in human beings:

- Many social-control mechanisms (short of law) are increasingly ineffective when brought to bear on corporations.
- In an increasingly complex society, there may be such widespread, legitimate failure of consensus as to what values ought to be pursued, that laws—with their mandatory, across-the-board solutions—may be neither feasible nor desirable in major problem areas.
- Even where societal values can be agreed upon, they often can be agreed upon only in the most general way, not adequately for translation into effective rules.
- Even to the extent legal control over corporations can be made effective, "federalist"-type values might lend us pause as to how far the government should assume control over their decisions.
- In many instances corporations (and trade associations) have available, or can have available in advance of legislative bodies, information directly bearing upon where legislation is needed.
- Some traditional legal sanctions developed to control human behavior are inapplicable where the corporation is the actor (imprisonment, the death penalty) or may be practically unavailable for other

reasons (lack of effective jurisdiction over some operations of multi-national corporations).

- Even where legal sanctions are theoretically available, both our counterorganizational strategies and the measures aimed at key personnel are less than perfect in bringing about the needed institutional responses.

- Corporations are so often moving ahead of the society that at no time will present legal rules (and even, perhaps, present moral rules) be adequate to provide them with satisfactory standards.

Thus, the functions for which we need responsibility in human beings have distinct counterparts in the realm of corporate beha-ior. But what does it mean to be responsible? What does being responsible involve?

Once we start to examine what responsibility consists of in an ordinary person, we can see more clearly why there is something so unsatisfactory about current discussions of corporate responsibility. The notion is so open-textured that people who might plausibly claim to be "responsible" in one sense of the term could be made to appear, with no disagreement as to the facts, "irresponsible" in another. For example, some people undoubtedly consider Daniel Ellsberg's releasing of the Pentagon Papers "irresponsible," while others, without any significant disagreement as to the facts, or even as to a position on the Vietnam War, could support him as a paragon of responsibility.

The problem is that judgments of responsibility can be ascribed according to two schemes that are superficially distinct, if not in outright opposition. The first sense of responsibility, Responsibility 1, emphasizes following the law—abiding by the rules of one's social office: carrying out the authoritatively prescribed functions of a prosecutor, judge, soldier, or citizen. The second sense, Responsibility 2, emphasizes cognitive process, and, in a way almost diametrically opposed to Responsibility 1, puts a premium on autonomy, rather than rule obedience. Specifically, responsibility in the second sense emphasizes that a person's deliberations include the following elements:

- Viewed in its cognitive aspects, responsibility involves a degree of repression. The responsible person does not immediately implement his initial desires or impulses, his "gut reaction." It is in this sense that one who, for example, simply vents his rage, is not being "responsible." Thus, reflection is always an ingredient of responsibility in this sense.

- Responsible behavior begins with perception. The responsible person observes phenomena the irresponsible person ignores; more than this, his perceptions are stamped with moral categories. The responsible person looks for certain morally significant features of his environment: other persons (and other creatures), harm, pain, benefit to the social group.

- A responsible person takes measure of the full range of his freedom. It is in this sense that a man is not responsible if he adopts the posture that his decision is predetermined by forces in his environment, institutional or physical. He acts with an awareness that he will be accountable for what happens.

- To be responsible in this sense emphasizes a person's taking into account the consequences and repercussions of his actions. Thus, a person who drops a lighted match in a forest would be deemed irresponsible not because he wanted to cause injury to others (in which case we would be more inclined to say that he was venal or malicious) but because he did not think of the repercussions of his actions.

- He must consider and weigh alternatives.

- Being responsible involves reflection in all the above senses, but reflection per se is not enough; the reflection must be structured by reference to the society's moral vocabulary—that is, by characterizations in terms of "good," "bad," "just," and so forth, by thinking of "obligations," "rights," and "duties."

- One must have, in addition to a moral vocabulary, a moral inclination—a desire, probably as much internalized as conscious, to "do the right thing."

- Closely related is the fact that one must be prepared to give some justification for what he is doing. Overlooking for a moment the variation among traditional ethical theories, by and large they hold in common the view that to be responsible involves being prepared to explain, to give good reasons for one's actions; the responsible actor is willing to generalize the grounds for what he has done. This preparedness to justify, and especially the preparedness to do so in terms that admit of generalization (the Golden Rule, Kant's Categorical Imperative), is an important step toward the socialization of one's actions, inasmuch as it forces awareness of the social setting and the socially sanctified grounds of behavior.

If we return now to my earlier illustration, we can see that someone who called Ellsberg irresponsible probably meant it in sense one, the charge being based upon allegations that he failed to *abide by* the most apparent authoritative code applicable to those provided top-secret documents. By contrast, those who supported him as responsible were probably relying more on sense two, with emphasis on his having—in their view— *reflected thoroughly* (as described above) upon the connection between his actions, his capacity for choice, and certain significant features of his environment.*

Which of these two notions of responsibility—that which emphasizes following rules or that which emphasizes cognitive process, with some allowance for autonomy—would we ideally want to implant into corporations? The answer is both. For where it *is* feasible to design relatively unambiguous rules for corporate behavior—not to include nonskeletal meats in frankfurters—all we want is the responsibility of the rule-following, role-adhering sort. But as I have stressed throughout, there is also a large range of cases where rigid rules are increasingly ineffective, and perhaps even counterproductive, as instruments of corporate control. To

---

* It may seem odd that the same term should connote two such apparently disparate ways of approaching a problem. The disparity seems less odd, however, if one considers the shifting function of responsible behavior as societies mature. Early societies, with fairly routinized methods of production and generally stable conditions, can fairly successfully organize social relationships by reference to fixed, all-inclusive codes of behavior that are embedded in the religions, customs, and folkways. Responsibility is largely rule following. But as societies mature and become increasingly complex, responsibility in the sense of unquestioning obedience to rigid, pre-established rules becomes increasingly impractical. The specific directions of fixed rules must yield to a more open-ended direction that trusts to the individual's "autonomous" choice, although obviously, in practice, the "autonomous" choice is going to be constrained by internalized notions of socially proper behavior. The shift is now to a responsibility based not in carrying out rules per se, but in approaching problems through taking into account a broad range of socially appropriate considerations.

This shift in the meaning of responsibility as societies mature—societal maturation—has a clear analogue in the psychological maturation of the individual—Kohlberg's "stages" in the child's developing attitude toward morality and rules.

meet the problems in those areas the responsibility that is needed
—whether we are talking about corporations or persons—is a
responsibility of the "mature" sort, emphasizing cognitive processes, rather than blind rule obedience.

But what sense is there in speaking of a corporation—the entity
—being responsible? What would it even mean?

Let me illustrate my approach to corporate responsibility this
way. Responsible behavior in the human being, viewed in its
cognitive dimensions, begins, we saw, with perception. The person we deem irresponsible simply does not inform himself adequately about aspects of his environment that the responsible
person observes—especially regarding his own impact on it.
Our question then must be, is there, in the arena of corporate
behavior, an analogue of an "irresponsibility" that owes to inadequately perceptive corporate behavior? And if so, are there variables associated with the organization's "perception" that can
be identified and manipulated in such a manner as to increase
the corporation's responsibility? A cartoon that appeared in *The
New Yorker* affords an amusing jump-off point. In the cartoon,
two men, apparently public officials, have led a third, a high
corporate officer, to a wall of his plant which abuts and overlooks a waterway. From this prospect, the officer can look down
to see three huge pipes from which his company is dumping
pollutants into the water. With a look of perfectly ingenuous surprise, he remarks, "So *that's* where it goes! I'd like to thank you
fellows for bringing this to my attention."[1] Some viewers of the
cartoon will interpret the corporate officer's remarks cynically:
Surely he must have known all along. But the fact is, the intel-
ligence-gathering operations of any organization have to be
limited, and, at present, the areas in the corporation's environment from which it seeks data are typically those that will inform it upon prospective sales volume, demand shifts, competitor
behavior, and the like. Of its own accord (and, as we saw, even
under the law's implied threats) the corporation is not readily
prepared to find out where, say, its pollutants are going, or to
evaluate systematically what harm they may be causing over an
extended period of time. Yet, if the processes through which the

corporation perceives can be identified, is it not possible that the society can structure the organization's information net so the corporation will get feedback on the harm it is causing through pollution? Or consider another example. The National Institute of Mental Health has estimated that American pharmaceutical companies are manufacturing between 8 and 10 *billion* amphetamine pills each year—vastly in excess of the amount required by legitimate medical use. Much of the excess—destined for consumption by illegal drug users—is shipped to Mexico, then smuggled back into the United States via an elaborate underground.[2]

My point is, even though it may be difficult to make one of these companies legally responsible for how its products are ultimately used, there can be little doubt that a corporation that was responsible in the cognitive sense I have been discussing would, in the first instance, undertake some systematic efforts to determine the ultimate destination of its shipments. Consider the case of a Chicago company that in a period of a few years had shipped 15 million amphetamines to the post office box of an alleged drugstore in Tijuana. A congressional committee later discovered not only that the supposed purchaser was fictitious, but that the address given for the store would have placed it on or about the eleventh hole of the Tijuana Country Club golf course.[3] All the pharmaceutical houses are aware that this problem goes on and must be aware that, statistically, some of their own products are probably involved. But it is one thing to know in principle what is happening and quite another actually to track out one's particular shipments. The latter involves not only an expense, but worse, the introduction of systematic changes in the company's information net—changes in the direction of finding out information it might rather not know.

Certainly I am not saying that traditional legal measures can do nothing in this area of drug abuse: The government can set industry-wide production quotas; gross shipments to foreign countries can be curtailed. But there are obvious limits to each of these approaches. As the House Select Committee on Crime observed,

No amount of Government regulation can be as effective as private enterprise carefully monitoring its own sales. Manufacturers . . . realizing the dangerousness of their products when abused, have a duty to the public to see that these products are put to their intended legitimate use. . . .[4]

In other words, when costs and benefits are considered, responsible self-policing—in which the company, as a first step, designs its own information network appropriately to find out where its products are going—may be part of a solution that is preferable to across-the-board, and possibly futile or even self-defeating legal measures.

What these illustrations suggest is that the perception element of responsibility in a human being has a counterpart in problems we might want corporate responsibility to solve, and that changes in the organization's perception—its information-gathering system—would be a step, if only a first step, toward alleviating some of the problems. But there is a host of questions that remain to be answered. Are there counterparts in the organization's other internal variables—its authority structure, its reward and advancement criteria, its information channels—to the other cognitive processes that we saw to be associated with responsibility in the human being—holding action in abeyance pending an analysis of consequences, assessing contemplated behavior by reference to socially "moral" categories, and the like? If so, and if the responsibility model indicates that changes in them are warranted, how can we get companies to go ahead and implement them?

# IV

## Controlling Corporations: Putting the Model to Work

What is the corporation problem, I asked at the outset, and how is it to be solved? Unfortunately, there is no single answer, for, just to start with, there is not one corporation problem, but many. In each of its roles—as employer, resource consumer, product innovator, distributor—the corporation presents a range of problems that are, from the point of susceptibility to regulation, distinct. There is no reason to suppose that measures reasonably suited to realize social goals in some areas will be adequate in others; a breach of warranty action may help the man who buys a defective toaster, but neither the law of warranties nor any other law can provide him with a comparable remedy against the multitude of organizations that, perhaps without anyone's knowledge, are destroying his chest linings. What is more, corporations vary among themselves in such ways that even where the underlying problem is the same, solutions relatively effective against some corporations will be relatively ineffective against others. As we have observed, small corporations, in which the managers and the shareholders are essentially the same people, are likely to be more sensitive to profit-threat strategies than are the giant broadly held corporations, in which the managers are basically employees, their salary and tenure more or less independent of the corporation's legal damages.

For these reasons, one should be cautious to put forward *a* solution to *the* corporation problem. Yet, despite all the important variances, both the major lines of inquiry I have undertaken raise some significant features that corporation problems share in common, features that point us in a distinct and important direction.

First, in the analysis of existing sanctions we have seen that the traditional legal strategies have an only limited success in bringing about, within the organization, the internal institutional configurations that are necessary if some problem is to be remedied—that is, to induce the ideal authority structures, patterns of information flow, and the like, without which the corporation is not likely to "go straight" in the future.

Second, in the analysis of corporate social responsibility we have seen that the problem goes even deeper: Many corporate social problems do not feasibly lend themselves to the traditional legal treatments even to start with. In those cases, what seems needed as a "remedy" is some institutional analogue to the role that responsibility plays in the human being, guiding action toward certain values where the ordinary legislative prohibitions are unavailable or, on balance, unwise.

These two lines of development coalesce in the following way. Both suggest that to steer corporations we cannot continue to rely as heavily as we do on threats posed to the organization as a whole, allowing the corporation to adjust to the law's threats as "it" sees fit, according to "its" calculus of profits and losses; nor even to trust to threats aimed at key individuals in order to induce them to institute the changes they see fit. It isn't that these strategies should be abandoned. But what we shall have to do, increasingly, is augment them with a new approach. The society shall have to locate certain specific and critical organizational variables, and, where feasible, reach into the corporation to arrange them as it itself deems appropriate. In other words, if we can first clarify what ideal internal configurations of authority and information flow would best ameliorate the problem of, say, corporate pollution (configurations suggested either by the model of corporate responsibility, as I have used the term, or by an organizational analysis based on what institutional configurations we would have hoped the legal sanctions to bring about if they operated perfectly) the society might then consider programs aimed at mandating such ideal internal configurations directly.

Thus, what I have in mind is a legal system that, in dealing with corporations, moves toward an increasingly direct focus on the *processes of corporate decision-making*, at least as a supplement to the traditional strategies that largely await upon the corporate *acts*. Instead of treating the corporation's inner processes as a "black box," to be influenced only indirectly through threats laid about its environment like traps, we need more straightforward "intrusions" into the corporation's decision structure and processes than society has yet undertaken.

But what are the internal variables that we might select to impact directly? How would we go about influencing them? And why, if traditional legal mechanisms fall short, should we expect more success if we proceed by manipulating these internal variables?

# 13. Structural Variables: The Room at the Top

*Roles and Role Definitions*

The corporation, like any modern complex organization and, indeed, like the entire social order viewed as a whole, is built upon an elaborate network of institutional roles, or offices. This division of functions—into legislators, prosecutors, judges, juries, in the broader social system; into directors, chief executive officers, vice-presidents, project managers, in the corporate world—involves specifying such matters as who is to develop and evaluate what data, what sorts of things are to be considered by whom, and who has the authority (preliminarily and finally) to make what classes of decision.

In some measure, the aim of such systems is to provide predictability and stability of organizational performance in the face of constant changeover of personnel. If the system is working well, it has purely procedural virtues—that those with a problem will know where it should be taken for redress. But it is important to remember that such vital "procedural" matters as which threshold questions will pass into the decisional system, and how each of them will be defined—matters inseparable from how the organizational roles are established—have an obvious influence on outcome: what the organization's final decision will be. Thus, it should not surprise us that, at least in the public arena, one of the important ways in which we influence the direction of our society is through structural and procedural changes in the government.

Consider the National Environmental Policy Act[1] for a contemporary example of policy being implemented through the design of decisional procedures. That is to say, the act does not legislate particular substantive outcomes—for example, that all pollution into Lake Erie must stop at once, or that companies engaged in timber cutting over and above some defined amount shall be subject to a fine. Contemplating environmental problems where no such clear-cut legislative remedies now seem advisable, the act proceeds more cautiously, and perhaps more sophisticatedly: It seeks to affect decisions by shaping the structure of the decision process itself. Section 202 creates a Council on Environmental Quality; it places the Council in the Executive Office of the President; it provides for three members to be appointed by the President with the advice and consent of the Senate; Section 204 specifies the "duty and function" of the Council as:

(1) to assist and advise the President in the preparation of the Environmental Quality Report . . . ;

(2) to gather timely and authoritative information concerning the conditions and trends in the quality of the environment . . . , to analyze and interpret such information . . . , and to compile and submit to the President studies relating to such conditions and trends;

(3) to review and appraise the various programs and activities of the Federal Government in the light of the policy set forth in . . . this Act for the purpose of determining the extent to which such programs and activities are contributing to the achievement of such policy, and to make recommendations to the President with respect thereto;

(4) to develop and recommend to the President national policies to foster and promote the improvement of environmental quality . . . ;

(5) to conduct investigations, studies, surveys, research, and analyses relating to ecological systems and environmental quality;

(6) to document and define changes in the natural environment . . . ; and to accumulate necessary data and other information for a continuing analysis of these changes or trends and an interpretation of their underlying causes;

(7) to report at least once each year to the President on the state and condition of the environment; and

(8) to make and furnish such studies, reports thereon, and recommendations with respect to matters of policy, and legislation as the President may request.

The act operates, in other words, not by saying—at least in the first instance—that this or that can or cannot be done, but by saying that, whatever outcome is arrived at, it must be channeled through such-and-such a system, one designed to insure that certain types of facts have been gathered and considered, and that certain values have received their due weight.

Oddly, while the influencing of policy through mandatory structural and procedural requirements is commonplace in the design of public agencies, we only rarely and marginally use that approach where corporations—our "private governments"— are concerned. At present we leave it almost entirely up to the corporation to determine what offices it shall establish and how the functions of the various offices are to be spelled out. This is not to deny that the corporation's choices undoubtedly reflect, albeit indirectly, the pressures of the outside world. The passage of labor legislation, for example, may cause the corporation to create, after a period of time, a vice-president for labor relations. Social protests may bring about, amid much fanfare, the appointment of a vice-president for social policy. But when we rely on such indirect pressures, there is no reason to be confident that the corporation's response—the roles "it" chooses to set up, and the way "it" chooses to define them—will neatly conform to the socially ideal solution; anyone who feels that it will is taking too little account of the corporation's ability to buffer its core processes from the puny threats we strew about its environment.

We thus have to consider the possibility of impacting corporate behavior directly by, for example, mandating the addition of specified roles, e.g., laying down by law that companies of a certain class *must* establish vice-presidents for environmental affairs, or vice-presidents for consumer affairs, and undertaking to establish—ourselves—the functions for these various roles so as to make them effective.

If, we feel reasonably confident that computer-aided frauds like the Equity Funding scandal could be headed off if someone within the corporation were performing certain specific audit functions, we might require the corporations to establish the appropriate role, spelling out the desirable activity as part of the "job description" (and, in ways that I shall explore, making failure to abide by the specified functions an offense answerable to sources outside as well as inside the company). Are there corporate problems of such a nature that it would be fruitful to mandate roles and role requirements for various positions in the organizational hierarchy? Could "graftings" of either sort "take," that is, would the balance of the corporation produce antibodies to reject or circumvent these alien intrusions?

## The Board of Directors

The best place to begin a consideration of these possibilities is with the board of directors. For one thing, the performance of the board is often linked to some of the most important "conscience" functions that I alluded to; specifically, there is a tradition that the directors, whatever else they might do, should and could operate as a sort of corporate superego, adjusting the id desires of the corporation to the reality and morality demands of the outside world. It is in part for this reason that directorships are the one internal role on which corporate activists have been focusing their attention, periodically demanding a publicly elected director for corporations over a certain size, or for a member to be selected, as in some European countries, from among the workers, or even, presumably, from some other constituency, such as consumer or environmental groups.

Such ideas are, if naïvely optimistic, not without merit. But it is safe to say that if concrete proposals for improved board representation are going to emerge in this area, they will have to be drawn with a more realistic sense of what, given both the traditions and the commercial realities, directors could feasibly be required and expected to do. In other words, one must combine the proposals for representation with concomitant proposals for reforming the very functions and responsibilities of the directors; it is simply not enough to thrust a public nominee onto the board, while leaving the framework—the rules, understanding, and practices—untouched.

Let me approach the situation this way: What is it that directors are *doing* that putting a black, woman, or worker on the board can be deemed so important by corporate activists? Start with the legal requirements.

In examining what the law demands of directors, there is at least one encouraging point: The very existence of legal requirements in this area is evidence that the corporate world can live with some intrusions into its "internal" organization, at least in principle. Every state demands in its laws that there *be* directors (while leaving the corporation free to create or not, as it sees fit, such lower-level functions as vice-presidents for marketing, legal counsel, quality-control engineers); almost all lay down some minimum number (usually three) that there must be; and all take *some* steps toward establishing the functions that directors must fulfill.

Some, but not many. And this is an important point that those who clamor for public directors fail to consider adequately. True, state corporation codes typically require that "the business and affairs of every corporation shall be controlled by the board" (California);[2] or that "the business and affairs of every corporation . . . shall be managed by a Board of Directors" (Delaware)[3]. Were this literally true, then of course any corporate reform program could make large strides by placing the "right" men on the board. But it just isn't so. No one can really expect the board to attend to all the details of corporate governance, any more than one can expect the President's cabinet to, in the fullest sense, "manage" and "control" the affairs of the country.

Indeed, a corporate director—especially of the sort we are contemplating here—is apt to know a lot less about what is happening throughout his company than a cabinet officer knows about his department. By "the sort we are contemplating here," I mean to underscore an important distinction businessmen make between "inside" directors and "outside" directors—a distinction that, although common today, would have made no sense in earlier times.

Traditionally, all directors came to the board from "outside" the company—that is, they were men whose principal employment was with some company other than the company on whose board they sat. A budding machine tool company might reach into its commercial environment to secure a local bank officer or two, a manufacturing executive, a lawyer, or an officer of a potential customer. It was this "outsidedness" that assured the business community that management's actions were being scrutinized with a modicum of objectivity and independence.

This century, however, has seen the spreading practice of

"inside" directors—that is, men serving as directors of the very companies that employ them as managers.[4] Viewed from a historical perspective, this development is a sort of managerial *trompe l'oeil*, for the more a corporation moves to a preponderance of "inside" directors, the more the "internal" management affairs are under no scrutiny but that of management itself. Thus, if there is any hope of getting from the board some of the special functions we are after, some input over and above that which management alone can provide, it lies, obviously, with outside directors of some sort.

What about the outsiders? Why should one be skeptical that, so long as the present framework remains intact, not much is going to come even from them? The answer lies, largely, but not solely, in the fact that vastly too much happens within the corporation for anyone to expect the directors to be in touch with it all. Worse, these are men with no independent staff, whose primary responsibilities ordinarily rest elsewhere, who meet only once a month, or perhaps even quarterly, whose compensation for serving as directors is ordinarily quite nominal, and who themselves compound these problems by serving on five, ten, fifteen, or even twenty boards at the same time.[5]

In such circumstances, the outside directors, unfamiliar with the ongoing details of the corporation's operations, dependent on such data as management gives them—neither predigested nor critically analyzed by any independent source—are by and large going to hear the problems management wants them to hear, and dispose of them in accordance with management's prior recommendations. As Stanley Vance has observed, "only in the rarest instances do outside directors have even the faintest idea of the technical processes, the competitive strains, or the real financial status of the host company."[6] This is a state of affairs that is likely to get only worse as the typical company grows, diversifies its product lines, becomes conglomerate and multinational, and thus increasingly gets involved in more and more problems that have fewer and fewer common features that any single group of men can effectively comprehend and direct.

The failure of the typical board of directors to be an effective force in running—or in even touching upon—most of the affairs of a modern corporation is rooted in problems that go deeper than even lack of time, familiarity, and expertise. Myles Mace of the Harvard Business School, who has done a study of directors in large and medium-sized, widely held companies, points out that the typical outside director, having been placed on the board by management (rather than, as historical theory would have it, the other way around), is particularly reticent to rock the boat with discerning questions. It is "plain bad manners," one company president chided, in private and after the meeting, an aberrationally inquisitive director who had done nothing more rude than ask what was being done to correct steadily declining earnings.[7] Mace acknowledges that some special sorts of outside directors—presumably those who represent dominant stockholders or who have been pressed onto the board by major creditors, such as banks, in connection with loan agreements— are inclined to be a little more probing (at least as regards financial well-being). Nonetheless, Mace concludes that the composite picture one gets of boards of major companies is one in which presidents "generally do not want to be challenged by the questions of directors."

The lack of active discussions of major issues at typical Board meetings and the absence of discerning questions by Board members result in most Board meetings resembling the performance of traditional and well-established almost religious rituals. In most companies, it would be possible to write the minutes of a Board meeting in advance.[8]

Nowhere in recent years is there more striking testimony to board impotence than in the collapse of the Penn Central. A tragic panorama of ineptness, deceit, and self-dealing had been going on under the directors' noses from almost the moment the Pennsylvania and the New York Central merged. Management, instead of giving its fullest attentions to the floundering rail operations, and at a time when the railroad was in dire need of cash to replenish rolling stock, was toying around with an ill-conceived empire that ranged from a hockey team to real estate ventures, to a downright hokey if not unlawful airline subsidiary (Executive Jet Aviation), to their own "private" investment trust (Pennphil).[9] Tens of millions of dollars were funneled to the airline without the outside directors, so far as anyone can tell, figuring out what was going on.[10] The insiders arranged, for example, for the railroad to advance $16 million to a subsidiary, American Contract Company, which, also under the insiders' control, inconspicuously slipped it over to the airline. The treasurer's report to the Penn Central showed the $16 million figure; yet the reports never disclosed what ACC was using the money for—and apparently nobody at the Penn Central board ever asked.[11] As the true situation at the Penn Central worsened, management, presumably as a way of putting a good face on things, and keeping the financial community and public unaroused, recommended increasingly higher dividends. The directors complied—so far as the minutes reflect, without any discussion—so that as the company was becoming more and more desperate for capital, money was more and more freely being pumped out.[12]

Reviewing the fiasco, the House Committee on Banking and Currency observed, "It was as though everyone was part of a close-knit club in which the Penn Central and its officers could obtain, with very few questions asked, loans for just about everything they desired . . . where the bankers on the Board asked practically no questions as to what was going on, simply allowing management to destroy the company, to invest in questionable activities, and to engage in some cases in illegal activities."[13]

There are, in the Penn Central debacle, a number of instructive lessons for anyone who wants to rely on boards as control devices. But none is more sobering than what the Penn Central board failed *about*: Theirs was not a failure to ask discerning questions about, say, what the Penn Central was doing in the area of environmental pollution, or the workers' well-being, or how it was responding on some other avant-garde social consciousness issue. Here was a group of financiers, primarily, and the one thing one might have hoped they could understand, and, God knows, as representatives of the financial community, had it in their interest to avoid, was the financial sickness of the railroad.*

If, in other words, a board of apparently "eminent" directors cannot, or will not—for whatever reasons—effectively attend to the matters that were critical in the Penn Central's demise, how can we suppose they will be effective in advancing "softer" values less consistent with the interests of the financial community?

## The Prospects for Change

Some of the weaknesses in the board do seem remediable, which both explains and supports some of the agitation for board reform. To the extent that the difficulty lies in the directors' being outmanned in terms of expertise and information-handling ability, one can ask that they be provided with staff (a proposal that ex-Supreme Court Justice Arthur Goldberg made in resigning from TWA's board recently,[14] and one to which I shall return in a moment). So far as no one on the board has been placed there to represent the public interest, it is tempting to suggest that the public elect, or public agencies appoint, a director responsible to the public. This is already the case with three of the fifteen Comsat (Communications Satellite Corporation) directors, who are presidential nominees, and was the case earlier in American history with the Union Pacific Railroad.[15] In other words, isn't all this just evidence that what is needed is a public

---

* The House report shows that the following financial institutions were represented on the board of the Penn Central through directors who also interlocked with their own respective boards:

| Name of Institution | No. of Interlocks with PC Board |
|---|---|
| Chase Manhattan Bank | 1 |
| First National Exchange Bank of Virginia | 1 |
| Philadelphia Saving Fund Society | 2 |
| First Pennsylvania Banking & Trust Company | 3 |
| Bankers Trust Company | 2 |
| Provident National Bank, Philadelphia | 2 |
| New England Merchants Bank | 1 |
| Suffolk Franklin Savings Bank | 1 |
| Morgan Guaranty Trust Company | 2 |
| Girard Trust Bank | 1 |
| Marine Midland Trust Company | 2 |

director on the board, who will be the one to ask the discerning and well-informed questions that are presently lacking?

The answer is, not quite. For even if we placed such a well-intentioned and well-staffed fellow on the board, at least three major problems, in addition to those I have already cited, would remain.

The first has to do with the overbreadth of "the public" as a constituency. Instructing someone to advance the "public interest" is simply too ill-defined and open-ended a mandate to be very effective: witness the patchy performance of administrative agencies that are charged with issuing certificates "if the public interest and necessity" so requires. If what the "public interest" dictated in some matter were clear, the appropriate disposition would presumably have been engendered—or should be engendered—in legislation. Moreover, as I shall argue more fully, it is not well-meaning generalists that the boards need, nor is it they who are likely to command the respect of the men whose cooperation they will have to depend on.

Second, even if such a person were placed on the board, we have to consider the sorts of discussions that he would participate in. Given the present institution, matters that rise to the board—and about which he could presumably ask demanding, relatively well-informed questions—largely involve finance (dividends, executive salaries, funding programs), proposed organic changes (mergers, consolidations), and new ventures (establishing a foreign subsidiary). Mind, I am not deprecating the significance of these matters for the general nonstockholding public —especially as huge companies that go under increasingly look to taxpayer funds to bail themselves out with. As regards, for example, the Penn Central failure (which, on the basis of some estimates could cut total U.S. economic activity a whopping 4 percent[16]), one could certainly wish that some well-informed and aggressive public director had been present throughout. The point is merely that a great range of the matters with which the corporate activists are concerned—environmentalism, consumer problems, transnational conduct, employee well-being—rarely rise to the board level in any significant form.

But, someone will ask, if a well-informed, inquisitive, public-spirited director is placed on the board, won't it be his task to assure that these matters are brought up? Isn't he going to return the board to performing as a vital and meaningful institution? The question brings us to the third problem. Given the present social and legal fabric, the effect of placing such a man on the board might well be the opposite: to *reduce* the amount of important business conducted there. To understand this paradox, one has to take another close and cynical look at the corporation codes, to discover the absolute minimum the company can get away with having the directors do.

The problem is this. Partly in response to the unfeasibility of having the boards really oversee everything that is going on, the power the codes give to the directors with the right hand ("the business and affairs of every corporation shall be controlled by the Board . . .") they immediately provide for delegating away with the left (" . . . subject to limitations of the [corporation's] articles of incorporation" [California]; " . . . except as may be otherwise provided . . . in the certificate of incorporation" [Delaware]).[17] As a result of these laws, specific provision can be made for various powers of the board—in fact, most of the powers of the board—to be transferred to executive committees consisting of only one or more directors. Thus, if the company (which for these purposes we can pretty well identify with the management and its cooperative directors) chooses, almost all the powers of the board can be shuttled over to some such clubby subcommittee. The nondelegable exceptions for the most part involve matters like declaring dividends, which lie outside the concern of most of the present corporate critics.[18]

Thus, if (let me fantasize for a moment) Ralph Nader or one of his associates were suddenly to be put on the board of a major auto company, the result, rather than to make the board a more vital forum, would at least as likely result in the following: (a) management would bring even fewer of its decisions before the board; (b) problems that management felt for one reason or another had to be brought to the attention of *some* outside directors (such as nominees of major credit institutions) would be increasingly discussed—as many "sensitive matters" are discussed today—discreetly outside the board room; and, (c) many matters that require formal "board" approval would be consigned to executive committees from which the "outsider" would be frozen out. Quite possibly all that would remain for the full board to consider would be those core matters that by law cannot be delegated to an executive committee (declaration of dividends, proposals to merge)—and even these could be brought to the board after a prior caucusing, to be officially approved in a way even more ritualistic and uninquiring than at present.

Thus, if there is any hope of valuable reform at the board level, it cannot rest with assigning some new members to the board. It has to involve a revision of key features of this whole system.

# 14. Reforming the Board

Would board-level changes be worth the effort? In light of the problems I have reviewed we have to recognize that nothing we do at the board level is going to cure all or even most of the corporate problems people are concerned about. What is more, because of the mystique about the board—the public's misconception as to its real influence—anyone who proposes reforming it risks inspiring an undeserved confidence that everything is being brought under control.

Notwithstanding these reservations, I have become increasingly convinced in the past few years that there are fundamental board-level reforms that should be implemented. These changes, particularly if reinforced by, and carefully linked with, changes elsewhere in the corporate system, could become an integral part of a major and significant reevaluation of the ways in which we control corporations.

What we have to do, though, is enter upon this task with some realistic sense of what we should and should not expect board reform to accomplish. If there is absolute consensus that some corporate activity, like price-fixing, is objectionable, then we do better to place our first line of trust in stiff laws, rigorously enforced by the government, rather than in the hope that an enlightened directorate will put its house in order. But as we saw too, it is not always feasible or wise to rely solely on the lawmaking and law-enforcement processes as a solution to corporate problems. As a force for controlling corporations, the traditional legal and market forces leave a gray area—a gap between what we can rely on these forces to get corporations to do, and what we might ideally want of them. Thus, when we talk about board reform it is with this gray area that we are concerned.

Even within this narrowed area, we have to mark a distinction between two sorts of corporate behavior. The first, which I call Class A behavior, is relatively feasible to deal with through moderate changes in the character of the board. The second, which I call Class B behavior, is considerably harder to get at through board changes—or, for that matter, through any other of the internal restructuring approaches I shall discuss.

## Class A Behavior

Class A behavior is behavior regarding which there is a minimum of conflict between what the public at large would want, and what would likely be approved by a cross section of businessmen such as are sitting on the boards of typical major American corporations, *if the board were fully informed of the facts* (which puts aside for a moment the question of whether they *could* or even *would want* to be fully informed under our present system). I recognize that in speaking both of the "public at large" and of such a typical cross section, I am invoking broad constructs. But behind the generalities there is a core of some substance and range. What I have in mind is that neither the public nor the executives wants a thalidomide scandal, or fabrics that will burst into flames. It is hard to believe that a representative sampling of board members, fully informed of what was happening to animals in Richardson-Merrell's laboratories, would have voted to push ahead with MER/29. To have done so would not only have run counter to moral views that are held by the general public and general business community in common; it would not have made sense financially, all the risks considered. The same can be said of the Equity Funding scandal, and some of the grosser acts and omissions behind the Penn Central collapse. These are things that tend to occur, or be abetted by, the sorts of institutional defects I pointed out earlier in the book. And one should not lightly assume that either the occurrences, or the underlying defects, would have the support of an informed board with any but the most speculative, short-term financial stake in the enterprise.

I expect, indeed, that there is a whole range of matters on which, at least insofar as values and ends are concerned, there are not large differences of opinion between what the public would disapprove of and what would be disapproved of by a representative sampling of the financial-commercial community from which outside directors are traditionally drawn. Specifically, I would expect that if the issue were put to them, an informed, disinterested cross section of businessmen would put their weight against* (if only because they would be ashamed, among a group of their peers, to put their weight behind):

- gross financial and inventory manipulations;
- an overt policy of racial discrimination in hiring and promotion;
- violations of criminal laws;
- the production of adulterated, unsafe, and shoddy products (although, we should observe, the business community's definitions of "adulterated" and "unsafe" are apt to vary from the general public's);
- corporate espionage;
- in general, a number of environmental and consumer abuses that businessmen incline to classify as "stupid"—that is, the sort of behavior that good management would spot as contrary to the long-run interests of the corporation, if only because if not remedied, they are likely to bring forth more "crazy" and "repressive" legislation.

Not all Class A behavior involves, like the above, unwanted acts. There is certainly an area of Class A positive behavior as well—that is, where there is a theoretical congruence between what the public wants and the long-run interests of the general financial community. Both ideally wish a company to develop products in anticipation of future consumer needs; both want it to have alternative sources of energy it can turn to in the event of disruptions in its traditional sources. Classic (precorporate) economic theory suggests that such a congruence between public and private interests is so inevitable that there is no need to worry up special structures to assure its realization. But this

---

* A director's willingness to vote an action up or down, or approve a board policy, is, of course, a considerably different matter than his demanding valid assurances that the vote is being carried—a distinction I am overlooking here for the purposes of defining classes of behavior.

faith is misplaced—not only because of the possibility that management may be too inept or unimaginative to capitalize on long-range social needs. Worse, there are any number of reasons why, absent some reform of the present system, special short-term interests may distort and overwhelm the theoretical long-term harmony. One is the fact that major shareholders are often speculating on short-term gains, not necessarily inconsistent with their countenancing, for example, the denuding of timber lands or their letting a half-tested but highly touted drug go to market (and then selling out their shares before the roof caves in—both on the remaining corporation and the society). Another is the proclivity of the most active and hysterical forces in the stock market to measure corporate performance on the basis of quarterly earnings reports which, when combined with the legal strictures against a company's projecting its future earnings, places a disproportionate emphasis on the present. This stock market atmosphere, in turn, can translate into a hurried and shortsighted vision within the corporation.

What these considerations mean is that while there is a broad range of "solutions" desired jointly by the general financial-commercial community, the public, and the corporation ("the corporation" considered as an abstract, ongoing entity) it does not follow that the particular forces who come to control any board will necessarily advance them.

## Class B Behavior

By contrast with Class A behavior, Class B behavior involves cases where the public interest and the business community's interests are less overlapping: A cross section of businessmen such as are sitting on a typical major American corporation's board, *even if fully informed of the facts,* would quite likely *not* put an effective damper on the activities the public was against, nor put their weight behind those that the public favored.

Among Class B negative behavior, one might expect to find:

• consumer deception that businessmen are apt to view more as "puffing" than outright fraud;

- pollution and other environmental harms, not clearly unlawful, and which the corporation cannot remedy consistent with a felt need to "turn a fair profit";
- a host of "citizenship" problems, ranging from a corporation's removing from some locale without prior consultation with local officials, to labor and investment policies abroad that may have adverse, long-range effects on our international policies.

In making these distinctions between Class A and Class B behavior, I am aware that at the edges they most assuredly overlap. What one group of businessmen might view as Class A, such as grossly deceptive advertising, will be "mere puffing," or Class B, to another group. Products that some men will view as unsafe will be, to others, necessary compromises with "reality," given the profit constraints they are under. ("After all," one of my executive friends is fond of saying, "the ordinary household pencil, if abused, is a dangerous weapon.")

Nonetheless, I think the distinction introduces some valuable contours for our analysis. For wherever one might guess the boundaries to lie, it can be said that there is some class of problems—Class A in my terminology—that we can hope to improve through relatively modest reforms, reforms that leave the corporation fairly autonomous in the director selection. But as we move deeper and deeper into the Class B problems, changes of a more radical sort seem called for. I will turn to these more intrusive measures in the chapters that follow.

## Getting at Class A Problems

The key toward some successful reform in the Class A area lies in the fact that, by definition, these are the matters on which a cross section of businessmen are apt to be in minimal conflict with the public at large, at least insofar as values and ends are concerned. This is not to deny the room for—nor the significance of the room for—differences of judgment between these camps: on calculations of risk, on relevance, on how the costs of various means should be balanced. But it means that at least insofar as these problems are concerned, we can hope to reduce the disparities by first conforming the makeup of the board to a more and more representative cross section of businessmen, and then reinforcing the changes in representation by changes in the institutional design of the board—in the information it receives, in the incentives under which it operates, in its effective authority to carry out prophylactic and remedial programs.

Such a program would include the following measures.

1. *Inside directors should be eliminated in corporations of major impact.* In the present framework the contribution of directors is such that it does not matter terribly whether the board is permeated with insiders or not. But if we are hopeful of making the board a more meaningful institution, we have to begin by reconsidering a practice that puts onto the board the very people it is supposed to be keeping under review. In the typical small, family, or otherwise closely held corporation, the practice might as well be allowed to pass.* But in corporations above some threshold level of impact—those, say, with annual sales of $50 million or more—it is well worth asking, as Mace puts it, "How does an insider on the board serve as a discipline on himself? . . . How does an officer-director with aspirations of continued employment evaluate the president except in favorable terms?"[1] Indeed, the practice is no more defensible when approached from the other side of the coin: Why is there even a *reason* for insiders to serve on the board? Surely managing officers can maintain whatever board contact and presence is required without actually being formal voting board members. If some insiders on the board are to be tolerated in some circumstances in order to preserve their prestige or to "legitimate" the board's decisions in the eyes of the corporation's staff, there is no reason why sliding scales cannot be adopted, so that, while small companies can have whatever mix of insiders and outsiders they desire, companies with increasingly more and more potential social impact must have proportionately more and more out-

---

* Except, perhaps, in special cases where the company has been a repeated law violator or is engaged in an undertaking particularly likely to give rise to a certain class of objectionable behavior, a problem discussed in Chapter 16.

siders. Why, for example, should we allow companies in Equity Funding's position to have—as Equity had—a mere minority of outsiders to keep tabs on what the insiders are up to? The more that our concomitant reforms endow the board with the potential to be a viable source of review, the more reason there is to call the predominance of insiders to question.*

2. *A percentage of the directors should be financially disinterested.* So far I have made no distinction among outside directors as between those who are financially interested in the success of the corporation, such as officers of institutions holding large blocks of the company's stock, and those not so interested. For many purposes, financially interested directors may be thought preferable, because their stake in the host company's well-being should provide an incentive for them to keep operations under tight review. Unfortunately, this is probably but half the truth under the present system: It depends on the situation and it depends, most importantly, on how easily the interested directors can bail themselves out of their holdings. Consider, for example, the scenario that took place as the Penn Central was going under, specifically as to the continued payment of dividends. The more cynical interpretation of what happened is that the directors who represented the major stockholder interests *did* become aware of the situation earlier than they now allow, but that they continued the dividend payments both to "get while the getting was good" and also, by keeping a good face on things, to hold the price of the stock up while the parties they represented dumped their shares on an unsuspecting market.[2]

Thus, while interested directors may be looked to to ameliorate some of the Class A problems, we have to recognize that when affairs promise to take a really serious turn, it is only the rare investor who will stick around: He is more likely to get out of a worsening situation, unobtrusively, than to publicize the problem by demands for remedial change. It is therefore evident

* Even the New York Stock Exchange's December 1973 white paper has recommended that all companies listed on the Big Board include at least three outside directors, and that the company set up an "audit committee" of such directors to deal closely with the independent auditor (*Wall Street Journal*, December 17, 1973, p. 9, col. 1).

that while an interested outside director board would, in most respects, be an improvement over an insider board, neither would provide the corporation with the cross-sampling of American businessmen such as the problems of the Class A area require. At the least, there must be some provision for a complement of directors who are not only outsiders, but who are not directly interested in the financial affairs of the company. "Directly," I grant, is not easy to define and police in our present financial society, given the pervasiveness of interlocking interests. But for these purposes, we could almost certainly improve our situation if we provided that in corporations of threshold impact (annual sales of $50 million or more), at least two or 10 percent of the directors (whichever were larger) could neither personally own, nor be a director or officer of a firm that owned shares in the company.

3. *The functions of directors should be defined.* One of the most incredible features of the present-day board system is that, beyond the bare-bone and vague requirements of the corporations codes, there is almost no authoritative guide as to what, exactly, the directors are supposed to be doing. In fact, in the modern corporation elaborate, formal job descriptions exist for just about everybody *except* the directors. When a man assumes, for example, the job of data control manager at a certain California manufacturing corporation, there is a written "position guide" that lays out the job's specific duties, including:

- Develops plans and schedules for all tasks and personnel under his cognizance and presents these regularly to the Program Manager.
- Hires (through Personnel Administration), reviews, promotes, demotes, and terminates personnel under his cognizance, subject to approval by the Program Manager.
- Measures and evaluates task progress and personnel performance against schedules.
- Originates workload priorities for all subordinates, including secretaries.
- Enforces adherence to approved company policies and procedures among subordinates.
- Monitors training of new personnel by subordinates.

All this tells the data control manager what is expected of him. Yet, as Mace points out, where directors are concerned the job descriptions, if any, are typically "broad, vague, meaningless, and usually unknown to the members of the Board."[3]

Mace proposes, as a remedy, that the specific functions of the board should be discussed and agreed upon by the chairman, the president, and the outside board members, and reduced to writing as a sort of "board charter."

I think that setting forth such job descriptions for directors would be meaningful (especially if some liability is attached to nonperformance). As long as there is no clear understanding of what they are supposed to be doing, the directors are the more apt to do the least they can, or else be swept along to do only what management wants of them. Given this void, the directors feel they lack a certain "right" (I mean an important social as well as a legal right) to ask provocative questions, to demand reports and explanations.*

What might help, in other words, is a job description that *mandated* that the directors, for example, receive and evaluate explanations of all loans to subsidiaries. For men in such a position as the outside directors, often serving at the pleasure of the insiders, the job description becomes a sort of an "out"; it not only stiffens their backs to do what they know should be done, it also enables them to do it in a way that preserves vital working relationships. Armed with such a job description, the director can always plead, "Of course I'm sure everything's in good shape but, as you know, I've got to file with the finance committee my independent appraisal of. . . ."

---

* The SEC's inquest into the Penn Central collapse is especially telling in this regard:

> Both before and after the merger [the directors] relied on oral descriptions of company affairs. They failed to perceive the complexities of the merger or the fact that appropriate groundwork and planning had not been done. After the merger they claim to have been unaware of the magnitude of the fundamental operational problems or the critical financial situation until near the end. They did not receive or request written budgets or cash flow information which were essential to understanding the condition of the company or the performance of the management. Only in late 1969 did they begin requesting such information and even then it was not made available in a form that was meaningful or useful. S.E.C., *Staff Study of the Financial Collapse of the Penn-Central Company* C.C.H. *Federal Securities Law Reporter* (1972), 82, 012.

While I thus agree with Mace that a delineation of directors' functions would be an important step forward, I am not sanguine about having the guidelines established by the directors and top management in whatever detail *they* can agree upon. My skepticism has several roots.

First, one has to appreciate why most corporations are so vague in delineating their directors' functions. Looked at from the view of inside management, the very promise of a well-defined job description for directors—to get the outsiders poking around more than they are doing at present—is exactly what they don't want. (In the present system, what management wants of the outside directors is, as much as anything else, prestigious window dressing, an inside track to important financial institutions when credit is suddenly needed, and some very broad financial policy input.) Looked at from the point of view of the outsiders, for them a too clearly defined job description threatens to require more time for their directorship activities than they are presently putting in, and, worse, could increase their liability in the event they don't do what they are specifically required to do.

Thus, it is unlikely that the parties, if left to their own wiles, are going to come up with detailed job descriptions that have much real bite to them. And even if they gave it a try, given present board constituencies, the descriptions they came up with would almost certainly be framed with the interests of major investment institutions not only the paramount, but probably the exclusive concern. In other words, even supposing a self-determined job description to be capable of ameliorating financial and operating collapses like the Penn Central fiasco, it is not likely that they will be so shaped as to call to question even the bulk of the Class A activities that, albeit socially undesired, are most profitably—or at any rate, most manageably—left unquestioned by the executives. What is more, insofar as the job description is a mere "compact" arrived at by the participants among themselves, breaches would not automatically give rise to any liability.

For these reasons, we should not simply trust to what the directors and management might come up with among themselves. The answer lies in society's identifying core functions the

directors ought to be performing and then providing for them *by law*; the federal government has adequate power to do so by general legislation under the Commerce Clause. In delineating such functions I would certainly embrace many of Mace's suggestions, such as that criteria be established by which the board is required to evaluate the performance of management annually.°
But I would advocate that matters of high social concern, not adequately factored into corporate decision-making under present circumstances, be worked into the statutory job requirements as well. If, for example, worker safety was deemed a particularly exacerbated problem in some industries, and environmental problems in another, and capital ratios in another, then directors of companies operating in these particular industries would be appropriately instructed to keep in touch with these special problems, setting targets, gathering information, and demanding progress reports. We might well demand that the directors of a railroad company specifically assure themselves that the non-railroad operations of the company do not so drain capital away from enterprise that the company cannot fulfill the purposes for which its charter and franchise were granted. It ought to be noted, however, that in order to tailor job descriptions to particular companies, or industry groupings, general legislation may be too inflexible, and thus the task of proposing and reviewing specially designed, top-level job descriptions might be one function for a Federal Corporations Commission.

4. *Changes have to be made in the standards for directors'*

---

° One of the smaller companies Mace interviewed, Omark Industries, had even undertaken a step in this direction, specifying job requirements for directors in areas including shareholder relations (". . . approve policy regarding tender offer strategy . . ."); financial structure and actions (". . . approve changes in capital structure and basic changes in debt policy . . ."); purposes, objectives, policies, plans (". . . approve long-range corporate objectives normally initiated by the chief executive officers . . . receive annually a special R & D report listing major projects by divisions . . . receive on request periodic compliance audits concerning conformance to major corporate policy . . ."); management (". . . appraise performance of the chief executive officer and the chairman, and review with them their annual personal objectives . . ."); control (". . . recognize and identify the Board's need for company information, and arrange for its timely supply . . . inquire into causes of measured deficiencies in performance . . ."). Myles L. Mace, "The President and the Board of Directors," *Harvard Business Review* (March-April 1972), p. 47.

*liability*. It is one thing to lay down a set of standards establishing what, ideally, we want directors to do. It is another thing to get them to do it. Indeed, the difficulties are so large as to constitute another independent roadblock in making directorships effective vehicles for social control over corporations.

The problem is this. Generally in the commercial world we get people to do what they are supposed to through a system of rewards and penalties. The ordinary worker who does his job well can look forward to promotion, pay raises, and the respect of his co-workers; the man who is lax will be passed over, demoted, fired, or even, in gross cases, subject to some public sanction through the courts.

Where directors are concerned, however, we are in a strange and distinct situation. Much of what we want the directors to add to a corporation involves their closely scrutinizing—even second-guessing and, if necessary, exposing—the management. This would not be so bad if the directors were really, as the legal theory has it, the agents of the far-flung shareholders, most of whom would strongly encourage a certain amount of vigilance. But realistically it is the managers themselves who, at least in the giant companies, decide upon the board "candidates" whom the shareholders will elect only pro forma. It is the management, too—and, in all events, not the far-flung shareholders—who constitute the peer group whose approval and disapproval has the most effective social impact. Thus, the director who does his job "well" (as the general society would judge it) is not destined to win the approval of his colleagues. Nor will his excellence win him added financial rewards and promotions. Quite the contrary. More likely than not, an "overly" conscientious director will be dropped from the board slate or, as with Arthur Goldberg at TWA or Norton Simon at the Burlington Northern, he will ultimately do the "gentlemanly" thing in those circumstances: tender his resignation.

Thus, there is not much hope of influencing directors through positive reinforcement, and as a practical matter we are forced to come at them from the other and less generous direction—with legal threats.

This approach barely stands us any better, however. For one

thing, penalties are never an adequate substitute for a system of positive rewards. Even at their best they are effective to bring forth *minimum standards* of performance—not to elicit from people the best of which they are capable. But even worse than this is the fact that the present legal rules that purport to make directors liable for negligently attending to their duties probably do more harm than good.° To begin with, they are toothless. As I observed in Chapter 7, such suits against directors are rarely pressed to a successful judgment. The standard of attentiveness the courts enforce is low;† corporate bylaws generally protect directors if they relied "in good faith" on reports, such as audits, that management presented them; and in all events, judges are little inclined to second-guess businessmen in matters of business judgment. Further, even in those rare cases in which some plaintiff does come up with a judgment (or, less rarely, a settlement) it is almost never the director who will bear the brunt of it, anyway. Settlements tend to be worked out in such a way that "the corporation," rather than the directors, picks up the tab (usually a payment to the plaintiff's lawyer); or the director, if he has to pay something, is immediately indemnified by the corporation; or he is covered by directors' liability insurance, the

° I am distinguishing here between directors' liability for negligence and the liability of a director for self-dealing—that is, a director's harming the company on whose board he sits by improperly swinging deals that benefit him personally, or benefit his "home" company. I make no recommendations to alter directors' liability in the latter area.

† See, for example, the opinion of Learned Hand in *Barnes* v. *Andrews*, 298 F. 614 (S.D.N.Y. 1924). There the defendant director had attended only one of two directors' meetings that were held between the inception of the company in 1919 and its demise two years later; his only attention to the affairs of the company consisted of talks with the president as they met from time to time. It was "entirely clear . . . that he made no effort to keep advised of the actual conduct of the corporate affairs, but had allowed himself to be carried along as a figurehead. . . ." Nonetheless, Hand ruled he was not liable on the theory that the plaintiff had the burden of showing both that the director's performance of his duties would have avoided the loss, and also what loss it would have avoided. Mere inattentiveness followed by the collapse of the business was not enough even to shift the burden of proof back onto the director. More recently, the Second Circuit has decided that an outside director has only limited duties under Rule 10b-5 (one of the principal antifraud rules of the Securities and Exchange Commission) to look over the company's financial information that is being conveyed to prospective stock purchasers.[4]

premiums for which have been paid for by the corporation.[5]

If this were all, if the law in this area were merely, in the last analysis, toothless, perhaps it would not be so bad. But the situation is worse. In bending over backwards to protect the directors, top-level management is inclined to shield them from "bad news" of potential corporate vulnerability—the very information we most want the directors to receive. This may seem odd to the layman, given, as I have just said, the low risk that the directors, even if sued, will ultimately suffer any out-of-pocket loss. But there is a special sort of conservatism that I have personally witnessed to operate in this setting. Everyone recognizes that the directors did not bargain even for the "hassle" of a lawsuit; no one wants to get them involved. What they don't know is often judged potentially less embarrassing than what they might discover.

Under these circumstances, we would do better to recognize in law what is already, effectively, a fact: that directors' liability for ordinary negligence is a dead letter, and even worse. But this does not mean that directors should be let off all legal hooks. I suggest that the traditional ordinary negligence standards be withdrawn and emphasis be transferred to a three-point program to keep the directors "honest."

A. The directors should continue to be liable to the corporation for losses owing to their "gross negligence" (as well, of course, as for their self-dealing); in addition to what this term might now encompass, it should be prima facie evidence of the gross negligence of any director that (a) the corporation sustained losses from criminal or civil liability; (b) evidence of the likelihood of such jeopardy had been received by the director in advance (I shall show how the likelihood of their getting it can be increased); and (c) the director did not take the steps a reasonably prudent director would have taken in those circumstances to head the problem off.

B. In the place of liability for ordinary negligence, and as a supplement to liability for gross negligence, we ought to attach liability, by statute, to failures to perform those of the mandated directors' functions (paragraph #3, above) that are deemed most vital. Indeed, beyond gross negligence, the only way to make the legal liability of directors a viable threat is to rest it upon non-performance of fairly narrowly defined, rather specific statutory duties. Directors have become increasingly concerned about the accuracy of any stock registration statements they have to sign, because the Securities Exchange Act specifically threatens liability against "any person who signed the [misleading] registration statement."[6] Similarly, notwithstanding the experience at the Penn Central, directors are ordinarily quite concerned that they are not so lavish with their dividends that they leave the corporation insolvent—for to do so transgresses one of the few specific duties for which a director can be sanctioned under the corporations codes.[7] For transgressions of these specific duties a suit should be maintainable either by the state (the attorney general) or by a shareholder for the corporation's benefit.

C. We have to reconsider the type of sanctions we are prepared to mete out to the directors. If some of the duties we assign seem critical enough, and nonperformance of them so shameful and improper, we may want to make the directors civilly liable, or even answerable criminally. We must remember, though, that wherever that much pressure is warranted, the liability is going to be meaningful only if we stop the directors from turning right around and getting indemnified by the corporation, or reimbursed by insurance. Limits must be placed on these practices, which have long since been mocking the law to the point of absurdity.[*]

In general, though, I think it would be best if for all but the most serious violations we moved in the opposite direction, relaxing directors' liability by providing that any director adjudged to have committed gross negligence, or to have committed nonfeasance (of one of the statutory duties mentioned in paragraph #3 above) shall be prohibited for a period of three years from

---

[*] Representative Wright Patman has urged that states adopting the Model Business Corporation Act delete the provision (5g) which invites such a practice which, in his view, "undermines essential safeguards of federal and state law." Joseph W. Bishop, Jr., "New Problems in Indemnifying and Insuring Directors: Protection against Liability under the Federal Securities Laws," *Duke Law Journal* (1972), p. 1160 and n. 34.

serving as officer, or director, or consultant of any corporation doing interstate commerce.*

Why is this better than what we have now? For one thing, the magnitude of potential liability today has become so draconian that when we try to make the law tougher on directors the more likely effects are that corporate lawyers will develop ways to get around it, judges and juries will be disinclined to find liability, and many of the better qualified directors will refuse to get involved and serve. The advantages of the "suspension" provision, by contrast, are that it is not so easy to get around (notice the "or consultant" proviso); it is not so severe that, like potential multi-million-dollar personal liability, it would strike courts as unthinkable to impose; but at the same time it would still have some effective "bite" to it—the suspendees would be removed from the most prestigious and cushy positions ordinarily available to men of their rank, and would, I suspect, be objects of some shame among their peers.†

5. *The directors will have to be accorded staff.* Assuming, as I am now, that the director himself will be an outsider, there is all the more reason that he be provided with some staff permanently assigned to assist him in his duties with the company. Staff are vital not only in preparing the directors to make informed decisions—gathering information, analyzing management proposals—but also in enabling them, once decisions have been made, to follow up on their directives and ascertain whether they are being adequately carried out.[8] To fulfill this function it is

---

* It would be necessary to provide, too, that in the event of a suit being settled (rather than brought to final judgment) the judge approving the settlement has the power to make such a penalty a condition of the settlement, if the facts warranted.

† It has always struck me as incredible that if, say, a jockey is caught "bumping" at Santa Anita, he is suspended from riding. At present, a director who does not attend meetings, and whose company goes down the drain under him, can carry this same vigilance to some other corporate victim. And they usually do. Indeed, the few top officers convicted of antitrust and other criminal offenses seem traditionally either to stay with the same company or play a sort of corporate musical chairs. See "Sandy Guterma Puts Prison Behind, Emerges as Corporate Chieftain: Convicted of Fraud, He Still Finds New Backers in Deal to Develop Bahamas Land," *Wall Street Journal*, November 15, 1973, p. 1, col. 1.

necessary that the staff be responsible to the board members, and not unduly subject to the influence of management. Toward this end, the compensation of staff, as well as its hiring and firing, ought to be a matter for the board members to determine. In companies that employ five to ten thousand workers, it is not unreasonable to insist that ten or twenty-five more be brought on board in this capacity—and it is simply unreasonable to suppose that directors' effectiveness will be much improved if we don't.

6. *Steps must be taken to assure that certain critical information gets to the board.* Was the board of Richardson-Merrell aware that its "prize" drug was inducing cataracts in animals in its own laboratories? Were the Southern California Edison directors aware—before they read it with the rest of us in the press a month later—that its San Onofre nuclear power plant had suffered a breakdown in one of its most important safety features?[9] Indeed, is it likely the Edison directors were made aware of any preliminary "mishaps" that may have occurred—clues to the need to demand special action? The answer is almost certainly not.

Why should this be so?

We have to recognize that there are several factors that conspire against the board receiving much of the very information the public most wants the directors to have. First is the problem of information overload: Too much information is generated within the company, and about the company, that it all could possibly be gathered and passed to "the top." Second is the fact that, given the traditions of the board, and given the expertise and expectations of those who presently serve on the board, there will be a tendency to bring to the top those items most reflective of the company's short-term earnings prospects. Third, as we just saw, there is a tendency to screen the directors from evidence that might taint them with liability in the event of subsequent litigation, or, at the least, embarrass them.

All these tendencies toward what management experts sometimes call "communication constipation" can be countered—somewhat. Giving the directors a better-defined function is one step in this direction; so is according them staff; so would be some of the changes in directors' legal liability that I mentioned.

But even with these changes, something more will be needed. What I propose is that certain designated categories of information *have* to be brought to the board's attention by law. As this proposal is part of a broader program of control over internal information flow that I deal with in Chapter 18, I will just remark here that there is nothing farfetched about *requiring* that the directors receive certain classes of information and backing up the requirement with effective sanctions, both as regards the directors (for failing to demand it) and as regards underlings (for failure to provide it). A unique provision of the California Insurance Code, for example, provides that each insurance company must designate some particular officer whose function it is to receive the report of the insurance commissioner; the law then insists that "such officer shall . . . inform [the company's] members that a copy of such a report is available for inspection" by them.[10] Then, intruding even further into the corporation's information processes, it adds, "there shall be entered in the minutes of each such meeting the fact that such officer did so inform the members present." In other words, certain data critical to the company's health have to go to the board—and no room for anyone to plead, later, that he "never saw it."

Why should there not be comparable provisions regarding the forwarding to the directors of a company that operates a nuclear generating station information regarding safety audits? Of companies suspected of seriously jeopardizing worker health, of health and safety audits?

# 15. General Public Directorships

The reforms of the preceding chapter would influence the makeup of the board, through, for example, specifying the number of outside directors there need be. But I stopped short of questioning the society's underlying premise that, in the ultimate filling of the board seats, the company, not the public, is to have the only say.

Where would reforms that went so far—but no farther—leave us? Probably the best we could hope for would be amelioration of some of the Class A problems, particularly those of a sort traditionally brought to the board's attention, and in which the congruence between the public's interest and the long-range financial interests of the corporation can be made most apparent. But the more we concern ourselves with problems beyond the traditional province of the board, and the less evident this public-private connection is—in other words, the deeper we move into the Class B area—the more problematical it is that the reforms outlined above will effectively change the way the corporation behaves.

If we aspire to go beyond this, we have to return to the question of public directorships. Should the society demand that, at least in some cases, there be directors actually appointed by, and in some sense "responsible" to, "the public"?

There are any number of reasons why one ought to approach public director proposals skeptically. I have already indicated some of these, both theoretical (How does anyone presume to represent "the public"?) and practical (Given the limited impact of the *ordinary* directors in most areas of corporate operation, how much less influence can we expect of one or two special directors who can always be outvoted?). What is more sobering still, the experience we have had in this country with public directors, although limited, can certainly be read as unpromising.

## The Union Pacific Experience

Our best-documented experience with public directorships in the United States involves the Union Pacific Railroad.* The railroad—the first complete rail link between east and west coasts—could not have been constructed without enormous public support, both in land grants and government funds. Desirous of getting its money's worth, and concerned about the monopoly power of the creature it was fathering, Congress wrote into the original 1862 legislation a provision giving two of fifteen board seats to presidential nominees. The act did not, however, give the government directors much in the way of mandates, powers, or duties.[1]

Almost immediately there was recognition that the proposal was bound to be ineffective, for within two years the public directorship provision was amended. The board was enlarged to twenty, five of whom were now to be presidential appointees (in other words, there was a slight percentage increase in voting power). But little was done to straighten out their functions, other than to clarify one or two powers in their direction (the right to inspect books and records—which I rather suspect they had anyway—and, quite sensibly, the right to have a representative on each standing committee). They were also given the duty of filing an annual report with the Secretary of the Interior, on what not being wholly clear.[2]

---

* I am leaving aside for the moment true public enterprise like TVA, in which public and private directors are not mixed. Also, during and after World War II, stock of corporations subject to enemy influence was seized by the U.S. government and vested in the Office of Alien Property Custodian. Directors of these companies, which included General Analine and Film (now GAF), General Dyestuff, and American Potash and Chemical, were appointed by the Custodian. The directors were left to manage the normal operations of the company, but its officers were required "to consult with the Custodian, and with designated members of his staff concerning any proposed major changes in policy or any extraordinary transactions which required prior specific authorization by the Alien Property Custodian." Annual Report, U.S. Office of Alien Property Custodian (Washington, 1945), p. 66.

Did the public director system work at the Union Pacific? This cannot be answered unequivocally, for we lack an authoritative statement of exactly what the public wanted, as a standard against which to measure the company's (and, derivatively, the directors') performance. On the other hand, because the Union Pacific construction was so broadly debated, one can reconstruct, as from congressional testimony and speeches, some sense of what "the public," generally, was after. There was much interest, for example, in the company's repaying its $27-million government loan. There was interest, obviously, in the development of the West; there were expressions of concern that there be nondiscriminatory access to the road's services, that the project be developed with maximum speed and efficiency, and that financial abuse and scandal be avoided in the construction and procurement programs.[3]

Those who have reviewed the history incline toward a pretty dim view of the results. Herman Schwartz, trying to draw from the Union Pacific experience at the time of the Communications Satellite Corporation Bill, remarked:

The record shows that most of [the objectives] were not achieved. Rates were not kept down, the railroad management concentrated on short-run profits and paid relatively little attention to the long-run public interest in the development of the West; the road discriminated with respect to rates and access; there were so many scandals connected with its construction [including Credit Mobilier, the Watergate of the 1870s] that several congressional careers and reputations were ruined. Even when some of these aims actually were achieved, the government directors deserved little credit.[4]

By 1888 most observers, including a number of the presidential appointees themselves, had called for an abolition of the public directorships. In 1897 the road went into receivership, and when it emerged, the public directorships had been quietly laid to rest. But however unpromising the historical evidence, I am not convinced that the lesson one draws from the experience needs be unmitigated pessimism toward public directorships in principle. Rather, I think we cannot draw any final conclusions from the

Union Pacific experience without taking into account the following shortcomings of that particular arrangement.

- The directors' duties, functions, and objectives were never clearly defined. Even on what one would expect to be a major point of consensus—the repayment of the government loan—the very sponsor of the public director provisions, Senator James F. Wilson, had gone on record as believing the Union Pacific neither would nor should repay the debt.[5]
- Not only was there no authoritative guide as to how the public directors should vote, there was no clear mandate on the matters into which they should inquire. True, the directors' reports allow that they were "to have intimate knowledge of its affairs, and keep themselves thoroughly informed concerning all its transactions."[6] But this is just too much for anyone to bite off. Directors so instructed are apt to be less effective, even if only as gadflies, than directors accorded more modest and manageable instructions.
- There probably was consensus on one task: that the directors were to play some sort of "window-out" function—that is, to inform the outside world on what the corporation was up to. But here, too, a lack of definition is apt to be self-defeating. The 1864 Act limply instructed the government directors to "communicate to the Secretary of the Interior . . . such information as should be in the possession of the Department." Who could be certain what that meant? The Secretary of the Interior, for his part, addressed only one inquiry to the government directors: In 1871 he asked them where the eastern terminus was.[7] Under these circumstances, one ought not to be surprised at complaints that some major decisions went unreported: There simply lacked any clear and meaningful channels for the transmission of data.[8] Overbreadth of this sort has another important drawback. There being no agreed-on rules as to what information the public directors should be transmitting to whom, the insiders will all the more suspiciously "freeze out" the public directors from many discussions. (Which is, in fact, what happened; one government director testified that he first heard of a Union Pacific merger through the press.)[9]
- None of the government directors put full time into his directorship. Much less, of course, were they staffed. They were selected without regard for any special expertise.[10] As the experiment was coming to an end, the government directors themselves pleaded that this

left them simply too uninformed to do a creditable job.[11] There was, moreover, no effective machinery for assuring that the government directors would be invited—seasonally—to the directors' and committee meetings.[12]

There were all manner of what might be called personnel problems. The turnover among government directors was high; some were, at best, indifferent;* some, unfortunately, were corrupt. Part of these problems it is tempting to ascribe to the frustrations of such a questionably meaningful job, compounded by the want of compensation[13]—rather than to suppose it inherent in the nature of public director arrangements generally.

In addition to the institutional shortcomings in the Union Pacific arrangement, there is another consideration against which the episode must be judged. We ought to be realistic about the sorts of things one has a right to expect of government directors in the first place. True, rates were not kept down. And certainly rebates and other discriminations were rife. But are these matters the public should have been looking to the government directors to remedy?

The level of rates is a good example of the sort of thing that puts the corporation's interests most squarely at odds with the public's (especially where, as with the Union Pacific, the enterprise is an almost classic monopoly). In other words, as much as we may create a setting for an informed, enlightened exchange of diverse views, there is not much a public director can say that is likely to change the minds of those who represent the private investors. Rate discrimination, too, is a matter it is unrealistic to expect directors to influence, at least without the backing of tough legislation. As economists (and businessmen) know, price differentials are simply a classic exercise and manifestation of

---

* One of the nongovernment directors testified of his public colleagues, "They did not as a rule . . . take a great deal of interest. They generally sat by themselves, and generally refused to vote on a dividend, and hung back. We did not expect them to take any active interest, or express any decided opinion, but in order to be safe they would vote *no* against anything, when they knew they were going to be entirely voted down. That was about the attitude they took." 1 *Testimony Taken by the United States Pacific Railway Commission,* S. Exec. Doc. No. 51 (pt. 2), 50th Cong., 1st Sess. (1887), p. 710 (testimony of F. Gordon Dexter).

monopoly power.[14] The warning to us, in other words, is that there are some matters too squarely in the corporation's interests that anyone should hope a board—even a board fully informed of what was going on—will call them to a halt. In such circumstances, the practice will be too much for the government directors to buck through their powers of moral persuasion alone— unreinforced by some tough legal sanctions.

Thus, however unpromising the limited historical experience we have had, it is not grounds to conclude that mixed public-private boards *need* be all charade. We would do better to instruct ourselves from its failures.

Unfortunately, if the Comsat legislation is any guide, we are slow learners. From a historical perspective the Comsat board is, if anything, a step backward from the Union Pacific board. Americans may congratulate themselves that in sitting three public nominees on Comsat's fifteen-man board, we are engaged in "a very wholesome development in American life, of government and private enterprise harnessed together to advance the national interest."[15] But as Schwartz points out, as bad as the Union Pacific setup was, the UP's directors had advantages their Comsat counterparts lack.[16] The presidential nominees to Comsat— originally George Meany, president of the AFL-CIO; Frederick Donner, General Motors board chairman; and Clark Kerr, president of the University of California—have no special mandates, powers, duties, or responsibilities whatsoever. Once seated they are simply ordinary directors, owing obligations, under the District of Columbia Corporations Code, to no one but the shareholders.[17] This is the window dressing of public participation at its worst.

We can, certainly, do better. What I shall propose are two sorts of public director systems. The first, to be discussed in this chapter, involves general public directors, who would operate under a fairly broad mandate in all companies of very large size. In the next chapter I shall distinguish such general public directors from special public directors, whose appointment would be geared to meet the exigencies of special situations, and whose mandates and responsibilities would be tailored accordingly.

With these considerations in mind, what might a viable public director system consist of? Where would public directors be placed and how would they be selected? What functions ought we to expect of them? What powers and responsibilities ought they to have?

## Selection and Placement of General Public Directors

1. *Where they would be seated.* Every corporation engaged primarily in manufacturing, retailing, or transportation, in whatever state incorporated, should have 10 percent of its directors general public directors (GPDs) for every billion dollars of assets or sales (whichever is higher).* That is to say, a manufacturing company with a twenty-man board and $1 billion in sales would have two public directors; a company with a fifteen-man board, $1 billion in sales, but $2 billion in assets, would have three public directors. For corporations engaged in banking, life insurance, diversified finance, and utilities (in which the figures run much higher), 10 percent of the board would be constituted of general public directors for each $3 billion in assets, rather than each $1 billion.

As for the number of companies that would be affected by this plan, if we use the *Fortune* 1973 surveys it appears that 149 manufacturing corporations would be involved, 32 commercial banks, 14 life insurance companies, 15 diversified financial companies, 28 retailing companies, 15 transportation companies, and 9 utilities.

Most of these companies would be affected marginally, by having one or two GPDs only. It ought to be noted, however, that under the figures used, if one did not add a proviso such as, ". . . up to 50 percent of the board," or ". . . up to 90 percent of the board," thirteen American corporations would have public directors entirely (AT&T, General Motors, Ford, Exxon, BankAmerica Corp., General Electric, IBM, Texaco, Sears Roebuck & Co., First National Bank, Chase Manhattan Corp., Prudential

---

* If the appointment of the GPDs is not expressed in percentage-of-the-board terms, their influence will be watered down by the company's simply expanding its board.

Life Insurance Co., and Metropolitan Life Insurance Co.). Although only a small percentage of American corporations would be involved, they represent, of course, the most powerful in American commerce and industry. The 149 manufacturing corporations alone account for an aggregate $360 billion in assets and generate $400 billion in annual sales—about one third of GNP. They employ a total of 10 million workers, 70 percent of all employees engaged in manufacturing, and one eighth of the total U.S. work force.*

2. *Their selection and removal.* The public directors could be nominated by a Federal Corporations Commission, if one has been established, or otherwise by the Securities and Exchange Commission. Each nominee should have to be approved by a majority of the board of the company involved, and he should be removable by the company by a unanimous vote of the board without showing of cause, or by a two-thirds vote for cause (such as breach of one of the public director obligations discussed below). Otherwise he should continue in office even as the seats of the other directors are periodically reviewed by the shareholders in the ordinary elections.

I recognize that the powers of the rest of the board to confirm and remove the public appointees will strike some as unduly compromising. Yet without such provisions, I see no chance of their developing the working relationships they shall need. Specifically, if the public director and his staff are to succeed, the arrangement will have to be one that suggests to the other directors (and, through them, to the corporate organization) that their particular public director is there because they have approved his being there.

3. *Their compensation and related matters.* The general public director would maintain an office at the company's place of

---

* In addition, the 32 commercial banks would have aggregated (using 1973 figures) $325 billion in assets and employ 334,000; for the 14 life insurance companies, the figures are $145 billion and 270,000; for the 15 diversified financial enterprises, $77.8 billion and 249,000; for the 28 retailers, $32.8 billion and 2,070,000; for the 15 transportation companies, $33.4 billion and 623,000; and the 9 utilities, $100 billion in assets and 1 million employees.

business and be expected to spend at least one half of his time on the corporation's affairs. His remuneration would be that of a highest grade civil servant. There would be some obvious advantages were we to make the general public director full-time, rather than half-time. But there are disadvantages as well, which, in my view, suggest we try it otherwise, at the start. To begin with, half-time is far more than most outsiders put into their directorships today. Then, too, there is not an unlimited supply of men of adequate substance and experience to carry on such a task effectively. Nor are the best of these likely to be free and willing to leap with both feet into such an arrangement as I am proposing. Many candidates will be semiretired executives (a class of people whose number this system should encourage). Others will be academics, who might be able to arrange half-loads with their institutions. In other words, we may simply be able to get better people on these terms than otherwise. What is more, connecting the GPD with the company full-time might involve too much identification; working on such a basis, the public director would learn more facts, but at the risk of acquiring the very view of the world that he must be prepared to call to question. On balance, making his staff full-time should inform him enough.

Nor do I think that public directors being drawn, as they often would be, from business needs be a drawback. What the business-trained director may lack is perspective he will more than likely make up for in savvy, and in the respect he will therefore be able to command. Further, one should not discount the influence on people's behavior of the social role into which they step. I like to hope that if the GPD role can be given adequate structure, and carry the prestige, a person who steps into a public director slot will assume the ethos it demands.

## Functions of the General Public Directors

One can always point out that, in almost all the corporations that would be affected, the representation ratio is such that the GPDs could always be voted down. What good, then, can they do? The answer is that the functions of the GPD should be developed in such manner that his actual *vote* is not what the public is banking on. Instead, his functions should include the following.

1. *The superego function.* The first function is the least tangible of all; it concerns the atmosphere that a probing and vigilant mind can contribute to. We have to remember that the problems we are looking to the GPD to deal with lie largely in an area in which reasonable men can hold differing opinions. But as we saw also, this does not mean that the society should therefore be indifferent to how the corporation goes about deciding. What we are after is the corporation's exercising some "responsibility" in the sense defined in Part III: reflecting a bit before it acts in certain areas; considering a broad range of consequences that its actions may have; considering alternatives; extending its time horizon; bringing to bear on its analysis certain social categories of judgment; doing only things it would be prepared to justify publicly, in the socially approved rhetoric of responsible action; taking into account the fact that part of what the environment is, is of *its* making. These are the things we should expect a general public director to aim for generally.

Why do I think that such a public director doggedly pursuing such a "superego" function might meet some success today, where the idea had little impact in the Union Pacific experience? For one thing, there has been an evolution in business attitudes. The self-image of the businessman today is less individualistic and rapacious than that of his social-Darwinist predecessor. He is less glibly confident that if the public good is any concern of his at all, the market is its only arbiter. Too, the reforms of the preceding chapter, should they be accepted, would all influence the makeup and performance of the board in the direction of the public director being more attended to, and not as likely to arouse the hostility with which the government appointees to the Union Pacific were met. Indeed, the very nature of the Class A, and some of the Class B problems, is such that if someone has the bad manners to raise them, it is not easy for a group of directors (of the constituency I described in Chapter 14) to brush them aside lightly, consistent with the prevailing self-image, which I

genuinely believe most of the business and financial community
has, of being good and concerned citizens.

Let me give an example of the sort of thing I mean, where such
a public director could be quite effective.

Not long ago, a major American railroad began slipping behind in its track repair and replacement program. One of the
directors got wind of this (incredibly enough, through a letter
from an inquisitive shareholder, rather than from anything the
director had picked up from his inside connections). He raised
the problem with the board—no other members of which had
been aware of how bad the situation had gotten. The specter of
increasing derailments was not a pleasant matter to have to feel
responsible for. As a result of the discussion, top management
(how aware had *they* been?) undertook an inquiry. What they
discovered was that in the first six months of 1973 they had suffered twenty major derailments (excess of $10,000 damages)
caused by broken rails: a net cost of the railroad of $3.5 million.
The reduction in the rail repairing program had been occasioned,
a top officer explained, "to achieve a satisfactory level of earnings,"* but in light of the apparent consequences—which were
likely to get more serious in the years ahead—management, now
on the carpet, acknowledged it "questionable whether there is
any true economy."

In this case, the very fact that the incident was aired at all
was mere happenstance—the combination of an alert shareholder
and a pugnacious director. But in the system I am proposing, such
occurrences would, presumably, be more regularized. Especially
promising is that, given the liability rules I have proposed, once
the directors in the example had gotten wind of the reduced rail
repair program, and had been informed of its risks, their failure
to correct the situation could result in their personal liability in
the event of the railroad's being exposed to a civil or criminal
suit arising from a derailment. That, too, would most assuredly
reinforce the GPD's efforts to improve the atmosphere of the
board meetings.

---

* That is, by holding costs down, the per share earnings were dressed up.

2. *Assuring that laws are being complied with.* The GPD, to be effective, would need functions that are more sharply focused than just contributing to a responsible atmosphere. One of these would be to oversee programs designed to assure that the laws were being carried out in good faith. They often are not. That is, in addition to the sporadic and unpredictable law violations that any huge enterprise is going to get involved in (owing simply to its manifold, complex contact with the society), there is also in many corporations and industries a smaller group of law violations and law circumventions that are systematic and chronic—not the happenstance of some particular ne'er-do-well employee on the make, but products of the organizational system itself, its established ways of marketing and the like.

In the present system, as I have observed, the directors do not want to hear about such seamy problems (unless and until, as one executive said to me, they have reached the front pages of *The New York Times*). But one of the functions of the GPD and his staff would be to roam through the corporation, as it were, identifying areas where difficulties with the law seem inveterate. "Legal audits" of this sort would be undertaken by the GPD in association with the corporation's legal counsel, and, where appropriate, with the "outside" (independent) law firm that handles the corporation's affairs.[18]

Where "soft spots" were located, it would be the duty of the legal audit crew to propose a plan that provided reasonable assurances that adequate remedial steps were being undertaken.* If some area of product defect were suspected, a remedial plan might include placing a top quality-control person at a key production point and making him report directly to the GPD staff. The existence of the problem area, the remedial plan, and peri-

---

* After the electrical equipment price-fixing episode of the 1960s, Westinghouse instituted a system whereby, inter alia, *all* contacts between their employees and employees of competitor firms, even on golf courses, had to be reported to counsel; failure to do so was made an "offense" subject to discharge from the company. *A Report from the Board of Advice to the Westinghouse Electric Corporation* (1962), p. 8; Richard A. Whiting, "Antitrust and the Corporate Executive II," *Virginia Law Review*, 48 (1962): 9 and n. 26.

odic reports on actions taken under the plan would all be matters regularly reported to the entire board. In my estimate, such a working relationship would not be resented by the corporation's lawyers. On the contrary, many corporate lawyers are strongly in favor of legal audits, and being able to trace their authority to the board would be received as welcome support.

There is, I have to point out, a rather ticklish question about what the GPD staff should do with information of this sort that it uncovers. Should they turn it over to public authorities? It seems to me that the answer is no, at least in the first instance. As back-pedaling as this seems, to be realistic, if the GPD and his staff are viewed internally as an arm of, say, the federal prosecutor's offices, their information-gathering effectiveness will be cut down considerably. Only if the GPD felt that his recommended internal efforts to remedy the situation were not being carried out adequately and in good faith, would he be authorized, after prior reporting to the balance of the board, to notify the appropriate public authorities of his belief in the possible existence of a course of unlawful conduct.

3. *To serve as a liaison in the legislative process.* Another function for the GPD would be to act as a conduit to public agencies in proposing legislation and trade standards. The need arises from the point I noted in Part III, that one reason why a corporation's simply following the law is not enough is that, on any realistic analysis of the political processes, the laws regularly lag behind social requirements. Information signaling the need for legislative action is often available in (or can be readily developed in) the corporate sector far before the legislatures and agencies receive it. For example, the first social institution to receive information that a particular fabric is flammable, and should probably be banned from sale, is the company that makes it. (Where does such information presently languish? The corporation's complaints department?) When the papers announce that a pesticide is seriously injuring farm workers, can one doubt that there were clues in the producing company's laboratories—or even its packing areas—which, systematically pursued, would have brought the dangers to light several years and thousands of injuries earlier?

The GPD could oversee the gathering of such data, and make public recommendations of areas in which legislation might be needed. He should be available, too, for comment on pending legislation. If the law is to rest, as it inevitably will, partly upon representations from the corporations to be regulated, we might feel more comfortable about the process if some of the testimony came from someone *in* the corporations, but not wholly *of* them.

4. *To serve as a check on the effectiveness of fundamental internal systems.* As I have already indicated, no one can expect any director, however well staffed, to keep abreast of all the activity that is going on in the corporation. But the performance of a corporation need not be analyzed and reviewed in terms of its *acts* alone. The organization is also a composite of *systems*, some of which are oriented toward research and design, others toward production, others toward the maintenance of internal authority, others toward the gathering and transmission of data. Even if it is impossible to keep tabs on everything that is happening in the corporation, it is not impossible to audit the effectiveness of the various systems. And once more, this is the sort of task in which the entire board (especially if constituted along the reformed lines of Chapter 14) would likely give the GPD its cooperation and backing.

As an example, take the problem that came up at Goodrich in its development of the brakes for the A-7D, a military aircraft. The brakes were designed by one of the engineers on the supposition that four discs would meet specifications.[19] One other of the engineers, however—junior to the designer—calculated that the plane could not be safely braked with four discs, only with five. Test after test in the wind tunnel bore out the junior engineer's doubts. But the senior man and others, whose investment in the four-disc concept was more vested, refused to reconsider. When on each successive test, the brakes didn't pan out, the test data were apparently fudged. Organizational inertia had taken hold, not because it was profitable for the organization as an entity to continue in this direction, but because the subunit's alliance with the overall profitability of the total organization is sometimes far looser than classic economics assumes. The engineer responsible for the design had assured his plant manager the brakes would work; the plant manager had passed this good news "up." When bad news develops, it doesn't move upward as fast, all the more so when good news has prematurely preceded it.

A congressional committee that later investigated the incident indicated that, to its satisfaction, Goodrich's top-level management was innocent of what had been going on in its plant.[20] And if we view what had been going on as the *act* of producing a defective brake, and the attendant coverup, then the congressmen were almost certainly right. But what this overlooks is a defect in *system* that is not so easily excused—the testing of the brake was entrusted to the same personnel who had designed it. That is the very sort of basic systemic flaw that a GPD who undertook to review operations and development systems could be expected to catch. And it is the very sort of organizational shortcoming (and plain bad business) one might hope the full board to understand and be concerned about, if only someone could bring it to their attention.

As to which internal systems the GPD might be assigned to audit, it would depend in part upon the GPD's sense of the nature of the enterprise (in other words, a financial institution as opposed to a manufacturing concern) and his sense, on an initial sampling, of where the most serious weaknesses might lie.°

5. *To fill a "hot line" function.* The GPD and his staff would be specially designated to receive, from anyone within the organization (or out), notice of things that were going seriously wrong, and which the ordinary organizational systems for detection were not uncovering. I cannot overemphasize the importance of this function. In almost all the cases my task groups analyzed, *someone* down in the corporate hierarchy was aware that the company was headed for trouble. This was obviously true of the A-7D brake affair at Goodrich. Consider, too, the

---

° I would allow, too, for the possibility of a central clearinghouse for the receipt, development, and transmission of various matters the GPDs should be concerned with. This and the management of priorities for GPDs of various enterprises could well be further functions for a Federal Corporations Commission.

Richardson-Merrell, MER/29 affair. At a stage relatively early in the development of the drug, a lab technician became aware of its potential dangers. Mice were developing eye opacities; monkeys were losing weight. When she called this to the attention of her immediate superior, he told her to falsify the data. When she reported his demand, and her reluctance to follow it, to a higher-up, she was instructed to do as she was told. So far as the documents we can turn up indicate, no one on the board was notified of the problems with the drug until many months later—when, in fact, all the institutional inertia was solidly committed to the drug's promotion, the institutional point of no return. In the Equity Funding scandal, it is quite possible that nearly *everyone* in the corporation (I am including secretaries and office boys) knew something of the fraud—except the outside directors and, I am told, the lawyers.

Is there no way to get such information to people who will have both the interest and the power to do something about it?* Of course, in theory, any concerned employee can always look up the names of his company's directors in the phone book, and give them a call or drop them a postcard. But absent some affirmative organizational action, all the psychology of the institution makes such breaches of protocol unthinkable (not to mention the employee's fears that his immediate superiors might retaliate). The ordinary outside director, whose primary employment lies elsewhere, is too distant in every sense—not only physically and hierarchically, but usually even in terms of what the employee presumes him to be concerned about.

In part, then, the answer must be to change the protocol—expressly to authorize the special director and his staff to be the recipients of "bad news," and to advertise this as one of their functions. If we did so (1) there would be some higher-up to

* There are undoubtedly some cases, such as, allegedly, the Equity Funding scandal, in which the highest-level management may have been approving the wrongful policy, in which case getting the "bad" news to the top would presumably not have changed the corporation's performance. Even there, though, if the board had been a sort described in Chapter 14, it could have been expected to correct or expose the fraud, or face, under my proposals, substantial liability.

whom in the regular course of events personnel aware of developing trouble areas could turn; (2) the person to whom they would be turning would be someone not so closely identified with "the organization" and its ethos as to be angry with them for raising the point; and (3) it would be someone who was high enough up in the organization both to right the situation and protect the source from harassment.

It is tempting to believe that had such an institutionalized "whistle blowing" system existed in Richardson-Merrell or Equity Funding, or Goodrich, a lot of trouble would have been nipped in the bud.

6. *To oversee the preparation of impact studies.* One of the major problems in controlling corporations is that neither they nor the legislating agencies have adequate information as to the impact of contemplated corporate action. Did any of the soap companies undertake to examine, in advance, the effect their detergents were going to have on streams? Or pesticide manufacturers, what their products would do to the ecological cycle? Do the companies that are unleashing the foods and beverages we consume undertake to assess the impact they may be having on the human gene pool? Do companies that bring in industrial psychologists to measure ways to increase productivity undertake parallel studies to measure the impact the recommended changes will have on worker emotional and physical well-being?

We ought to see that in an increasing number of areas private corporations, like governmental agencies, be required to make their own impact findings. How these findings would be made, and in what areas, are all subjects to be examined in Chapter 19. In the meantime, let me just observe here that the ultimate authority for the preparation of these reports would rest with the GPD and his staff, at least in those corporations that have GPDs.

7. *To act as an information interface between the corporation and its environment.* Viewed from one perspective, the corporation is an information system that consumes, digests, and produces data. How adequately the corporation discharges its social functions depends, obviously, upon the validity of the information

it takes in and the validity of the information in turns out. But truth and falsehood are gross as categories for evaluations information systems. The adequacy of the system depends upon a lot more: where in its environment it reaches to gather information; the categories of abstraction it employs (i.e., what it "looks for"); to what points, within itself, it dispatches the gathered items; how it "translates" data as it moves from one subunit to another; which items it decides to store for recall; which items it tends to remit to the outside world, and in what form.

Anyone interested in the social control of corporations must attend to the details of this information net. Whether, for example, a court's decree is obeyed by the corporation may well depend upon how adequately (and in what good faith) someone in the company translates the legalistic terms of the judge's order into language likely to have an impact on, say, the salesmen. To "translate" effectively demands a knowledge of the corporation's affairs that one wholly outside the corporation does not have—but which the GPD and his staff would.

These internal information arrangements are dealt with in more detail in Chapter 18. In the meantime, one aspect is particularly appropriate to mention here: the potential of using the GPD to monitor the exchanges of basic information between the corporation and its environment (as distinct from overseeing the internal information systems). Some information that is coming out of corporations is coming out distorted (claims from pharmaceutical companies regarding drugs); other information is not coming out at all (some of the dealings of our multinationals abroad); some may be coming out, but too late, or in a form that lends no confidence (some of the oil company data regarding the energy crisis). One of the tasks one might look for in a GPD has to do with the gathering, verification, and dissemination of "boundary-crossing" information of various sorts: the "window-out" function. There is no need for the government to be scurrying after the facts about oil reserves and refining capacity *after* a crisis is upon us. The underlying estimates are the very sort of thing a competent board, pushed by a GPD, should have had in each company in advance. And there are no predominating reasons of secrecy for not allowing it to be passed on, on request of the appropriate governmental agencies.

There is room, too, to develop a "window-in" function for the GPD. Are corporations effectively getting the information the society wants them to have? Are there data available in governmental agencies—respecting, say, projected needs and shortages—which the corporation is either not gathering or not gathering at a high enough level? To the extent this is so, the GPD could be used as a conduit by agencies to bring to the corporation's attention (for relaying, for example, to the corporation's R&D branch) matters that it ought to know about. And for which the society at large is the ultimate beneficiary.*

8. *To monitor the directors' adherence to the reformed board system.* The success of the general board reforms I proposed in Chapter 14 depends upon a number of miscellaneous factors: that information of designated categories be brought to the board's attention, that dissents and reasons therefore be recorded, that the appropriate ratios of inside and financially disinterested directors be maintained, that the official minutes of various meetings truly reflect what transpired, that attendees of meetings are receiving agendas and matters to be discussed adequately in advance. It would be a function of the GPD to assure that these and related features of the board system were being observed in good faith.

9. *To act as director for the corporation.* Odd as it may sound, we would do well if the GPD considered it one of his functions to serve as director for "the corporation." For in our present circumstances it is not inevitable that anyone on the board is primarily concerned with the financial long-run well-being of the entity itself. The most dominant outside directors are typically keeping an eye out for major shareholders, major suppliers, major financial institutions. In *most* corporate action, what is in the best

---

* My guess is that even if the information is available somewhere in the public domain anyway, if it comes to the board and management through "their" GPD, who can relate it, in turn, to his monthly conference with, say, an Assistant Secretary of State, the flavor of inside scoop will give the information added credibility—as well as add to the prestige of the GPD among his peers.

interests of the corporation, over the long haul, does not come clearly in conflict with their narrower interests. But there is always some corporate action, and usually major corporate action, which potentially sets the directors' home interests at odds with the corporation's.

Consider, for an important example, what happens when the company needs to raise new capital. The one on the board to whom the other directors look for guidance in these matters will be their investment banker colleague. This presents, however, an obvious conflict. His bank will almost certainly be selected to head up the very syndicate that is going to market the bonds to the public. Not only will his bank get an enormous fee, the propriety of which will be passed upon only by the other board members, but they all know that the higher the board prices the bonds (and/or the lower the interest yielded) the more money is in it for the corporation. But the lower it prices the bonds, the more margin there is in it for the bankers (when they resell them to the public).

In these circumstances the other directors should be extra cautious to prevent the investment banker-director from playing too strong a hand in the pricing. True, neither they nor the interests they represent have anything to gain in the investment banking director's lining his company's pocket at the corporation's expense. But the present situation is one of gentlemanly reciprocity. The director from the steel company knows that if he keeps quiet now, the director from the investment banking house will adopt the same trustful stance when a proposal comes up that the corporation enter into a long-term steel purchase agreement from you-know-who. Thus, in matters such as these, someone ought to be on the board exercising a more vigilant scrutiny over the corporation's financial health than it is now receiving.

## Special Powers of the General Public Directors

Let us turn, finally, to note something of the powers the GPDs ought to be accorded if they are going to be effective.

First, they should have the power to hire staff of their selection, who will, though paid by the corporation, be responsible to the GPDs in their duties. In addition, the GPDs should have the power to retain consultants as they may from time to time need.

The GPDs and, where specifically authorized by them, their staff should have the power to inspect all corporate books and records.

They should have the power to requisition from general corporate staff reasonable surveys, reports, and the like not otherwise on hand.

They should have the right to be seated on all corporate committees whose work is relevant to the furtherance of their functions.

They should be given reasonable notice of all appropriate board and committee meetings.

They should have the right to stay the firing or any other punishments of an employee on account of his cooperation with the GPD and his staff.

They should be given voice in the reward and advancement system for the corporate system as a whole, so as to hold out the possibility of rewarding lower-echelon workers who pursue goals not presently credited, and protecting others whose cooperation with the GPD might put them in disfavor.

In the event of management's recalcitrance in carrying out the board orders, or obstruction by anyone within the corporation of the GPD in the performance of his duties, the GPD should be authorized to go directly to court to seek an order, noncompliance with which would be punishable by contempt. The order should run not against "the corporation," but against the key corporate individuals whose obstructionism the GPD identifies.

None of the powers noted above should be exercisable by the GPD absolutely (except the access to court and agencies to force compliance). Certainly the balance of the board, and management, have a right to object if the GPD budget is getting out of line, or if particular demands on corporate staff are interfering with the balance of their expected duties. In all such cases, if a dispute arises, the corporation would be allowed to appeal the GPD's demand to the proposed Federal Corporations Commission for adjudication; if still unsatisfied with the commission's rulings, the corporation could perfect an appeal to the courts, as it can from the ruling of any other federal agency.

Nor should the GPD be himself without obligations. If he should engage in self-dealing, or be grossly negligent, he ought to be subject to the same liabilities as anyone else on the board. One obligation of the GPD, in particular, ought to be singled out and considered in advance. This has to do with discretion regarding corporate deliberations. Some corporate secrets the public should know about—that workers in vinyl chloride plants are coming down with liver cancer, for example. But there *is* a class of matters that cannot be cavalierly broadcast—where to do so would have disruptive effects not only within and upon the corporation, but in the outside world as well. In such situations, for the GPD to be a "leak" would destroy his working relationships without any outweighing virtue. I have in mind cases such as where the corporation may have evidence of a possible mineral discovery, or may be contemplating an acquisition or the opening of a new market. "The truth" about such matters (in whatever degree) makes the stock market gyrate badly enough when the stories flow from ordinary corporate officers and directors. The effect of such announcements coming from the GPD, if not well timed and wholly authoritative, would be no less disruptive. Thus, I would suggest that early in the GPD's tenure, he (or they) work out with the balance of the board and management guidelines for secrecy and the release of information. If substantial disagreements arise over the guidelines, the dispute would be taken, in the first instance, to the Federal Corporations Commission. When such a charter had been agreed to, then breaches of it by the GPD—like gross inattention to his duties—would constitute grounds for his removal by the balance of the board "for cause."

# 16. Special Public Directorships

How well would the system of general public directors work? Obviously we cannot tell in advance, although considering what we get out of boards presently, it is hard to argue against at least giving it a try. The companies that would be affected are as large and powerful as states. When one gets right down to it, if the *only* virtue of the general public directorship system were the symbolic one—a more obtrusive, nagging reminder of these companies' obligations to society than the American flag over their plants—the system would, to my mind, have justified itself.

Where my proposals are weak is in the breadth and magnitude of what the GPDs are asked to do, even after their functions have been more narrowly defined than just advancing "the public interest." I like to believe that as time went on, and experiences with the system built up, the participants would be able to analyze and further clarify their functions themselves, recommending development along whatever lines they find they can do best. In the meantime, however, there are some highly critical areas of need that call for more immediate and certain action. This brings me to the third and final level of board reform that I should like to propose: a system of special public directors (SPDs).

Unlike the GPDs, appointment of the SPDs would not hinge upon the largeness of the company per se. Instead, the process of placing these special public directors would be begun by identifying critical areas of social concern that are deemed most likely amenable to their influence—for example, problems associated with technological innovation, product safety, environmental pollution, foreign relations. The SPD would be a person whose expertise was suited to the particular area, and he would be given an appropriate, more sharply focused mandate.*

To be more specific, from my point of view the special public director weapon should be reserved for cases in which the forces of the market and ordinary legal mechanisms seem inadequate, on their own, to keep the corporation within socially desirable bounds. There are at least two general sorts of situations in which such "gaps" might call for the implementation of special public directors. The first situation I call the *demonstrated delinquency situation*; the second, the *generic industry problem*.

## The Demonstrated Delinquency Situation

The key feature of a demonstrated delinquency situation is that some company has been so repeatedly violating the law that it is apparent traditional legal mechanisms are not adequate to assure compliance. Let me give as an illustration the Holland Furnace Company, a Michigan corporation that seems almost to have been born crooked.

Holland, with gross annual sales of approximately $30 million, was the only home heating equipment manufacturer that sold through its own salesmen direct from factory.[1] A Holland salesman would make his way into a house by claiming himself to be an inspector from the gas company or the city, or claim he was making a "survey" of furnaces. Once inside, he would use his ostensible authority to dismantle the furnace, then flatly refuse to reassemble it on the grounds that to do so would involve grave dangers of an explosion. If the furnace was that of a Holland competitor, the salesman would inform the homeowner that it had passed its useful life, was not worth the expense involved in repairing it, or that the manufacturer had "gone out of business" and necessary replacement parts were unattainable. At this very moment, though, the solution presented itself miraculously

---

* We might say that the appointment of an SPD to a company whose size required three or more GPDs would reduce the GPD requirement by one; but not otherwise.

at the door: A Holland furnace man (the "inspector's" buddy who had been waiting around the corner) rang the bell and made the sale.

Now, the interesting thing about Holland's sales techniques is that they did not develop overnight. As early as the 1940s complaints about Holland were rife. In 1946 the company had been dragged before the federal courts for making such unnecessary sales in violation of rulings of the War Production Board.[2] In 1951 the Michigan Corporation and Securities Commission, outraged by this style of salesmanship, instituted proceedings that led to the suspension of Holland's license to do business for sixty days. Complaints continued. A high company officer was told that one of its branch managers was selling used furnaces as new; the offender was quietly elevated to position of division superintendent. In 1954 the Federal Trade Commission instituted a large-scale investigation of Holland. In 1958 it condemned the practices and issued an order to cease and desist. Holland, in response, set up a Product Service Department supposedly to assure compliance. But the practices continued. In 1966 Holland, the company's seventy-four-year-old president and board chairman, and two corporate vice-presidents, were held in criminal contempt. The president was sentenced to six months' imprisonment.

The courts, obviously, had lost patience—twenty years of this sort of trumpery is more than the society should have to put up with. But I think the law is going about it the wrong way. There may be some vindictive satisfaction in seeing an old man sent off to prison. But it is naïve to suppose that what developed sprang full-blown from the evil mind of any top executive, or was even within the capacity of a single man to remedy. The practices had become rooted in the whole institutional design—in the way the salesmen were trained, the way they were commissioned, the decentralization of authority into sales regions, the patterns of supervision. It does not seem to me inconceivable that the old man simply could not, or did not know how to, bring the sales force to heel. What is more, putting him in prison for six months does not do any good to the consumers who, for about twenty years, were boondoggled this way. What I would recommend in such a situation is that we recognize the defendant corporation as a recidivist and assign a special public director to it. How such a director would be selected, and what his precise functions would be, I shall return to. Let me first outline the other situation that calls for a SPD.

## The Generic Industry Problem

The key feature of the generic industry problem is that a matter of considerable social concern has arisen, although unlike the demonstrated delinquency situation, none of the companies involved has engaged in repeated law violations. Indeed, a frequent characteristic of this second situation will be that the problem is one not presently amenable to any of the traditional law-sanction solutions.*

As an illustration consider the tragic worker health situation that has recently come to light in the asbestos industry. According to estimates from Mount Sinai Hospital's Environmental Sciences Laboratory, one out of every five deaths among asbestos insulation workers in the United States is caused by lung cancer; almost one out of ten deaths is caused by mesothelioma, a rare cancer of chest and abdomen linings; another one out of ten deaths is caused by asbesteosis, a scarring of the lungs.[3] Nearly half of the men studied were dying of some form of asbestos disease.

In 1954, one small plant operated by Union Asbestos Company in Paterson, New Jersey, was shut down (operations were moved to Tyler, Texas). By coincidence seventeen of its workers were patients of a Dr. Irving J. Selikoff, who has an interest in tuberculosis. The seventeen workers having remained in New Jersey in other employment when the operations were transferred, he maintained a follow-up study of them. In 1973, less than twenty years later, only two were still alive. Seven had died of lung cancer, two of stomach cancer, four of asbesteosis, and one

---

* This might be so for any of the number of reasons I discussed in Part III. The government does not have adequate information upon which to legislate, the "costs" of absolutely eliminating the activity through traditional strategies may exceed the benefits, and so on.

of malignant mesothelioma. The fifteenth death was heart disease.

Perhaps even more astonishing are the data on asbestos insulators. The insulators, unlike asbestos factory workers, spend only half their time working with asbestos, and often work in relatively airy, out-of-doors job sites. Fibrosis of the lungs was found in fully half of 1,117 members of two union locals whose membership was examined. Among 392 men with more than twenty years' experience, 339 had developed asbesteosis—to a moderate or extensive degree in fully half the cases. Among workers who had twenty years' exposure, the mortality rate was 25 percent higher than normal. Where standard mortality charts would have indicated six or seven deaths from cancer of the lung, pleura, or trachea, there were actually forty-five. Where nine or ten fatal gastrointestinal cancers were to be expected, there had in fact been twenty-nine. Indeed, statistics that are now being developed indicate that just living in the vicinity of asbestos mines, dumps, or factories is a significant health hazard.

Chronic problems of this sort are not peculiar to the asbestos companies. Plastics workers have their liver cancer.[4] Paper mills and steel companies create vast amounts of water pollution. Oil refineries are typically air polluters. Multinationals present peculiar problems relating to our foreign relations and monetary stability. Manufacturers of consumer products, like automobiles and televisions, present special consumer safety problems. Companies that produce nuclear energy present special threats to nearly everyone.

In many such cases a SPD should be appointed with a mandate and functions especially tailored to meet the particular problems that are presented.

### Appointment of Special Public Directors

By what procedures would we place the appropriate SPD on the board?

By the very nature of the demonstrated delinquency situation, the company will be before a court or agency. In such a case, the appointment could and should be by the court, with the advice and consultation of the company, the prosecuting agency, the court's own probation staff, and perhaps even (for reasons that will be clearer as we progress) a management-organizational consultant.

The idea of a court appointing such a director is not as far-fetched as it may sound. Many state corporation codes provide for court appointment of directors, although the power is reserved—typically, as we have seen—when the corporation's shareholders need protection, rather than its consumers or neighbors.[5] For similar reasons courts are empowered to appoint highest-level management when a company is in bankruptcy or reorganization. In August 1974, a federal court in Washington, D.C., in settling a civil fraud action against Mattel Inc., forced the toy manufacturer to appoint two additional directors to its board, neither of whom is to have any other affiliation with Mattel, and their selection is to be subject to SEC and court approval.[6] But in the Mattel situation, again, it was the shareholders who inspired this extra measure of judicial compassion. In extreme cases of corporate recidivism like the Holland Furnace affair, why shouldn't a director be appointed whose primary concern is to achieve compliance with the law where people other than investors are being abused?

In the generic industry situation, where the companies involved will not typically be before any court or agency on the problem at issue, the original impetus for appointment would have to come from some corporation's GPD, or from the regulatory bodies with primary concern over the industry or problem—perhaps via a Federal Corporations Commission. (My suspicion is that problem-oriented agencies, e.g., an Office of Technology Assessment, Occupational Safety and Health Administration [OSHA], the Environmental Protection Agency, are apt to be more inclined to move in this direction than the agencies oriented toward, and thus "close to," particular industries, e.g., the Federal Power Commission, the Interstate Commerce Commission.) If, for example, in the asbestos industry problem, a government information-gathering source (HEW, OSHA) becomes aware of the health hazard, it could then apply, to the proposed Federal Corporations Commission, or directly move before a federal court (again, under legislation easily drafted) for a hearing on the appointment of a special public director. At such a hearing, trade association and corporate representatives would be called to discuss the nature of the problem and to deal with the likelihood and mechanics of its being ameliorated by a special director.° If the appointment of a director seemed advisable, his functions would be proposed and, as in the appointment of a trustee in bankruptcy, those interested, including the company, would submit recommendations for the post—subject, though, to final approval of the court.

## Functions of the Special Public Director

Just as the SPD would be distinguished from the GPD in terms of the occasions and mechanics of appointment, so too would the SPD have somewhat distinct functions—mostly but not all flowing from the sharper focus and narrower limits of his mandate.

In the exercise of the general superego functions, for example, the SPD's performance would be enhanced by his being able to present himself to the balance of the board as a man of special expertise—not just a well-meaning generalist. That is, if water pollution problems occasioned the appointment, we would expect the SPD to be a sanitary engineer; in the asbestos industry, a doctor or public health figure. We would anticipate his questions and recommendations carrying that much more weight. Further, if a nuclear engineer concerned with safety were on the board, those preparing board presentations will be forced to anticipate and prepare for questions of a different character. Putting such people on the board may give a useful "lift," too, to those employees throughout the organization who can ident-

---

° One outcome of the hearing—other than dismissal of the motion— might be to compromise on the appointment of, say, a corporate vice-president or even divisional executive, as distinct from a director. See Chapter 17.

ify with the SPD professionally. The placing of an environmental engineer on the board of a paper mill company, for example, would signal to the entire organization that, in terms of the organization's values, from now on the environment was to be taken into account seriously—and that those engineers throughout the organization who were engaged in that effort were being specially recognized.

There are other reasons to suppose that a SPD would be more effective than a GPD. As an insurer that the laws were being complied with, the SPD would know just what he was looking for, and have ready access to the court or agency that appointed him to get meaningful powers to back him up. In the Holland case, for example, he and his staff would presumably have established for themselves the right to receive all complaints that came in from customers, the Better Business Bureau, and local authorities. He would have demanded the power to put suspect sales areas under effective surveillance, and the power to fire any salesmen who persisted in the improper techniques. His staff would have made sure that complaints were being followed up on, and even interviewed noncomplaining customers (via random samplings of sales slips). If the SPD thought the wrongdoing was inherent in the organizational structure, he could recommend, for example, a less decentralized structure, or a change in compensation plans so as to take some commission pressure off the salesmen.

Or consider, once more, the Richardson-Merrell case. Judge Friendly felt himself in a box. The company had caused, he was willing to grant, some grievous harms. Yet, if he assessed the company punitive damages, it could "end the business life of a concern that has wrought much good in the past and might otherwise have continued to do so in the future, with many innocent stockholders suffering extinction of their investments from a single management sin." Without challenging here Judge Friendly's analysis, let us just observe that MER/29 was not, as he says, Richardson-Merrell's "single management sin"; just prior to that it had marketed a drug it called MER/24 but which the public knew by its generic name: thalidomide. Were a system for the appointment of an SPD available, the best solution would have been for the court to have assigned an SPD to Richardson-Merrell, a company where the top management was so ignorant of pharmaceutical matters that its president was to explain that, since he did not understand scientific papers, his practice was either to scan them or read a summary. (As for departmental reports: "A lot . . . went over my desk and I didn't open the cover. . . . At other times, I opened it to get an impression of the fields in which we were working. . . .")[7] How much more likely are the employees to express their misgivings to the staff of a director with whom they can identify—a fellow chemist, say—than to a president who cannot understand, and isn't terribly interested in, what that pharmacology stuff is all about.

In the generic industry situations, where no law has been violated, the emphasis of the SPD's work would be only somewhat different. There—as in the asbestos situation—his activities would lean toward recommending new laws and industry standards. He would oversee the work of the company's chief medical officer (who could often use some high-level support), direct studies of worker health histories, correlate information with SPDs at other companies in the industry, and gather and disseminate data to public health authorities in the United States and abroad. He would also report regularly to the company's board on the gravity of his assigned situation and on the steps taken to ameliorate it. This latter information would put the board "on notice" of the situation, with all the implications discussed in Chapter 14.

## Powers of the Special Public Director

The powers of the SPD would be essentially of the same character as the GPD's, but exercisable within the SPD's narrower range of authority. In other words, the SPD in the asbestos manufacturing company would have the power to inspect records, but the records he would assess would include X-rays and other medical data, rather than cash flows through subsidiaries.

In many cases, however, special powers ought to be agreed upon at the time of his appointment. These might well include the absolute power to suspend or fire an employee in appropriate situations (for example, in the Holland case). His effectiveness would be enlarged, too, if he was known to have the power to veto promotions. Another special power—drastic, but perhaps *the* effective power we might vest in someone in appropriate cases —is the power to halt production. If, say, the SPD in a product safety position was convinced that agreed-upon quality-control measures were being circumvented, we might give him power to suspend the production process until the situation was righted. (He could be empowered to go to court for a temporary restraining order if necessary.) Other special powers that might be appropriate in diverse situations include some influence over internal budgeting—to demand an increase in safety R&D, for example.

# 17. Managing with Management

The possibilities explored thus far have singled out the directors as the focal point of internal corporate reform. But working through the board is not the only way to bring about the organizational reforms we are after. Nor, given some practical and political considerations, is the "top" necessarily the most feasible or effective place to begin. Some further, and I think very viable alternatives are latent in a few recent developments in the federal courts.

The first case arose when ARCO (formerly Atlantic Richfield Oil Co.) was charged with spilling oil into the Chicago Sanitary and Ship Canal.[1] ARCO's response was to do what companies so charged almost inevitably do—plead *nolo contendere* (essentially a euphemism for guilty). And no wonder: The fine ARCO was liable for under the sixty-five-year-old Rivers and Harbors Act was a mere $500 to $2,500. "Just," ARCO said in effect, "send us the bill."

But Judge James B. Parsons, who had heard this response too often, was fed up. The very same leaky ARCO plant had already been convicted of the very same violation.[2] He proposed that instead of the fine, he would suspend sentence and place ARCO on probation; a condition of the probation should be, they urged, that within forty-five days the company set up and complete a program to handle the oil spillage.

The government lawyers had very little previous law in support of the position Judge Parsons was urging them into. But they came up with an imaginative and persuasive analogy:

It seems obvious that a district judge could remove a minor from the custody of a guardian who is interfering with his probation and rehabilitation. Why may not the court remove a portion of corporate activity (pollution control) from the control of officers interfering with corporate probation and rehabilitation?[3]

Now, a human being would ordinarily be quite pleased to submit to an argument like this—to have sentence suspended in favor of probation. For the human being, probation looms as a better alternative to prison. But ARCO—as a corporation—was not imprisonable anyway. The worst it could be sentenced to was the paltry fine. Thus, although it may sound ironic, ARCO, sensing a dangerous trend in the law, brought in a whole new staff of lawyers to fight for its "right" to turn down probation and be sentenced. Only persons, ARCO's lawyers argued, can be put on probation.

Judge Parsons seemingly acknowledged that a corporation could not, like a person, pay visits to a probation officer; but, *a probation officer could pay visits to the corporation.* And, indeed, Judge Parsons went on, if within the forty-five days allowed,* the company had not satisfied the spillage program condition of the probation, he would then hold a hearing on the appointment of a special probation officer. The "probation officer," with powers of a trustee under supervision of the court, would go right into the plant and make good and sure that ARCO was doing whatever was necessary and feasible to abate the pollution.[4] (The idea would be more effective, I might add, if the man appointed as probation officer was in this instance a sanitary engineer.)

The second case arose in 1973, when one of the twelve largest accounting firms in the United States, Lavanthol, Krekstein, Horwath and Horwath, got in trouble with the SEC. The ordinary punishment that can be visited on accountancy firms—expulsion or suspension from practices before the SEC—is so serious a penalty that it is rarely invoked, especially if the misdeeds can be pinned (as they usually can be) on just one or two "errant" employees. Nor does a suspension, per se, unearth and cure the underlying defects that got the firm in trouble in the first place.

---

* Later amended to sixty days.

Thus, neither the SEC nor the companies are satisfied with suspension of the whole company as a remedy. In the Lavanthol case, therefore, Judge David N. Edelstein worked out what the *Wall Street Journal* called "an unusual settlement intended as a model for disciplinary proceedings against accounting firms."[5] The order required Lavanthol to adhere to a thick set of "supervisory and control procedures" worked out by the firm under SEC supervision. Then the court got the American Institute of Certified Public Accountants to select an inspection team from among its members, to go into the company and report on how well the procedures were being carried out. Lavanthol will bear the expenses. According to the *Journal*, accounting sources reported that the Lavanthol-type settlement pattern "is under active consideration for other cases."[6]

It seems to me that if we put the *ARCO* and *Lavanthol* cases together, the principle they suggest has farther-reaching possibilities than anyone has yet realized.[*] For one thing, in both cases the action was taken only *after* some wrongdoing had occurred. That is, the appointments were invoked to remedy demonstrated delinquency situations. Why should such comparable procedures not be available prospectively in generic industry situations, that is, where some social problem, probably amenable to internal checks, can almost inevitably be predicted throughout an industry?

Further, both cases suggest that the law might effectively inject people into the corporation, in appropriate situations, at

[*] In this same context, one ought to consider also *S.E.C.* v. *Koenig*, which involved Ecological Science Corporation (ECO), a company that was being ballyhooed so successfully that the price of its shares actually doubled between July and December 1969. A series of charges by the SEC ensued. Some of its European subsidiaries seemed to be involved in questionable financial activities, and ECO's reporting of the tortuous path of cash from shell to shell was so confusing that no outsider could be certain of what had been going on. What was needed—as in the ARCO case—was some way to inject *into* the corporation someone responsible to the court, someone who could remove from the officer that portion of the company's activities (here, financial disclosure) that the managers had shown themselves unwilling or unable to handle. Judge John M. Cannella came up with a rather innovative concept—a "receiver with limited powers"—not to take over the business in its entirety, but to go in and handle the part that wasn't working, the investigating and clarifying of its financial affairs.[7]

levels well beneath the board. Indeed, in the ARCO situation the outside overseer was to be installed right into the lawbreaking plant—that is, at just about the lowest operating level in the organization. True, in both these cases the person injected was purely an officer of the court, rather than of the corporation. But there is no reason why his duties could not be structured to include whatever mix of corporate line functions was deemed appropriate to the situation. It is not hard to see many practical advantages to zeroing in on a problem this way. This is especially true the more precisely the problem and its handling can be defined at the time of the appointment, the more diversified the corporation, and the less significant the problem looms in the overall scheme of things that is likely to occupy top-level management's attention. For example, to revert to the asbestos example, to the extent a corporation is wholly or primarily engaged in asbestos manufacture, then the special director approach has plain merit. But to the extent that asbestos is one of many operations in some corporation's far-flung empire, an agency might prefer to approach the problem by inserting someone in the company at a lower level.

How successful a lower-level appointee would be depends in part upon how adequately he can be shored up with the necessary reinforcement and powers. A director inherits certain powers—inspection and so forth—just by virtue of his office. But where a special officer were appointed beneath the director level, all his powers would have to be specially provided for in advance. These arrangements could be made easily enough, though, so that a lower-level management appointment could succeed without having to connect him with some director concurrently appointed "upstairs." In the ARCO situation, for example, had an appointment been made,* there would have been a prior hearing. At the hearing, the parties, together with environmentalists, engineers, and others who wanted to appear, could have worked out with the court such matters as the extensiveness of the officer's power to inspect, the circumstances, if any, in which

---

* The judge was satisfied that ARCO had adequately complied within the time allotted, and the probation hearing never had to be held.

he would be able to halt production,* and any limits of the costs that his recommendations might impose on the company.†

Then, too, even if the courts stop short of designating particular corporate personnel, it is not unthinkable that the society should establish by law that corporations (or certain classes of corporations) include in their management structure certain specified offices. Indeed, when state corporations codes require that corporations, as a condition of enjoying the corporate privileges, have a board of directors, the society is doing just that. The law may occasionally demand that the corporation establish at least one vice-president and perhaps a secretary and treasurer. But it does not go beyond that to insist, as it might, upon the creation of designated medium-level and lower-level management positions. We allow a company that is operating a nuclear generator to decide, wholly on its own, whether to have an

---

* The Soviet factor's inspection department reportedly has the power to stop production not only on individual machines but even in entire shops. David Granick, *The Red Executive: A Study of the Organization Man in Russian Industry* (1960; rpt. Garden City: Anchor, 1961), p. 277.

† It is questionable whether, under the law as it now stands, a corporation could legally or practically be subjected to a probation order that imposed on it more onerous costs than it would be liable for if fined. That is to say, if the most ARCO could have been fined were $2,500, could the probation officer demand that it take such steps to abate the pollution as would cost the company $10,000?

A court might regard such a condition as "unreasonable" and beyond the intention of the drafters of the Probation Act. On appeal of the ARCO decision, the Seventh Circuit, while agreeing with Judge Parsons that the corporation could be put on probation, thought his conditions unreasonable, perhaps (the Court of Appeals is not terribly clear) on these grounds. *U.S. v. Atlantic Richfield Oil Co.*, 465 F. 2d 58, 61 (7th Cir. 1972).

In all events, even if the probation officer's request for corporate remedial action were not legally unreasonable, it would face a further, practical difficulty. If a person on probation violates a condition of probation, probably the worst one can do to him is to revoke probation. This throws the court back to where it started—that is, it can invoke no larger sentence than would originally have been available—in the ARCO case, $2,500. Thus, if a defendant were shortsighted enough, and a potential fine low enough, it could disregard a costly probation recommendation and take the fine. In responding this way, however, my guess is that the company would inspire the authorities to institute a new lawsuit against it every morning. What is more, there is no reason why federal law could not be amended to empower a court to hold in contempt a company that deliberately disregarded a reasonable probation request. The contempt order could not be treated so lightly.

executive in charge of safety, and if so, where he should be placed in the management structure. Similarly, there is no legal requirement that companies operating in heavily polluting industries establish, say, a vice-president for environmental affairs.

Is this legal vacuum defensible? Strong defenders of laissez-faire will urge that if the damages a polluting company causes are large enough, or if fines for pollution are raised, then, at the point where a special officer in charge of environmental matters is the best way for the company to cut its losses, we can be confident that it will, of its own, institute the "right" officer to perform the "right" internal checks. But we have already seen in how many ways the self-interests of the situation—both the corporation's and the top executives'—is no guarantee that the companies, on their own, are going to establish officers with power to implement the most effective internal monitoring and control. Thus, in the many situations in which a special public director may be less effective than someone located closer to operations, we must seriously consider requiring corporations to establish the appropriate roles. Such a move would, indeed, be rare. But it has been done. The recent *Mattel* settlement took the step of imposing into the corporation both a financial controls and audit committee and a litigation and claims committee; the latter was charged with determining, among other things, whether the company should institute action against present or past officers. (The order specifies that the first committee be composed of four directors and the second committee of three, all subject to SEC and court approval.)[8]

Of course, making a company establish an office is not enough, if all it comes to is painting a name on a door. To make the office truly effective, there must be attached to the office well-defined and meaningful powers and duties, as well as a place in the organization that guarantees the appointee's not being closeted away from the critical action. Which powers and duties are attached will depend upon the problem. In the Holland Furnace situation, for example, the company, in an ostensible effort to comply, established a products service department under a products service manager—supposedly to check out complaints. As we saw, this system failed to keep the salesmen within the law. But this was not, I think, because the idea of a products service manager with compliance responsibility was a bad idea in principle, but because he was not given the power to suspend or fire anyone, or even effectively to contribute to those decisions.[9] One major utility corporation told me proudly that it had hired an environmental engineer. But on close examination it turned out that its touted environmentalist was slated to report directly to the vice-president for public relations! He had no formal authority to review the decisions of the operating engineers, nor did he even have input to those working under the vice-president for planning. The management structure was such that his task could be little more than to justify to the public decisions that were going to be made without any uncalled-for help on his part. These situations suggest a sort of organizational resistance and foot-dragging that could, and should, be anticipated in advance.

Once the law establishes job definitions for critical offices, then liabilities should be attached for the inadequate performance of those functions. The point is central to the theme of this entire book: As corporations increase in size, and production processes become more complex, and more and more persons (and machines) have a hand in the finished product, it is increasingly difficult to locate responsibility on any one particular individual *for that end product:* the defective car or the building that collapses. But if we make a system of punishments *task*-oriented (in addition to our *product*-oriented punishments), it is much easier to locate responsibility—on the person who failed to perform the critical task—and thus to head off problems before they occur.

There are already a few stabs in this direction. The amendments to the Food and Drug Acts that followed in the wake of the thalidomide and MER/29 cases provide that there be an "investigator" for each drug under development, and lays down certain functions for the office. By law—not by the company's choice—the investigator is required to prepare and maintain adequate and accurate case histories designed to record all observations and other data pertinent to the investigation on each individual treated with the drug or employed as a control in the investigation.[10]

The gist of such provisions is that while no one may feel responsible for some distant, contingent wrong—the possible damage to some still abstract drug taker—someone can be made to feel *immediately* responsible to a specified role performance; thereby the law can more effectively induce the sort of behavior it needs.

Let me give another illustration. All the auto companies have test drivers and safety engineers. But what is their responsibility? And to whom? After repeated accidents involving the Corvair, an ex-General Motors employee revealed not only that the staff had known of the car's tendency to roll over, but that there was a document recommending a relatively inexpensive way to remedy the situation. (GM personnel are said fraudulently and dishonestly to have kept the document out of the hands of the plaintiffs' lawyers.)[11] Now, the point is, were the office of, say, chief test engineer one established and defined not only by the companies but by the society at large, in such a way that it was his legal duty to keep a record of tests, and to report adverse experiences at once to the Department of Transportation, we would be far better off. A superior who asked the chief test engineer to "forget that little mishap" would not only be asking him to risk some unknowable person's life and limb at some undefined time in the future; he would be asking him to violate the law, which is a far more serious and immediate liability for both of them.

Not all the punishments for failure to abide by required role performances would have to be exacted by the state in a criminal trial. Another possibility is to make an individual who failed to abide by his job description legally answerable to anyone who was injured by a product that passed through his control, without putting the injured plaintiff to the task of proving actual negligence. The nonperforming employee would be what lawyers call "absolutely liable" to the injured party, perhaps even in circumstances in which the company itself would not be liable. Or we could make nonperformance a condition calling for immediate discharge of the employee. The Federal Trade Commission is beginning to adopt an approach like this, although still in a very narrow area. Companies whose employees have been engaging in fraudulent sales practices have been forced to discipline or fire employees who do not conform to assigned ground rules.[12]

## Requirements for Holding Office

Another "intrusion" into management autonomy involves society's laying down qualifications for performing certain highly critical corporate tasks. Like the other proposals, it sounds more radical and unthinkable than it really is. Right now, we don't allow just anyone to examine and approve a company's financial reports. Various laws (and stock exchange regulations) demand that the person who performs that role must be a certified public accountant. Other functions—for example, giving certain opinions relating to a financial prospectus—can be done only by a lawyer. In both these cases, however, as I have stressed throughout the book, these sorts of intrusions into corporate autonomy are reserved for the protection of the corporation's investors. What about the consumers of the company's products? Or its neighbors? Should they not have, and is it not feasible to accord them, comparable protection?

For illustration, let me revert once more to the Richardson-Merrell MER/29 case. There, it developed that when the director of the company's toxicology and pathology laboratory resigned he was replaced as toxicology director by one "Dr." William M. King. It was thus "Dr." King—whose degree was as imaginary as the graphs on invented monkeys[13]—to whom fell the task of reviewing and evaluating such matters as blood changes in the laboratory animals.

I submit, it is nothing short of incredible that with our pharmaceutical houses developing drugs that will enter the bodies of just about everyone in America, no one even seems to think about requiring the sort of qualifications for key tasks in the drug production process that we require for key tasks in the issuance of the companies' financial prospectuses.* Only men admitted to the bar can appear for a corporation in court, but anyone it chooses can evaluate its laboratory data.

The other side of this coin is disqualification. Lawyers can be suspended or disbarred. Under the Landrum-Griffin Act, persons convicted of various crimes are disqualified from being labor union officers for five years after conviction.[14] But insofar as the criminal record of corporate officers is concerned, the law couldn't care less.[15] The union crook caught under Landrum-Griffin can turn around and swing a job with management.

I am not urging that every executive or other corporate employee who has been convicted of a crime be automatically debarred from serving in a corporate post. On the contrary, if a man has served in prison the maximum time the law lays down for the offense, I think it questionable to put further disabilities on him. But we have to recognize that white-collar criminals rarely are given anywhere near the maximum sentence the law provides—if they are sentenced at all. In cases where they are to be "let off light" it would seem appropriate in some circumstances to disqualify them from immediately returning to control over the vast resources and powers that their corporate positions can command.

Consider in this regard the aftermath of what is known in California as the Sylmar Tunnel disaster. Lockheed Shipbuilding (a division of Lockheed Aircraft) was building a tunnel in the San Fernando Valley. The possibility of encountering gas was

---

* The farthest the FDA seems to have gone in this direction is to require in various drug application forms that the drug's sponsor include a statement of "the scientific training and experience considered appropriate by the sponsor to qualify the investigators as suitable experts to investigate the safety of the drug." There also are requirements to include "the names and summary of the training and experience of each investigator . . . charged with monitoring the progress of the investigation and evaluating the evidence of safety and effectiveness. . . ." 21 *Code of Federal Regulations* 130.3 (a) (2) 8, 9. What influence the FDA could or would bring if it deemed the qualifications inadequate is not made clear. Will it *reject* a drug application if the principal investigator appears inadequately qualified?

(in the words of the court) "clearly forecast."[16] Yet almost none of the available gas-detection technology—standard in modern shaft mining—was put into operation. Rumors of danger were rife among the workers. On July 23, 1971, a flash fire raced through the mine, injuring four men. One group swore it would not return to the tunnel until a monitoring system had been installed. Even in the face of this and other portents, the company refused to suspend work and do something about the situation. The next day the mine exploded, killing seventeen men and injuring three. Two others were injured during rescue operations.

The state brought criminal actions against Lockheed and its two safety engineers in charge of the project. Judge George W. Trammel, on sentencing, observed an incredible string of safety code violations and said,

The evidence reflects that little was done to adopt or use practices . . . which would render the San Fernando Tunnel safe in the event that, as anticipated, gas and/or oil was encountered. This is borne out as to the two shifts that worked the night that the flash fire occurred. . . . We have a complete corporate breakdown as to safety in this case [including] inadequate geological workups and investigations, inadequate testing and testing procedures in an area where gas was clearly anticipated to be encountered, an inadequate ventilation system, inadequate ignition protection. . . . How Savage could stand by and watch almost identical circumstances develop on the night of the fatal explosion as developed the night before . . . is almost beyond belief. I can't imagine any other case where so many warnings of impending doom could be so callously ignored.[17]

Callous. Almost beyond belief. Yet, what was the upshot? Lockheed was fined $85,000.* Lee was sentenced to eighteen months in the county jail; Savage, to twenty years. But in the next breath, the court suspended sentence and placed the men on probation. The probation reduced their confinement periods

---

* Lockheed had to pay an additional $120,000 into a State Victims Indemnity Fund; an unusual provision of California law requires those convicted of "crimes of violence" to pay into the fund $5,000 per victim of their crimes, for the benefit of dependents. Judge Trammell reasoned that what Lockheed had done amounted in the circumstances to a crime of violence.

to six months and five years respectively. And then, continuing, *the terms of the probation do not even preclude the two men from returning immediately on release to "safety engineering," to positions of authority and control over the lives of hundreds of men.* All the court did was to demand that "in any situation in which you have direction, management, control, or custody of any employment, place of employment, or employee," the two do so in a reasonably safe and adequate way.

In a case like this, would it have been so unreasonable to disqualify the safety engineers from returning to safety supervisory posts at least for the periods of the fullest sentences they might have received? How can we reconcile the fact that a lawyer who violates the law is likely to be suspended or disbarred, but not a safety engineer, or a chemist in a pharmaceutical house? Can anyone believe that an inept or immoral lawyer threatens more lives than an inept or immoral toxicologist? Or that an overzealous jockey is a greater threat to society than the men who were mounted on the Penn Central?[18]

## Review of Entire Management Systems

Thus far the "intrusions" into management autonomy that we have considered have all been piecemeal—a change by placing a new office here, by adding a new function or obligation there. Might it ever be advisable for an outside source to pass upon entire management plans?

I think that the answer, in general, is most certainly no. Each organization evolves into its own unique organizational patterns, both formal and informal. What is the best organizational mode for one company—given its history, its resources—is not necessarily the best for some other, even one producing the same product on the same scale. For this reason, the traditional reluctance of courts to second-guess management on "managerial" matters makes a lot of sense; the piecemeal intrusions I have already outlined would themselves put the law in a largely new and uncertain area.

But I would be remiss to close the chapter without some remarks on the possibility of outside review of larger segments of the company's entire management plan. Let me use as an example the Penn Central merger. I do not want to suggest that the collapse of the railroad was in any simple sense "caused by" the major organizational deficiencies, but absolutely no one is satisfied with the manner in which the two huge companies were slapped together. Daughen and Binzen, in *The Wreck of the Penn Central* observe:

When two railroads that had been bitter rivals for 100 years combined, human conflicts were inevitable. Yet they were never dealt with openly and honestly. They weren't even anticipated. One could read 40,000 pages of merger testimony before the ICC without encountering a hint of impending trouble in meshing "red" PRR people with "green" Central People. Even after the collapse, Stuart Saunders considered reports of red-green feuding "greatly exaggerated." The reports, if anything, were understated. . . . James Symes to the contrary, the PRR and Central were not like "two peas in a pod." In operating style, in marketing philosophy, in personnel, they differed sharply. The Pennsylvania, stolid, steady and traditional, carried ore over mountains. It was "volume oriented," and its operations were highly decentralized. It generally promoted from within its own ranks. The Central was smaller, scrappier, hungrier, more inclined to abandon the book and innovate. Perlman once said: "After you've done a thing the same way for two years, look it over carefully. After five years, look at it with suspicion. After ten years, throw it away and start all over again." The Central carried manufactured goods along its "water-level route." It was profit oriented and centralized. . . . In addition to major stylistic differences between the two rival railroads there were many minor operational ones. . . . The two railroads even used different kinds of railroad spikes. And then there were the incompatible computers. . . ."[19]

Why these problems inherent in the Penn Central merger are of particular interest is that the merger was many years under review for any number of problems by any number of agencies. The Antitrust Division of the Justice Department (as well as the ICC) reviewed the merger for the effects it was likely to have on competition; the ICC reviewed the merger for its impact on commerce. Would it have been asking too much that those proposing the merger to have elaborated in advance the organizational plans of the proposed company, and to have had their proposal reviewed for overall management feasibility by a staff that included management experts and retired officers of other roads? Are the railroad mergers presently contemplated going to go through in the same manner—without any consideration for the possibility (or even likelihood) that the private compromises among the parties to the merger are going to create a managerial, organizational monster?

Having an outside source pass upon the overall organization of some entity is—like my other suggestions—not as incredible as it first sounds. To some extent, this is done by courts when they have to judge the feasibility of a reorganization plan. But what is even more intriguing as precedent are various procurement rules of the Department of Defense. The day is long past when those companies bidding to build a ship or plane submit plans for the final product only. Today's military specifications demand that the would-be defense contractor set forth the management and organizational procedures that it is proposing to get the job done. The Department of Defense (and NASA, under like regulations) goes over and works out compromises in the structural proposals just as it does the proposals for the final product. In so doing it is regularly exercising influence over large segments of what is ordinarily thought inviolable management prerogative: Design-review committees have to be established, rules for information flow are specified, and offices are established and defined.

Defense companies have come to accept these "intrusions" as a matter of course. Why, then, would it be unthinkable occasionally to demand the same of other sorts of corporations whose actions are highly charged with a public interest? The ordinary commercial lender that comes to some company's aid will often demand a strong hand in the management, even a place on the board of directors. Where the government's financial support gives it a proprietary interest akin to that of a bank or other lending institution, why should it demand less? Indeed, at the time the government was bailing out Lockheed, Senator Alan Cranston (D. Calif.) would have required a change in the entire board and the whole management team as a condition of the government's loan guarantees.[20] The bill that finally emerged, The Emergency Loan Guarantee Act, actually gives the Emergency Loan Guarantee Board the authority to "require before guaranteeing any loan . . . that the enterprise make such management changes as the Board deems necessary. . . ."[21] It remains to be seen whether the government will have the courage to exercise this sensible, if limited, power.

# 18. Mending the Information Net

A few years ago, columnist Jack Anderson got his hands on an ITT house memo in which one of the company's Washington lobbyists, Dita Beard, intimated that the company had pledged funds to the Republican National Convention in exchange for favorable settlement of some antitrust suits then pending against ITT. When the row had settled, what was the "moral" that the corporate community had drawn from the affair? That corporations ought not to meddle with the law? That boards should demand assurances that no one in *their* company was engaged in similar activities?

Perhaps. But the real, immediate lesson is one that was buried in the financial pages. "Dita Beard's now-famous memo somehow escaped the crunching jaws of an office shredder," the *Los Angeles Times* reported, "and the document-shredding industry has been working overtime ever since. . . . To avoid any possibility of embarrassment, big and small firms alike have scrambled to find a convenient method to shred, cube, pulp or otherwise maim any documents they consider too sensitive to toss in the office wastebasket."[1] If you were looking for a good investment, the Pacific Paper Cutter Co. was the place—"sales definitely went up after the Dita Beard affair," one company spokesman assured the financial community.[2]

The fact is that while imposing direct requirements and controls on a company's internal information processes would be one of the most effective ways of influencing corporate behavior, we leave our corporations pretty much free to gather, disseminate, and shred whatever data they choose. Such informational controls as have been adopted are piecemeal and inadequate exceptions, at best. Once more, we run into the effects of the law's notion that the corporation is just another "person": a person's thought process being regarded as sacrosanct, and a corporation being a person, we can barely bring ourselves to think about a whole variety of ways to take advantage of direct intrusions into a company's "inner thought processes."

As an example of how this mentality operates, there is an article in a recent *Trial* magazine on consumer product safety. The piece, by the chief of the Epidemiology and Investigations Branch of HEW, spells out "a new and innovative strategy of data-gathering on products related to injuries."[3] Under the Division of Consumer Product Safety, a National Electronic Surveillance System (NEISS) is being set up "to establish, for the first time, a statistically valid means to assess community needs relative to hazards imposed upon the consumer." A thoughtful sequence of information-gathering operations is to begin when an accident victim enters a hospital emergency room for injury treatment; data are to be collected by hospital staff and coded. At the end of the day, a coder/transmitter will send the coded data into a Western Union Model 33 teletypewriter tied into the headquarters computer in Washington. There the headquarters staff will review the summary registers and, by statistical sampling, determine where further investigatory visits are advisable. This new system is hardly to be disparaged. It almost certainly is what the author calls it, "The most important epidemiological program in the field of consumer product safety and in the history of government activity in this area." But my point is that while the people who designed the program contemplated the gathering and dissemination of information among hospitals, injured parties, and the government, they do not extend their projected information net to the very institutions that are turning out the injurious products—the corporations.

If statistical samplings are to be gathered, isn't it obvious that data lying within the companies would be an important complement to what one finds in the hospitals? Yet, even the most advanced social thinking implicitly regards what goes on inside the corporation as "off limits" to public view.

What can be done to improve corporations' behavior by focusing directly on their information processes? There are two broad types of information-oriented measures to be considered. First, we could impose *information handling standards* on the corporation, while yet leaving the operation of the system predominantly in the hands of the corporation's own agents. Second, there are measures which would install government inspectors directly into critical points in the flow of data—most "drastically," within the company's own plants, if need be.

## Dealing with the Corporation's Information Net

The importance of a company's information processes cannot be overstated; they are as vital to the corporation as the nervous system of a human being to the body. What information the corporation seeks from its environment, where it looks for feedback (both within and without itself), where it dispatches what it learns, what it stores in memory, and what, for all intents and purposes, it "forgets" (or destroys)—all these features of its information system are fundamental determinants of the corporation's behavior. There is no reason why each of these information processes, in turn, cannot be influenced directly by the society.*

To begin with, there is, in the environment of each corporation, a great deal of information bearing upon its own activities that it never receives. This is part of a more general problem in the society—so often critical information is available, but simply is not being steered to the appropriate place for action. One of the more extraordinary facts we discovered in our "autopsy" of the MER/29 affair was that within three months of the drug's release the chief of cardiology at Los Angeles's Cedars of Lebanon Hospital had announced that he was discontinuing use of MER/29 because of its effects on his patients. There is no

---

* The key word here is "directly." Obviously, each time we pass a law of general application, we do something that indirectly affects the categories that the organization has to consider—"restraint of trade" with the Sherman and Clayton acts, the categories of unfair labor practices with the Norris-La Guardia Act, and so forth.

indication as to whether, and in what form, these doubts might have been relayed to Richardson-Merrell, much less the FDA. But we know that E. F. Hutton, the stockbrokerage house, picked up the story almost immediately and alerted its brokers across the nation—for it portended a possible decline in Richardson-Merrell stock.[4] In other words, *the information processes of our society are such that across America doctors were prescribing MER/29, oblivious to dangers that their stockbrokers had long been alerted to.*

Of course, every organization (like every human being) has to put some limits on the reaches of its inquiry. To try to pay attention to every corner of the universe at once could result in a sort of corporate schizophrenia. But it is by no means clear that the reach of corporate information nets at present is bringing about anything like an ideal information search. Consider again those American pharmaceutical companies manufacturing between eight and ten *billion* amphetamine pills each year—a number vastly in excess of conceivable legitimate medical use— with the result that a huge quantity is shipped to Mexico for smuggling back into the United States's illicit drug trade by an elaborate underground. Perhaps the companies involved really *do* know what is going on. But I think it at least equally plausible that giant corporations are not effectively aware of effects they are having. The tendency of business organizations is to focus their limited information-gathering resources on such matters as industry sales volumes, capital costs, market shifts, and competitor behavior. Their information nets are simply not designed to haul in other, "softer" data, less immediately relevant to profits, growth, and prestige. And even if information lands at the feet of someone within the company, there is no guarantee that it will be advanced upward to an executive with authority to do something about it. (Especially, as I have observed, if the higher-ups do not want to hear about "that sort of thing.") Thus, while the vital information about where their pollutants are winding up, or where their amphetamines are traveling to, may be somewhere in a company, it need not be in the company at a place and in a form conducive to corporate remedial action.

To improve the company's information searches will usually call for, in the first instance, the establishment of a corporate office whose special functions spell out both *where* the holder of the office is to go to collect data (the sources), and what *categories of abstraction* he is to use (what he is to look for).

As "unthinkable" as such action may sound in our society, there is a remarkably well thought out and sophisticated step in this direction in the consent decree entered into between AT&T, the Secretary of Labor, and the Equal Employment Opportunities Commission (the AT&T Anti-Bias Decree).[5] This decree, framed in the wake of numerous complaints that AT&T and its affiliates had for many years been discriminating against women and minorities, does just what I have been suggesting. The decree directly imposes on the companies a detailed Internal Reporting System. Under the system, the company must continually gather data on applicants by minority group and sex. The required information includes such categories as the number of minorities hired; number rejected; reasons for rejection; data on placements, upgrades, and promotions; resignations and dismissals. To make the system work, the decree pins down on particular officers exactly what their responsibility is to be in the maintenance and monitoring of the system. It provides, for example, that the companies set up equal employment opportunity coordinators and equal employment opportunity managers, with special duties in support of information gathering and monitoring. Why are approaches like this not extended to other areas?

We could well mandate that each auto company have one office responsible for gathering and collating the wealth of data "out there" in sheriffs' records, coroners' reports, hospitals, auto repair shops, and the Highway Safety Research Institute. Drug companies should have someone affirmatively responsible to gather follow-up data on drugs; the pharmaceutical houses themselves are in many ways more likely to get honest feedback from doctors using the drug than is the FDA. But at present, after a drug has been approved, the only contact between the producer and doctors is apt to be through the detail men, who typically have no scientific (or often even college) training, and whose interest in selling the drug inevitably leads to their playing down, or even fending off, any hints of danger that a doctor might try to relay to the company.[6]

Since many problems owe not to failures of the corporation to have the information on hand (somewhere), but to failures to process it upward to the people who are in a position to do something about it, we must also consider where the data, once gathered by the corporation, are to be transmitted.

No one supposes, of course, that just landing the right information on the right desk is a sure guarantee that the appropriate remedial action will be taken. In a case like the Equity Funding scandal, for example, a federal grand jury has had reason to suppose that the men at the top of the company were fostering, much less aware of, the wrongdoing. In such a situation, our steps to assure that the highest level management knows what is happening would appear bootless. But there are two important points to be kept in mind. First, there are many cases like the B. F. Goodrich brake affair, where the problems that the higher-level management never heard about were destined to work to the detriment of the corporation. In such cases one may legitimately hope that if the data can be moved upward, the top management will intercede to set the situation straight—in the company's own interests.

Second, even in those cases in which "the company" or its officers would rather not take any action upon the information, legally required pathways may yet be quite effective. If we *make* top executives know certain things they would rather not know about, the knowledge can be used to increase their (and the corporation's)* liability. For if the law says that the organizational pathways *have to* lay certain information at the feet of specified people, it can effectively do away with the various defenses of "ignorance" that the officers might otherwise subsequently raise.

---

* As indicated in Chapter 6, the reluctance of the courts to impose punitive damages on the corporation can sometimes be overcome by proof that the top management was aware of the wrongdoing.

Could the law lay down requirements effectively commanding certain patterns of internal information flows?

Indeed, it could.

One approach is simply to require the information system directly by law. Under California insurance law each insurance company must designate some officer to be the recipient of financial reports on the company; the law then proceeds to require that that officer (presumably the secretary) *must* report the findings to the board; and the minutes *must* reflect that they saw it.[7] A measure like this, though now the exception, could increasingly become the rule. Why should it not be an offense that corporations fail to establish reasonable routines for the internal communication of certain significant information? More effective still, we could provide punishments for failure of an underling to make a *written* report, to a vice-president level or above, of information bearing upon the possibility that his organization may be violating the law, or engaged in a course of conduct that a reasonable man would recognize as posing high risks to the public or any class thereof—consumers, investors, and so on. Would this really be so unthinkable?

Consent decrees can also be used to impose appropriate information systems as part of a settlement package. This approach allows tailoring of the information system to the particular company and problem involved—and failure to maintain the system would be enforceable by a contempt proceeding, both against the company and against key officers. The AT&T Anti-Bias Decree provides an example. The Federal Trade Commission, too, is increasingly utilizing this technique in cases where salesmen have been discovered systematically engaged in flagrantly deceptive sales practices. Rather than play the cat-and-mouse games they played with Holland Furnace, they are demanding that the employer corporation institute a program of continuing surveillance over its sales force, often spelling out some details of the surveillance.[8]

In addition, there are a number of "levers" the law could bring to bear on companies to induce them indirectly to seek out the information. Some of the alternatives include: (1) that in any legal actions against the company arising from injuries that might conceivably have been prevented had the information been on hand, the failure of the company to have gathered the data, and communicated them effectively, shall constitute prima facie evidence of guilt or liability; (2) that the failure to gather the information, as above, could result in double or triple liability against the company, in the event a wrong were traceable to the failure; and (3) perhaps even more effectively, we could deny insurance recovery to any company that had not established a reasonably adequate information system (i.e., make risks so caused noninsurable).

The internal information systems one will want to impose must be concerned not only with the flow of critical information upward to those in positions of authority to change corporate direction, but also with the flow of information *downward* to various operating levels. The AT&T Anti-Bias Decree provides for the vice-president–general counsel—the corporation's top legal officer—to be "responsible for assuring that the personnel relations department is properly informed about all local, state and federal regulations affecting equal employment opportunity."[9] The Federal Trade Commission is beginning to stipulate in its orders that companies require supervisory personnel to "fully explain the applicable provisions of this order to all sales agents, representatives."[10]

Of course, merely communicating an order downward does not mean that it will be obeyed. General Electric had a clear written Directive Policy 20.5, first issued in 1946, specifically forbidding employees from activities which violated either the spirit or the letter of the antitrust laws. Yet in the early 1960s it was disclosed that price-fixing was rampant in the company, and had undoubtedly been going on for many, many years. To make a message effective, the communicator must anticipate the mental set and context in which the recipient is destined to view it. Indeed, anyone concerned with monitoring communications within an organization must allow for the fact that a single message may have to be presented differently to different units within the organization if it is to have the same desired impact.

This suggests, for example, that the present practice of framing consent orders aimed for a general corporate audience (usually in lawyer's language) is almost certainly a poor idea. It might be more effective for courts and agencies, with the assistance of management consultants, to review the form of message that the corporation proposes to distribute to each group from the point of view of helping to bring about the "appropriate translations."[11] This would be especially useful where the practices complained of are subtle, not flagrant, or where the thrust of the decree is not to cease certain conduct, but to inspire affirmative action in a desired direction.

Finally, while it is harder to monitor than the flow of information, one has to consider the adequacy of the messages as well. Consider a company such as Richardson-Merrell, where the top level lacked scientific training. There the manner in which the scientific data are "translated" on their way upward is all-significant. At one point in the MER/29 experiments one of the lab reports described the condition of a group of test animals as "good, except for loss of hair and sight."[12] It is not hard to imagine this incredible characterization being passed upward simply as "good." Possibilities of this sort could be reduced by specifying forms for reportage, in situations in which that is feasible.

The last feature of internal information control involves placing limits on the storage and recall of data. The law has on occasion demanded that some corporate records be preserved for inspection, such as with data relevant to costs and prices under the World War II OPA regulations and, more recently, as a reinforcement of the wage-price regulations. But there is much more that could be done in this direction.

This seems so obvious that I want to comment here on just three features that we ought to concern ourselves with—all of which are pointed up forcibly in various cases we have "autopsied."

First, both the MER/29 and B. F. Goodrich episodes suggest that where retention is advisable, it ought to be imposed on the *raw* data. The "fudging" that goes on is much more easily accomplished if the company has to preserve only the final charts with the "right" indications, while the raw data, from which they were supposedly prepared, can be conveniently destroyed. There are at least two reasons for this. While an experiment is in progress, it is often difficult to anticipate precisely what significance some of the raw data will have when they are all put together. In addition, those who are recording the raw data are that much closer to the scientific end of the organization than the marketing end. For both of these reasons, the raw data are apt to be more "honest" than the second-level abstractions.

Second, in many areas all raw data, and even first-level abstractions, ought to have to be signed by the person responsible for preparing them. Key actors in both the MER/29 and B. F. Goodrich cases were willing to *prepare* distortive documents; but they drew the line at putting their names on them. There are obvious reasons for this balking. The signature can be used to pierce through corporate anonymity to locate some accountable flesh. This will be especially sobering to the signator if the information is required by federal law, with some possibility of perjury attaching. What is more, people feel a strong psychological connection between their actions and their names; signing is a symbolic gesture that itself lends pause to the would-be prefabricator.

The final major feature of storage-and-recall constraints that ought to be mentioned has to do not with the substance of what is to be retained, but with the form of retention. One of the many suggestions that comes out of the Equity Funding scandal is that all companies in an industry might be required to develop a uniform system of computer-use procedures. At present, only those people who deal directly with the computer can understand what truths it may be concealing. Most inspectors have had little experience in dealing with computer records to start with, and while this is a situation that will probably improve over time, the task of monitoring financial data—which Equity Funding demonstrates is becoming more and more vital—will require common bases of computer operation so that the various inspectors (inside and out) can find out what is truly going on.

(The same should be true with respect to indexing systems for files of basic material that companies keep outside their computer.) One ex-consultant for Equity Funding states that he had designed ways to better handle Equity's reinsurance programs on the computer. But he claims his systems were repeatedly rejected by management because they were too informative and revealing.[13]

## Public-Private Interfaces

Let me turn now from the flow of information within the corporation to the flow of information across the boundary between the corporation and its environment. Here there are three areas of interest: (1) regularized disclosure, (2) government inspection, and (3) the protection of the whistle blower.

There already exist scattered requirements that corporations remit to the outside world data bearing upon certain of their internal affairs. Most corporations are subject, for example, to laws that they be periodically audited, and that the required audit information be passed on to the shareholders, the SEC, and perhaps (depending on the corporation's business) certain other regulatory agencies. But it is interesting to observe that these, the precedents that most readily come to mind, involve once more *the investors* who are being safeguarded. Only rarely does the law demand that the companies gather and disseminate information in the interest of, say, consumers or neighbors and workers. The new Food and Drug Act amendments contain promising exceptions, such as that adverse findings be passed on to the FDA.[14] But such measures are few and far between.

The corporations are a prime—perhaps *the* prime—receptors of information about the adverse effects they may be having. It is to them that the first reports of dangerous chemical reactions are likely to come. It is in their worker absentee records that lie the clues to employment-related health hazards. Should these data, once collected and collated by the corporations along the lines discussed above, be a matter for their private use only?

The answer is certainly not; and increasingly we shall have to connect the corporations' improved internal information nets with centralized analytical facilities operating under the various federal and state agencies.*

The most direct route lies in bringing the government right *into* the corporation's information net. Consider building inspection. We don't say the contractor has a "right" to put up a building in secrecy on the grounds that his reputation and concern for liability are adequate guarantees that he will do the job safely. We put government inspectors right on the site to assure that he is in conformity with the applicable codes. Why are not such approaches extended to other areas? Instead of waiting for an auto company to produce a defective car, then to invoke sanctions after the harm has been done, we could put a government inspector in a position of discovering where weaknesses may lie, and thus, hopefully, to precipitate the necessary remedies in advance. Such an approach is especially appealing when we compare it with the alternative, after-the-fact solutions the law traditionally relies on. Its advantages include:

- the government inspector's primary responsibilities are to an outside agency, not to the company being inspected;
- the law's "after-the-fact" remedies do not really, as the law is fond of saying, make the injured plaintiff "whole"; what is more, they put on an injured party a burden of proof that becomes increasingly onerous as time passes and evidence fades—the freshest evidence and the best evidence is right in the plant at the time of design and production;
- the inspector, by his questioning, can institute reconsideration where it will do the most good—not in a court, after someone has been injured, but in the plant itself;
- the increasing time lag between planning and production, and the

* The new Occupational Safety and Health Act, I am glad to say, appears to be a long step in this direction. 29 U.S.C. §657(c)(2) provides:

The Secretary [of Labor], in cooperation with the Secretary of Health, Education and Welfare, shall prescribe regulations requiring employers to maintain accurate records of, and to make periodic reports on, work-related deaths, injuries and illnesses other than minor injuries requiring only first aid treatment, and which did not involve medical treatment, loss of consciousness, rstriction of work or motion, or transfer to another job.

enormous scale of investment, make it increasingly unlikely that defects will be discovered by the company itself, or, if discovered, set right.

It is true that these virtues of on-site inspection sound better in theory than they work out in practice. It is not always easy to agree what to inspect for,* and how to test it.† There is a general feeling that in almost all areas in which inspection exists today the government inspectors are "outmanned"—in terms of both numbers and professional expertise; and there is almost inevitably some degree of co-option, which comes down to out-and-out bribery in some cases.[15] Further, the more intensive the system, the more it costs, And, finally, when all the efforts are done, the procedures are hardly foolproof. A New York man died of botulism in 1971 after he ate some Bon Vivant soup. Afterward it developed that the United States Department of Agriculture had had two inspectors assigned full-time to the plant that produced the cans, and one of them, according to the *Los Angeles Times*, had monitored the plant's production line the day before it was packed.[16]

These criticisms most certainly show that on-site inspection is no panacea; but they are hardly proof positive against the system. If it were a fatal objection to government inspection that the inspectors have been known to receive bribes, we would on those grounds have to eliminate all policing activities—and is it

---

* The complexity of the task may generate more bureaucratic problems than it is ultimately worth. The deeper one looks into any problem, the more one finds an enormously complex set of variables that the society *might* be interested in, many of which point the inspector in inconsistent directions. For example, in inspecting food, one set of possible desiderata will involve nutritional standards, while another will involve culturally and aesthetically determined standards (color, taste, texture). In the tire industry, the tire that wears the longest or rides the smoothest may not be the one that brakes the best or corners the best.

† For example, one can take some substances that a producer is using in his goods, give it to mice, and see that it causes some disease; but we cannot be certain thereby that it would cause disease in humans. Or, again, there are expensive, highly complex machines available for testing tires by simulating road conditions. But there seems to be a view that all they really test is the ability of the tire to withstand the rigors of the machine; no one is certain as to how good an indication the machine is of actual highway performance.

not better to have a system where those we look to for protection are in the pay of the inspected occasionally, rather than (as with the company's own staff) in the pay of the company as routine?

Thus, notwithstanding all the drawbacks of an inspection system, the defects in alternate mechanisms should make us give serious thought to extending the areas in which government inspection is used, and to improving our present inspection procedures. Indeed, having an inspector present is a good idea if only to give some additional "justification" to employees within a company who are themselves against turning out shoddy products but are unable, on their own, to "buck" company pressures.

There are some steps that could be taken to improve our inspection system. First, and most obviously, certain changes in staffing should be considered, including an upgrading of the inspectors' status through pay hikes and otherwise; further, a system of inspector rotation, while involving some sacrifice in expertise, would help ameliorate the bribery problems.

But even more important, we have to take account of the fact that a basic problem many inspection systems face is that too often where inspection has been instituted, the inspectors are involved only at the end of the production process, to check over the final product. In highly technical areas, this is unwise. The further along a product is, the more "investment" (both financial and psychological) the company has in it, and thus the more resistance the inspector is liable to meet, by way of concealment or otherwise. Where appropriate, we should be prepared to "intrude" inspectors into the production process as early as the design stage, when resistance to making alterations will be lower, and where there will likely be indications of what "soft spots" will have to be carefully watched over during the balance of the production.

The second major step that should be taken to beef up government inspection systems is to have the inspecting agency monitor and tap directly into the corporation's own information system. Such a setup would involve several steps. First, the inspecting agency would have to approve the corporation's own information procedures. This is exactly what government military specifications now require for government contractors:

The Contractor shall perform or have performed the inspections and tests required to substantiate product conformance to drawings, specifications and contract requirements and shall also perform or have performed all inspections and tests otherwise required by the contract. The Contractor's inspection system shall be documented and shall be available for review by the Government Representative prior to the initiation of production and throughout the life of the contract. The government at its option may furnish written notice of the acceptability or non-acceptability of the inspection system.[17]

Then, instead of trying to have an army of government inspectors at every point in the plant, a smaller number of inspectors would monitor the inspection system (checking, for example, on test instrument calibration, and seeing that the company was gathering the relevant data). Periodic substantive checks would be reserved for the most vulnerable points in the process.

Consider those private companies now manufacturing nuclear generators for utility companies: Should we demand anything less than this?

Finally, anyone concerned with improving the exchange of information between the corporation and the outside world must pay serious regard to the so-called whistle blower. The corporate work force in America, in the aggregate, will always know more than the best-planned government inspection system that we are likely to finance. Traditionally, workers have kept their mouths shut about "sensitive" matters that come to their attention. There are any number of reasons for this, ranging from the intangible forces of corporate loyalty and peer-group expectations, to the employee's more solid fears of being fired or getting his source of income shut down for noncompliance with some law. And there is also at work, of course, the sheer indifference that workers may feel in a huge network of diffused responsibility.

Yet, despite all the various forces that operate against whistle blowing, there appears to be increasing evidence of workers placing their loyalty to the society above that of their companies.

The B. F. Goodrich brake case was broken when one of the company's data analysts went to the FBI. Much of what we know about the shady side of ITT owes to whoever is slipping Jack Anderson internal memos. Robert Rowen, a (former) technician at Pacific Gas and Electric, filed forty-nine charges with the Atomic Energy Commission alleging deliberate violation by the company of government safety regulations regarding the handling of radioactive waste.[18] Some years ago, when the California Public Utilities Commission was staging its usually uneventful hearings on a rate increase for General Telephone of California, one of the company's young employees, Jerry Finefrock, requested time to testify as a member of the public, and proceeded to tell what he knew. The company acknowledged Finefrock's right to testify (there is the annoying thing about the First Amendment), then fired him.[19]

These occasions would seem to an outside viewer few and far between; but they have sent enough shock waves through the corporate sector to bring forth from James M. Roche, former General Motors chairman, a sound damnation:

Some of the enemies of business now encourage an employee to be disloyal to the enterprise. . . . However this is labeled—industrial espionage, whistle-blowing or professional responsibility—it is another tactic for spreading disunity and creating conflict.[20]

People who feel *that* threatened by whistle blowing will inevitably seek to "make an example" of the whistle blower: by firing, demotion, or harassment. This is so even if the information that is divulged ultimately rebounds to save the company itself from huge losses.* For it is not so much *profits* that whistle blow-

---

* *Time* points out that had someone involved in the Corvair production made public noise about the adverse test results, GM would have saved itself millions of dollars ("The Whistle Blowers," April 17, 1972, p. 85). The same story reports that a few years ago a U.S. Steel marketing executive in Houston became concerned over possible safety failures in some new U.S. Steel pipe he was being asked to market; he wanted the company to hold off sales efforts until some further tests could be performed. His immediate superiors refused. He "rocked the boat" by going over their heads to the company's main offices, where tests were ordered performed. The product was withdrawn from sale, but he was fired for "insubordination."

ing subverts, but something more basic still: the hierarchical principles and role-playing niceties upon which all organizations are built.

This means that if ethical whistle blowing is to be encouraged, some special protections and perhaps even incentives will have to be afforded the whistle blower. At present there are almost none. Even those union contracts that contain a clause prohibiting firing "without just cause" are not likely to win an interpretation that helps a whistle blower.[21] And, of course, the bulk of white-collar professional employees have no union grievance machinery to start with.

Ralph Nader, Peter Petkas, and Kate Blackwell, in their book *Whistle Blowing*, survey a number of possible routes to develop orderly and sensible protections for the whistle blower. What emerges, most broadly, are two sorts of remedies.

The first would aim at protecting the whistle blower from losing his job. Various labor legislation, for example, prevents employees from being discharged for their union organization activity, or for complaining about violations of federal wage and hour laws. Although these laws do not in present form extend to cover the whistle blower, amendments in this direction could be easily drafted. The drawback, however, is that while the law can save the employee from being fired, it is a much harder matter to prevent the employer from making his life uncomfortable. In the traditional situation of the company's harassing a union organizer, the workers—and an organized team of labor lawyers— are on hand and inclined to stand behind their co-worker. In many whistle-blowing situations, this is not the case.

Thus, there is a lot to be said for the second approach: the development of a cause of action for "malicious discharge." Under this notion the employer would be allowed to fire an employee. But if the employee could then show that the discharge was for refusing to compromise professional ethics or to participate in immoral or unlawful activity, the worker would have a suit for damages—perhaps even punitive damages. Arthur S. Miller points out that rulings of this sort need not unduly hamper the employer, if only those actions considered "reasonable"—not motivated by malice or ill will or based on false information—give the discharged employee a cause of action.[22]

Surely these changes in the law will not bring forth from the corporations all the wrongdoings and jeopardies that its employees know about. No one wants to stick his neck out; and lawsuits are not certain, cheap, or fun. But as there spreads through the society an increasing consciousness about the environment, consumerism, and related matters, more and more troubled workers will be moved to the verge of speaking out. Some legal protections will give a few of them the courage to take the final, extra step.

# 19. Redesigning the Decision Process

For the reasons I explained in Part III, the proponents of corporate responsibility do wrong to put so much emphasis on *what* corporations are deciding rather than on *how* they are deciding—the corporate decision process itself. The sort of "responsibility" we ought to be developing in our corporations is not exclusively responsibility in the rule-following sense, but also responsibility in its cognitive aspects—the sense in which a person who is "responsible" does not immediately put his first impulses into action; surveys his environment to take stock of the consequences his decision will have on others; measures and weighs alternatives; is prepared to give justification for his actions.

Can we bring about changes in the corporate decision process so that the way corporations "think" conforms more nearly to the decision process of the responsible human being? The measures I have outlined to improve the corporation's information gathering are a step in this direction at the "lowest" cognitive level—that is, perception. What now about extending the idea to the corporate analogues of "higher"-level cognitive functions?

## The Level at Which a Decision Must Be Made

One of the most effective ways to make a corporation more responsible (in this sense of being more deliberative and reflective) is to take decisions of large social concern out of the hands of lower-level functionaries and insist they be put in the hands of others higher in the organization. Some precedent for this already exists in the corporate law area: Under most state statutes the decision to declare dividends must be vested in the board of directors, not in those at some lower level. Would it not be possible to adapt such a technique to problems in which the broader community is involved, and not just the shareholders?

There is a thought-provoking gesture in this direction in a recent ruling of the Federal Communications Commission. The commission had been receiving complaints about disc jockeys playing popular songs whose lyrics referred, usually by innuendo, to the pleasures of drug use. This is a particularly hard problem to deal with. The commission has no jurisdiction to intervene and stop a radio station from playing a particular record; indeed, such action could well raise First Amendment objections. And even the constitutional objections aside, how would you formulate a definitive and workable standard as to which records were play- able and which not, especially in the light of the nuances that the lyrics present? How—and at what costs—do you police such regulations? The area is one, in other words, in which "cor- porate responsibility" as I have used the term, seems the only solution—that is, the "costs" of trying to control the problem by traditional sanctions were quite likely not worth the benefits.

In the circumstances, what the FCC decided to do seems, if novel, quite appropriate. It simply brought the problem out into the open, and then proceeded to turn responsibility for handling it back onto the broadcasting companies. Whether a particular record promoted illegal drug usage, it said, "is a question for the judgment of the licensee. The thrust of this Notice is simply that the licensee must make that judgment and cannot properly follow a policy of playing such records without someone in a responsible position (i.e., a management level executive at the station) knowing the content of the lyrics."[1]

The decision caused a minor uproar in the industry. The law is supposed to spell it all out—what is legal and illegal, what one can and cannot do. The commission seemed to be speaking only of vague "responsibilities." The companies, it seems, wanted firm rules.[2]

Reacting to the criticism, the FCC issued a second opinion within a few weeks, this time elaborating on what the corpora- tions' responsibility might include:

As to the mechanics of licensee responsibility . . . disc jockeys could be instructed that where there is a question as to whether a record pro- motes illegal drug usage, a responsible management official should be notified so that he can exercise his judgment. It may be that a record which raises an issue in this respect is played once, but then the station personnel who have heard it, will be in a position to bring it to the attention of the appropriate management official for his judgment. The Commission is not calling for an extensive investigation of each such record. What is required is simply reasonable and good faith attention to the problem.[3]

How well this has worked exactly, no one can measure. My own survey of "rock music" stations in the Los Angeles area suggests a thoroughgoing, and not at all fractious, compliance. I was informed by one network affiliate that, while it had theretofore established a higher-level review for obscenities, it had never really given much thought to channeling the "drug lyrics" problem to managerial level; but that it had since established (as had all the stations I spoke with) regular procedures to do so. The problem, in other words, seems to be being adjusted to everyone's satisfaction—without the costs and confrontations of illusorily "firmer" measures.

A related approach is to require that certain actions cannot be approved except by a fixed, greater-than-majority percentage of votes. The law often influences corporate decisions this way, requiring, for example, that any major organic change such as a merger or consolidation must be approved by two thirds of the shareholders. But this sort of requirement has not been carried over into decisions on matters where the interests directly involved are other than those of shareholder and investor. Conceivably the law could demand that, in areas in which corporate decisions were likely to have a critical social impact, not only would the directors have to decide, but the decision would have to be by two-thirds vote; and perhaps if such a high degree of consensus could not be reached, the matter would automatically be referred for consultation with an outside agency for recommendations—for example the Environmental Protection Agency, the State Department, the new Consumer Protection Agency.

## Those Who Must Be Assimilated into the Decision Process

A second way in which decision-strategy variables could be used to make corporations more sensitive to particular features of their environment is exemplified in the federal labor laws. In requiring that labor and management have to sit down and "bargain in good faith," the law is not telling the corporation what wages it must pay, or what conditions of work it must establish. What we have done is incorporate the workers into the organization's decision process in those areas in which they are most acutely affected. This forced inclusion of workers has long been accepted. Yet there remain any number of other groups strongly affected by corporate actions who might with legitimacy be brought into the process as well.

There is, for example, the recurring problem of companies "picking up stakes" and moving out of some dependent community. I do not think companies should be absolutely prohibited from doing so; if the company cannot make a go of it in one place, and can in another, it is surely better for the whole society that it move. On the other hand, the company (meaning usually the top officers in some distant headquarters) may not have at their disposal all the information they ought to have, if they are to make a fully informed choice. And ending the relationship through the traditional notice of a corporate fait accompli stuffed in everyone's pay envelope is no good way of finding out whether some mutually satisfactory adjustment might not have been made. When the impact on some community of pulling up stakes is going to be significant, the law might well force high company officials to confront and negotiate "in good faith" with community leaders. In this way both sides may find themselves able to work out a give-and-take that the embarrassed, unannounced pullout renders impossible.*

That the law might impose such a procedure is in no wise far-fetched. There is a growing body of case law in which the courts are demanding that federal agencies take into account the groups they are affecting in just this very way. *Powelton Civic Home-owners Association* v. *HUD*⁴ was a suit brought a few years ago

---

* Another example: There can be no doubt that a decision made in Detroit as to auto emission devices has a profound impact on the Los Angeles County basin. Ought it not be possible that the companies at least have before them the "briefs" of, or even directly confront and "in good faith" deal with, representatives of Los Angeles?

by homeowners scheduled to be relocated by a housing project. The homeowners argued that in approving the project, HUD had failed to give them an adequate opportunity to demonstrate why the project did not meet the requirements of the law. The court, while holding that they were not entitled to a full-dress adversary hearing, nonetheless insisted that they had to be given some opportunity to present their claims to the agency—for example, the right to submit written and documentary evidence. A similar sort of ruling—again involving a federal agency—is to be found in *United Church of Christ* v. *FCC.*[5] There, an allegedly racist Mississippi radio station was applying for a renewal of its license before the Federal Communications Commission. The United Church of Christ (UCC) petitioned for a right to intervene to present evidence and arguments in opposition to the relicensing. The FCC refused to hear the UCC on the grounds that members of the listening public do not suffer any injury peculiar to them, and that to allow listeners "standing" would pose great administrative burdens. The court, however, agreed with the UCC, remanding the matter with instructions that the FCC provide for some "audience participation" in the proceedings. Broadcast licenses, it chided, are issued to serve the "public convenience and necessity." Unless the "consumers" could be heard, there might be no one to bring programming deficiencies or offensive commercializations to the attention of the commission in an effective manner.

Why not bring to bear on our corporations some of these new restraints we are—quite wisely—developing for federal agencies?

## Mandated Findings

One of the most significant ways in which we might influence the corporate decision process in the direction of greater responsibility is to require that before the corporation can act in designated areas, it has to make certain *findings.* Here, too, this is not the same as insisting that when all is said and done, the company must decide this way or that; it is just to say to the company that, prior to making "your" decision, you must make sure you have formulated and recorded preliminary judgments about certain specified matters.

There are already in the law scattered examples of this sort of control device. But most often they are brought to bear on public agencies without much thought that the same sort of regulatory measures could be brought to bear on corporations, our "private" governments. Most prominent is the requirement under the Environmental Protection Act that agencies prepare and deliver an environmental impact report whenever actions they contemplate (a new major housing development, a new coastal highway) are likely to have a "significant" impact on the environment. In 1971 the California Supreme Court, in the landmark Friends of Mammoth case demanded the same for agencies of the state: Before undertaking any project likely to have a "significant" impact on the environment, they must make a determination of what those impacts are likely to be.[6]

The exact nature of environmental-impact findings may vary with the circumstances. But in general, to have an adequate, acceptable statement, an agency must: (1) describe, and insofar as possible, quantify the goals to be achieved by the proposed action and the benefits that will be realized; (2) describe any feasible alternative means of achieving those goals (the so-called primary alternatives); (3) describe and weigh the environmental impacts and the irreversible commitments of resources that each alternative will cause; (4) set forth methods of mitigating the impacts of each of the primary alternatives (secondary alternatives) and designate for each primary alternative which impacts and commitments of resources cannot be avoided if that alternative is selected; (5) value the environmental factors in light of various sections of NEPA and describe how the values were derived; and (6) solicit consultation and comments on its draft impact statement from appropriate federal, state, and local agencies, as well as from the public, and then set out and respond to these comments in its final, revised impact statement.[7]

It is easy to say that when all the red tape and delay is done, the impact statement will have no real impact on its preparer— that it will amount to nothing more than a rationalized go-ahead for the original plan. But I don't think so. There are several points to keep in mind.

First, there is good reason to believe that putting a person in a position of having formally to justify his actions has a pronounced—and beneficial—influence on how he decides in the first place. This is one of the major reasons for having judges write and publish opinions. There is no reason why it should be otherwise with organizations. The task of preparing the statement makes the organization take into account, and even tell us how it weighed, certain factors it might otherwise not have thought of. What is more, it compels the reevaluation at the time when it can do the most good—when the costs of making changes in the plans are at their lowest.*

There are a host of other reasons why preparing an impact statement may lead to revisions in the company's thinking. Even if the statement indicates the company's actions will be within the law, the statement being a public record, it may give rise to more informal social pressures than the company is willing to buck. In addition, the impact approach may counteract the problem of organizational anonymity by pinning responsibility on the particular individual who assumes authority for preparing the report. That person knows he will become the focus of criticism if the impact turns out to be misleading.

Let me give an example of how these various considerations may combine, at their best. In early 1973, Orange County, New Jersey, was planning to build a new sewage treatment system. The *Wall Street Journal's* Jeffrey A. Perlman reported:

Questions were immediately raised. How would the new facility affect the aquatic life in the County's numerous lakes and streams? What would be the effect on vegetation that laces the County's miles of marshlands? What about animals? Houses? Local landmarks?[8]

He rightly noted that only a few years ago such questions would probably have received "cursory consideration and prompt

---

* It is important to remember that the issue the preparer of the impact statement faces is rarely of an either/or sort (i.e., either to build a dam or not) but more often one of how best to do the job, a broad range of values considered.

dismissal." But under the NEPA provisions it was necessary for the county to prepare and file an impact statement. The county officials, pursuant to the requirements, set the wheels in motion to do so. Soon a fisheries biologist, a terrestrial plant ecologist, and other scientists were examining the scene. The results, according to the *Journal*, included:

- certain of the County's marshes, discovered to be a major source for many fish species and much of the County's wildlife, were set aside as untouchable by the projects;
- siltation of an important lake was prevented;
- a 250 year-old house and a 150 year-old mulberry tree, both popular with local residents, were rescued from the bulldozer;
- the sewage authority, because of these and other changes recommended in the impact statement . . . found that its project would cost some $700,000 less than had been originally estimated.[9]

Not all impact preparers will, like Orange County, be induced to make alterations in their designs. But it is important to realize that the impact statement may be quite useful even in those cases where the company goes ahead exactly as it had originally planned. One reason is that the findings, circulated to various agencies in the society, can be used to prepare to meet some of the difficulties that the undertaking may cause. Consider, for example, the problem of detergents and their effects on natural waterways. Had the soap companies had to make impact findings, and had the findings given a clue of the difficulties that lay ahead, other agencies—for example, municipalities—would have had a "head start" in preparing antidetergent technology; legislatures, in preparing appropriate legislation; law-enforcement agencies, in knowing what to be on the lookout for. Consider, for a contemporary example, the forthcoming large-scale cracking of shale to produce oil. Does anyone really know what effects it will have not only on the environment, but on the whole of allied technologies? There are serious concerns that the shale wastes may even be carcinogenic. If we make the companies involved investigate these matters and publish their findings, we will be that much more ahead of the game in preparing to meet the crises that may be inevitable. No one supposes, of course, that their findings should be the last word; but it would not be a bad idea for their findings to be the first.

Concededly, environmental impact statements are too new a device for us to be certain how well they will work. But I suggest that as we evaluate their success, we do so with an eye toward extending *to corporations* such requirements—not only in the environmental area, but in other areas as well.

One prime area for consideration would be the newly developing field of technology assessment. Congress has recently established an Office of Technology Assessment[10] to (in the words of Sen. B. Everett Jordan) "provide an appraisal and 'early warning system' of the probable positive and negative impacts of the applications of technology, and to develop . . . analytical information which would assist the Congress in legislation."[11] In supporting the bill, Sen. Edward Kennedy gave the example of the tragic consequences of lead-based paint:

About 400,000 children suffer from lead poisoning and each year about 200 children die from it. Much of the problem comes from homes that were painted over 30 years ago with lead-based paints.

The Senate Subcommittee on Health will hold hearings on this topic. If Congress had had an Office of Technology Assessment 30 years ago, it is conceivable we could have anticipated this problem and enacted legislation which would have spared thousands of children from the grievous effects [of] this poison.[12]

Among other examples Senator Kennedy offered were evaluation of the atmosphere, economic, and health effects of the supersonic transport (SST), financial and regulatory issues relating to Civil Aviation Research and Development, deployment of antiballistic missile systems, and Congress's need for a "solid basis of facts" to deal with the erosion of U.S. technological competitiveness in world markets.

The act does not, in its present form, empower the Office of Technology Assessment to command "technology impact" statements, the way the Council of Environmental Quality can require environmental impact statements. It should, it seems to me, be given that power at least on an experimental basis.

As Senator Kennedy's lead-based paint example points up, many health problems traceable to corporate action can simply be regarded as problems of technology impact. Still, the health area is large enough, and closely enough identified with other, preexistent agencies (most obviously, HEW) that we might well want health impact statements to be handled as a separate procedure. Just consider this item: At a recent meeting of the American Society for Cancer Research, a group of scientists claimed that 80 percent of human cancers "may be derived, directly or indirectly, from chemicals in man's environment."[13]

The scientists said that the air we breath, the food we eat and the water we drink are increasingly being contaminated by cancer-inducing agents over which there is little federal regulation or control.[14]

One of the illustrations the scientists offered was the recently discovered fact—out of a B. F. Goodrich plant in Louisville—that a rare form of liver cancer is striking at workers who come in contact with vinyl chloride. If the companies engaged in the vinyl chloride productions had had to prepare impact statements, might the relationship not have surfaced earlier? There were early clues of the dangers all over the place.[15] It has more recently been suggested that the impact on the atmosphere of aerosol from spray cans (five million tons of it are up in the air right now) threatens to deplete the earth's protective ozone layer, with a concomittant increase in skin cancers.[16] Should not the spray can manufacturers (among others) be investigating this?

The possible uses of such impact statements are, it seems to me, legion. I will give one final example that brings out so clearly the close parallel between what we would call "responsible" behavior in a human being and the making of impact studies by a corporation. In 1973, news leaked out that there had been a failure of the core safety system in the nuclear reactor at Southern California Edison Co.'s San Onofre Nuclear Generating Station. In a story, "Atom Safety Study Left to Builders, Edison Says," the Los Angeles Times revealed that although Edison has its own nuclear engineers, they had made no attempt to verify the accuracy of the manufacturer's (Westinghouse) data.[17]

Under cross-examination, an Edison supervising engineer admitted that he had not even read "the relevant and controversial studies on emergency cooling himself." The story goes on to indicate that, according to Dr. Henry W. Kendall, a nuclear physicist with the Union of Concerned Scientists, utility companies generally have been purchasing nuclear power plants "in the face of a clear consensus among reactor safety experts that no one really knew the effectiveness of the planned safety features."

This is the very sort of behavior, in corporations, that we would condemn as "irresponsible" in an individual: a complete failure by the actor to recognize and assume accountability for the effects *his* actions may have on his environment. But it is not through vague and airy demands for "corporate responsibility," in the abstract, that we are going to reduce such behavior. We need to make a series of specific impositions on the corporation's inner, traditionally "private" processes.

# 20. The Culture of the Corporation

The various measures I have described would go a long way toward correcting some of the most serious limitations in our present system. But we have to remember that no laws, no matter how sophisticated in their design, can carry the burden of social control through their threats alone. To be really effective, the law has to be able to persuade, or at least make sense to, the community it is supposed to govern. And it must be kept in mind that the corporation (and the business world) is just that: a community. It has its own attitudes, norms, customs, habits, and mores. Even in enforcing present anticorporate measures, the law often runs into a widely held business view that the conduct it forbids is not morally reprehensible, "that it is the laws themselves that appear bad."[1] Indeed, it has been observed that

. . . typically the conduct prohibited by economic regulatory laws is not immediately distinguishable from modes of business behavior that are not only socially acceptable, but affirmatively desirable in the economy founded upon an ideology of free enterprise and the profit motive.[2]

The problem is a serious one, the more so for my proposals than for the measures in use today; for undeniably what I am recommending involves a more widespread invasion of corporate managerial autonomy than anything ever tried in this country. Then, too, I am proposing not merely that the corporation accept these intrusions; I am asking that it affirmatively cooperate—for example, to come forward and volunteer information that points up the need for tighter legislation—even if doing so involves a sacrifice of profits in some cases.

All this plunges us into the question, can we change those things that the corporation *cares about*? We can restructure the corporation's information processes so as to make it gather and channel vital data to those in a position to do something about it. But what is there to guarantee that the person in authority, supplied the information, will act upon it? What if he doesn't care that his company is running the risk of imposing long-range health hazards on the public? We can make companies install special officers in charge of particular problem areas. But what is there to guarantee that, the special executive having been instituted, the other officers will not undermine him in all the subtle ways available to them? We can provide arrangements to protect, and thus encourage, potential "whistle blowers" to come forward with information about the dangers and abuses that they see on their jobs. But what amount of protection will get the workers to come forward if they simply don't give a damn in the first place?

I do not want to leave the impression that the "internal reform" measures I have been proposing cannot be rested upon anything firmer than the corporation's good intentions. On the contrary, there are, as I have indicated, any number of ways to link legal penalties (and rewards) to bona fide compliance, both of the company and of key individuals. There is good reason to suppose, moreover, that the strategies I have been proposing can be more effectively policed and enforced than those the law has traditionally relied upon. For example, my recommendations, by zeroing in on and requiring specific tasks and procedures (rather than focusing on the final product) can much more effectively be used to locate and settle responsibility upon particular individuals. In addition, by impacting the organization as I have proposed, in advance, during its planning and production stages (rather than after the fact) we can be more optimistic about the company taking the requirements into account in its decisions.

But we have to recognize too that, in the last analysis, the most these measures can do is *reduce* the resistance of the pre-existent corporate cultures. So long as the underlying attitudes are left untouched, some measure of resistance—of circumvention, disregard, and foot dragging—is inevitable.

This leads me, then, to the final, most difficult and elusive problem of all: Should we hold out any hope of altering the very attitudes of corporate America? *Is there any chance at all?*

The answer, I am afraid, is that we are very limited in what we can do. It isn't just a matter of autonomy: No organization, of course, is going to hand control over gladly. There is, even beyond this, simply a limit to how many different, potentially competing aims and attitudes any institution can entertain. Universities aim to educate; armies, to fight; hospitals, to treat and cure. These shared, mutually understood goals provide a context against which commands are interpreted and actions synchronized. They provide a post against which the institution can measure its "success" and stabilize itself.

To be realistic, with the American business corporation the dominant orientation of the institution is going to remain toward profit, expansion, and prestige. Those who labor in it are going to remain concerned about providing for their wives and kids, about the approval of their peers, about "moving up" in the organization. What ideas can we gather up in our entire society that are powerful enough to set in competition with these, with "self-interest" as so many centuries of the culture have defined it?

To recognize these basic constraints is not to say we are powerless, however. We live with the fact that human beings are dominated by certain ego-centered goals/drives (sexual gratification, power, self-preservation). But through various acculturating mechanisms we have been able, not to do away with these forces, but at least to put constraints on them. On a parity of reasoning, even if we accept profit *orientation* as a basic and inalterable fact of American corporate life, we don't have to accept, or expect, sheer corporate hedonism. What I am asking of our chemical companies, for example, is not that they abandon profits. Producing fertilizers and chemicals that will get the world fed would be, and should be, a profitable activity. But what we want, too, is that the companies will manifest enough concern about the effects their products are having on the health of the field workers who use them, that they will accept the internal structures we deem appropriate; that in cooperation with the imposed systems they will perform some amount of follow-up; that, if suspicious circumstances are apparent, they will undertake appropriate studies and notify health authorities; that they will make data available to interested parties—rather than cover up the apparent risks and deny their very possibility.

We could, in fact, attempt a listing of various attitudes desirable in connection with each of the various social roles that the corporation plays.

### the corporation as citizen

- to be concerned with obeying the laws (even if it can get away with law breaking profitably)
- to aid in the making of laws, as by volunteering information within its control regarding additional measures that may need to be imposed on industry
- to heed the fundamental moral rules of the society
- not to engage in deception, corruption, and the like
- as a citizen abroad, to act decently to host country citizens, and not inimically to U.S. foreign policy

### the corporation as producer

- to aim for safe and reliable products at a fair price

### the corporation as employer

- to be concerned with the safety of the work environment
- to be concerned with the emotional well-being of its workers
- not to discriminate

### the corporation as resource manager

- not to contribute unduly to the depletion of resources
- to manifest some concern for the aesthetics of land management

### the corporation as an investment

- to safeguard the interests of investors
- to make full and fair disclosures of its economic condition

### the corporation as neighbor

- to be concerned with pollution
- to conduct safe and quiet operations

### the corporation as competitor

- not to engage in unfair competition, on the one hand, or cozy restrictions of competition, on the other

### the corporation as social designer

- to be innovative and responsive in the introduction of new products and methods
- not to close its eyes to the fact that the movies it turns out, the shows it produces, the styles it sets, have an impact on the quality of our lives, and to concern itself with that impact responsibly

Some will say it unlikely that corporations will ever do these sorts of things—that is, go much beyond whatever the law, and market competition, can absolutely force from them. How much do ordinary citizens meet some of these standards—report favorable errors on their tax returns, for example? Indeed, if Christianity "hasn't been tried yet" why should we suppose that it is corporations who are finally going to get it off the ground?

The possibility of something better is inherent, oddly enough, in the very development decried by Adolf Berle and Gardner Means in their famous *The Modern Corporation and Private Property* (1932). Berle and Means first called public attention to the fact that as the industrial sector was evolving from sole proprietorships to larger and larger corporations, the owners of the property in the traditional sense—the investors—were no longer the true managers of the companies. Formerly, the owner-investor had been his own manager, or had exercised tight control over the hired officers. But now the officers—the men who were calling the shots—were emerging with relative independence from the stockholders as the latter became increasingly passive and dispersed. The investors, moreover, were losing their link to the underlying corporate property; they sold their shares and bought stock in a new enterprise with perfect fluidity.

This situation, Berle and Means saw, contained the germs of a sort of "irresponsibility" that had not existed on such a scale before. But they were thinking of the relations between the managers and stockholders. This is the relationship that was of

paramount concern to those analyzing the "corporation problem" in the thirties, when widespread tragedy to investors was
very much a part of the intellectual and moral climate, rather
than "consumerism," "environmentalism," and the like. And
from this perspective, they were clearly right. But from the
other perspective—that of the management's relations to interests "outside" the corporation—the same historical development
provides at least a new wedge of hope for greater managerial
accountability. For when the interests of management and ownership are one (as, most purely, in the case of a sole proprietorship) all the compromises management makes with profits come
out of its own pockets. If the people who own the business decide to install an unrequired pollution filter, or establish day
care for mother-workers, or go out of their way to investigate
the health hazards of their products, *they* pay.* But it is not so
in the giant, broadly held companies. There, the "charitable"
gestures of management do not come out of their own pockets.†
Thus, in theory—and I think in practice as well—the giant,
broadly held company is more likely to be socially accountable,
and less likely to engage in sharp, irresponsible conduct, than
the small, closely held concern that served as Berle and Means's
historical model.

## Why Aren't Corporations More Moral?

"Well, then," someone may ask, "why isn't the corporation more
responsible than it is?" The answers are not all obvious; they
are, moreover, important because any program to change cor-

---

* Net of taxes; that is, the managers can in effect force the government to bear a share of their largesse because the corporation can deduct
the outlay on its tax return as a business expense.

† As I noted in Part III, this gives rise to concern—theoretically quite
legitimate—that over a long period of time, "policies of self-restraint [i.e.,
rather than legal-competitive restraints] may result in a serious distortion
in the pattern of resource use."[3] At present, I would say the benefits of
encouraging the limited nonprofitable activities I have advocated in this
book are well worth the theoretical possibility of long-run dislocations of
capital. As a practical matter, the risks of corporate "largesse" getting so
out of hand seem rather small.

porate attitudes has to begin by identifying the particular asocial attitudes that we are up against.

The first point to remember is that while the corporation is *potentially* immune from a single-minded profit orientation, in any particular company that potentiality is able to become reality only after some satisfactory level of profits has been achieved. A corporation that is operating "on the margin" is going to cut as many corners as it can get away with on worker safety, product quality, and everything else.

Then, too, it would be a mistake to believe that the desire to turn profits is the only attitude that causes us problems. We know, for example, that many companies—especially the major dominant companies—go through periods in which they are well enough off that they could put a little something extra into, say, environmental protection, and not have to face (what is a real rarity) a shareholder coup d'état. The true range of attitudes we have to confront is much deeper and more complex than "profits"—but not necessarily any the less intractable.

One range of attitudes we might call "profit-connected." Even when the company is achieving enough profits that the managers can protect their own tenure, they may continue to pursue much the same course of conduct, but now as a reflection of other motives. Prestige in the business world comes of being connected with a firm listed on the New York Stock Exchange, one whose sales are rising, or which appears in the *Fortune* 500. The problem here is a lack of most other measures of success, other guarantors of prestige, than those which can be read off the company's ledgers.

Some other of the attitudes we are up against are even further removed from profits. Consider corporate insensitivity to their workers. The received wisdom on "blue-collar blues" is a purely economic one: that the worker is crushed in the corporation's never-ending push for profits. In part, this is true. But any bureaucracy, and not only the modern corporation, evolves toward depersonalized relationships. Its very "success" depends upon the mobilization of personalities into roles—the better for the synchronization of behavior. Thus, if corporations appear insensitive (to the world as well as to their workers) they may be insensitive for many of the same reasons that many nonprofit bureaucracies are insensitive (a hospital is the first example that comes to my mind). I am not saying that we therefore give up on attempts to sensitize them. I am just suggesting that if we are going to confront such problems, we have to be prepared to deal with subtler and more pervasive features than "capitalist greed."

Or consider the lack of responsibility of assembly-line workers to dangerously ill-assembled units that move past them, or their even countenancing minor sabotage. This is ordinarily presented as a problem of worker "indifference" brought about by "boredom on the job." If so—to the extent it is mere boredom—some style of work motivation may be an appropriate remedy, or just a less demanding pace. But here, too, the real roots may lie somewhat deeper and harder to get at. Our project's psychoanalytic consultant, Dr. Joel Shor, suggests

It's not "just boredom," and it's not that the assembly-line workers "just aren't aware" that the faulty products they are producing will harm somebody. There has to be, among the workers, a level of downright hostility—not just to the employer, but to the entire society, which as they see it, has cast them in a role barely above, perhaps subordinate to machines. The whole milieu, in sum, is one antagonistic to any experiences of empathy.

In such actions as sabotage, we are involved, too, in very complex matters of group dynamics. In an institutional framework, men do things they ordinarily wouldn't. (The army is a dramatic example.) One reason for this is that the usual restraints on antisocial behavior operate through a self-image: "I can't see myself doing *that*." In an institutional setting, however, *that* isn't being done *by me*, but *through me* as an actor, a role player in an unreal "game" that everyone is "playing." The evidence in the electrical equipment industry's price-fixing case is shot through with this flavor of a huge game. So, too, is the entire Watergate affair. The Equity Funding scandal went so far as to involve role playing in the most literal sense—"forgery parties" at which people played the roles necessary to fake dossiers.

What I am getting at is that behavior that may seem on the

surface to spring from profits or even venality may actually involve, and have to be dealt with as, something as far removed from venality as play. An ideal examination of "the culture of the corporation" (which I can present here only in outline) would try to identify a whole range of underlying institutional attitudes and forces, and proceed to identify the particular sorts of undesired corporate behavior that constitute their symptoms. These attitudes would include, for example: a desire for profits, expansion, power; desire for security (at corporate as well as individual levels); the fear of failure (particularly in connection with shortcomings in corporate innovativeness); group loyalty identification (particularly in connection with citizenship violations and the various failures to "come forward" with internal information); feelings of omniscience (in connection with inadequate testing); organizational diffusion of responsibility (in connection with the buffering of public criticism); corporate ethnocentrism (in connection with limits in concern for the public's wants and desires).

## What Can Be Done?

This definition of the corporate culture is barely even a first step. And we have to face the fact that we really know very little about how to change it. There are, it is true, plenty of people (industrial and management psychologists, for example) who study and attempt to alter attitudes within this matrix. Much thought has gone into motivating workers toward increased productivity. Sensitivity training has been invoked with executives to eliminate "interpersonal frictions" that threaten the corporation's "solidarity."

But how about calling to question the organization's own values? How about motivating workers to recognize and report clues that a substance they are working with may kill fish, or farm workers? Or to adopt a more positive attitude toward the law—even when the chances of the company's getting caught are slim? What I have discovered is that there is almost no literature available on these matters; when industrial psychologists have been called into a company, it is always by management with an eye toward getting some group to perform more "effectively" from the point of management's preestablished aims —not to challenge those aims, or to try to work into the organization "extraneous" values favored by the society at large.

Nor are most matters of our concern amenable to established practices like sensitivity training, whose

target is essentially the individual and not the organization. When the individuals return to their old structures, they step back into the same definitions of their roles. What is more basic, these roles are intimately related with other organizational roles, . . . the expectations of superiors, subordinates, and colleagues have not changed, nor has there been a change in organizational sanctions and rewards.[4]

Thus, to a large extent, the territory we are striking out into is unmarked. To map our way, we ought to begin by learning more about why different corporations—like different political administrations—seem to permeate themselves with their own characteristic attitudes toward law abidance and "good citizenship" generally. "Lawbreaking," some sociologists have observed, "can become a normative pattern within certain corporations, and violation norms may be shared between corporations and their executives." The atmosphere becomes one in which the participants (as at Equity Funding) "learn the necessary values, motives, rationalizations and techniques favorable to particular kinds of crime."[*]

[*] Marshall B. Clinard and Richard Quinney, *Criminal Behavior Systems* (New York: Holt, Rinehart and Winston, 1973), p. 213. It is not only the institution's citizenship attitudes that are of concern. Companies that are not sufficiently curious and innovative in meeting real social demands are equally a problem, especially if they are tying up large social resources. There is a delightful write-up in the *Wall Street Journal* of such a problem on a small scale: a 119-year-old manufacturer of stiff paper collars for men's shirts. "The company's collars went out of style about 50 years ago," but "the company seemingly never got word and apparently alone in the country mass produces them." The company had, the *Journal* reports, a "very good year in 1913 but rarely since then." *Wall Street Journal*, March 5, 1973, p. 1 col. 4. On this scale, the problem is amusing. But when our auto industry continues to be tooled, psychically and physically, for enormous gas-consuming monstrosities in the face of energy shortages, it becomes a more serious domestic problem.

One would want to know, too, why different industries manage to evolve their own customs, habits, and attitudes. For example, the most recent and provocative survey I have seen involves a comparison of worker safety records in coal mines owned and operated by traditional coal mining companies with those owned and operated by steel firms.[5] The differences are striking. The ten major mining concerns experienced an average 0.78 deaths per million man-hours worked; but in the mines operated by the steel companies, there were on average only 0.36 fatalities per million man-hours. The injury statistics were more discrepant still. The ten major mining companies experienced, on average, 40.61 injuries per million man-hours; the steel-company-operated coal mines averaged 7.50. There are several possible explanations for these striking discrepancies. But one of the most common factors cited was simply an attitudinal one—that the steel companies have just not evolved what was called "a 'coal mentality' " that accepts a great loss of life and limb as the price of digging coal."

. . . Traditionally the steel companies' top corporate executives, being used to a relatively good safety record in their steel mills, have never been willing to tolerate poor safety performance in their mines. . . . "There's a paternalistic attitude [in the steel companies] that you don't find prevalent in [coal,]" admits the head of one large commercial coal operation.[6]

Why is it that different corporations, and different industries, exhibit these differences in attitude? Can we identify the variables that make some more responsible than others, and put this knowledge to work by directly manipulating those variables? We simply do not know the answer to these and many similar questions. But even in the absence of this knowledge we do have some good clues as to how attitudinal changes can be brought about—clues that suggest two broad approaches suited to two distinguishable situations.

The key characteristic of the first situation is that the attitudes we want to inculcate can be connected with, and find support in, norms and/or subgroups that preexist in the organization.

An example of this is provided in the aftermath of the electrical equipment conspiracy cases referred to earlier.

Price-fixing in the industry—certainly in the heavy-equipment section of the industry—had become so widespread as to constitute something of a behavioral norm. To change this corporate culture that had grown up within it, Westinghouse appointed an outside advisory panel.

The advisory panel insisted not merely on the company instructing its employees that price-fixing was illegal. Despite all the industry protests about the "vagueness" of the antitrust laws, none of those involved in the secret meetings had any doubts about the illegality of price-fixing. And that knowledge, of itself, obviously had not pulled enough freight. Instead, the panel decided to aim for an affirmative demonstration "that competition, properly pursued, can produce far more consistent profits than . . . conspiracy."[7]

In-house programs were established—management courses, workshops, conferences—all adopting the positive approach that the company's business success in the future, over the long haul, depended "to a considerable degree on the adoption . . . of policies of vigorous (and even aggressive) flexible, competitive initiative."[8]

The presentation, in other words, was not that the company had to "submit" to a stronger, outside force—that is, the government. Rather, the price-fixing was depicted as itself a foreign element, inimical to the more fundamental corporate ideal of increasing one's share of the market through better salesmanship, superior design, and the like—the norm of competition. In fact, I am authoritatively informed that at discussions among employees, a sentiment emerged that the price-fixing had been "the sales force's thing: a way to avoid the hard work of really going after sales." The same source reports that the design engineers actually resented what had been going on. Their self-esteem had been based on their ability to build better mousetraps; suddenly they discovered that their share of the market for heavy equipment had been fixed at a ratio that had no real bearing on their own contribution.

This brings me to the second point. Securing conformity to the compliance norm was not based solely on demonstrating its link to a preexistent, supposedly dominant, corporate *ideal*. In addition, there already existed within the organization certain *groups* potentially more supportive of the desired attitude than the corporation as a whole. Part of the trick of changing the attitude manifested by the corporation as a whole is to locate the critical support group and strengthen its hand. (The engineers have already been mentioned.) In the example at hand, lawyers were particularly crucial. Company lawyers "look bad," both among their peers and their co-workers, when something like widespread price-fixing is revealed to have been going on under their noses. What is more, along with their other functions, they, in particular, symbolize law abidance within the organization. In such a context, making the desired attitude more acceptable involves placing the symbolic custodian of the attitude more prominently in the corporate hierarchy. This was accomplished in the Westinghouse situation by requiring other employees to, for example, file reports with the lawyers whenever certain questionable activity was undertaken. The practical virtues of this procedure have already been mentioned; what I am emphasizing here, though, is that in addition to its practical aspects, the underscoring of the lawyers' role had a significant symbolic component that may prove equally important.

True, the Westinghouse situation is a special case in that no one there doubted that unless certain attitudes were changed the money damages to the corporation could be enormous. The directors, too, although saved from liability this time on the theory that they had "no reason to suspect" the wrongdoing, had now become an additional support group. They simply had to make some gesture of concern to "cover" themselves in case of a repeat performance.

Still, there are any number of roughly comparable situations where the same sort of approach should and could be invoked to alter unwanted attitudes. Insurance industry executives insist that a high percentage of worker injuries (and possibly product defects as well) are directly traceable to heavy drinking, and, increasingly, to drugs. The insurance industry wants, and management should want, to confront this problem and stamp it out. But the insurers have an almost impossible time getting the employer to discuss the problem. One in-house memo of an insurance company that I have seen, reporting on its alcohol program visits to companies with "drinking problems," states that in forty-eight of sixty-one companies visited "the material was received with indifference, and the following statement either made or implied: 'we do not have this problem in our staff.'" "They [management] regard the worker's drinking problem as part of his private life," an insurance executive informed me, "and it is none of their business; none, that is, until the worker stumbles into a press and loses his arm."

In a situation such as this, there is reason to hope for improving attitudes; the task is more one of changing perceptions and getting the problem into the open, rather than tampering with an underlying corporate goal (profits, prestige, expansion). And here, too, there are ready-made groups with which an alliance can be forged: the unions and insurance companies, especially. This does not mean that the task is easy. (If it were easy it would probably have been done.) But with some government encouragement, company bulletin boards could advertise and clarify the dangers, union executives could be called to Washington to discuss "their" interest in an airing of the drinking situation, in-plant worker meetings could be held (discussions among peer groups seem far more effective than hierarchical, "handed down" orders), and companies might set up alcoholic treatment programs (as some companies have done, but usually, to my understanding, solely for the executives).

In a second class of situation, however, the problem of dealing with the corporate culture is stickier. I am thinking now of the cases where the attitudes the society wants to inculcate are at odds with all the dominant norms of the corporation and can find no alliance with any of the attitudinal groups I mentioned (the work group, industry, business community).

For example, where worker-safety problems are concerned, we can at least consider mobilizing some internal alliance with the unions; for product quality and safety, with the engineers; for resource conservation (as through recycling energy), with the investors. But consider, by contrast, the problem of getting "insiders" to give notice of the company's pollution; to halt industrial espionage and campaign law violations; to keep clear of political adventures in foreign countries; to exercise concern for land use aesthetics. In these cases, the attitudes desired by the "outside" world have barely a toehold on the "inside."°

When we move into this area what we are faced with is nothing less than providing the organization with a new *internal rhetoric*—the special "vocabulary of motives" that every culture, and every cultural subgroup, provides its members with as its own "legitimate" reasons for doing things. These varying vocabularies involve more than just different ways of interpreting and explaining an act already completed. The range of available motives imposes boundaries on the alternatives a member of the group is prepared to consider. Today, a lower-level executive who recommended against a program on the grounds that "it will cause a lot of noise in the neighborhood" would be rather unlikely to get his recommendation advanced very far up the corporate hierarchy—unless he could convincingly append something about "we are likely to get fined (or zoned out)."

That is why any program to shift basic corporate attitudes has to involve, not replacing the profit motive ("will it sell?"), but at least providing respectable alternate vocabularies that can effectively be invoked, within some range of profit constraint, in special circumstances.

How can such a change be brought about?

A good deal depends upon the sort of gradual social evolution that is out of the control of any of us. As the general public becomes more and more informed and concerned about the

---

° Our problem in this area is analogous to getting the police to abide by "pro-suspect" rulings of the United States Supreme Court. The police are organized around a dominant organizational goal of apprehending wrongdoers and stopping crime. The court, in handing down such rulings as *Miranda* (police must inform interrogees of their legal rights) represents an attempt by an outside agency to intrude a value—fair play to the "criminal"—that is almost impossible to reconcile with the organization's dominant goal: "collaring" wrongdoers.

environment, for example, some of that concern will gradually work its way through the corporation's walls, with the result that explanations today unacceptable—"out of place"—will become persuasive in time.

On the other hand, while much is in the hands of this sort of evolution, there are some deliberate measures that we can take. These possibilities include the following.

### Rewards for Excellence

At present, just about the only positive reward corporations achieve is in the form of profits (or sales, or other measures of financial growth). Essentially, all other social feedback is negative—public criticisms or legal punishments for doing things badly. This need not be the case. During World War II, for example, "E" awards were bestowed on defense companies that had exceeded their allotted production. The presentation of the "E" to a qualifying corporation was the occasion of a high ceremony, at which government representatives, executives, and workers joined. The company would get a flag, and each of the workers an "E" pin. Why should not the Environmental Protection Agency, for example, be authorized to give out its own Environmental Protection "E"s to companies that accelerate beyond their "cleanup" timetables, or come up with ingenious new environment-protecting methods?

### The Social Audit

A great deal has been written recently about devising a "social audit" for corporations to supplement their traditional financial audits. Their aim would be to represent on paper the total social costs and benefits of a corporation's activities, over and above those that are now reflected in its financial statements.

The problem with the traditional statements is that they developed to reflect the interests of the financial community. Investors—and potential investors—have no particular need for a breakdown of figures displaying, for example, how much the company has put into quality-control systems or how much it has done to increase minority worker mobility. A paper company's statement will reflect the cost of the lumber it consumes; but if it uses the local river as a sewer to carry away waste, and does not have to pay for the damages this causes downstream, those social costs will nowhere appear on the company's books. They don't affect earnings.

A reporting system that measured these hidden costs and benefits would be—if we had it—quite interesting. But at present, the details of how to implement it are wanting. Much of the value of a true audit, for example, is that it has a set, prescribed structure, designed to display the answers to a series of questions which are the same for all companies.[9] This the social auditors are nowhere near achieving. And it may well be beyond their grasp.

Part of the difficulty is that many of the features that they want to reflect are not quantifiable. Moreover, even if they could agree on what internal company data were required, it would be hard to pry loose in a full and honest form.* And as for the external data, the effects of any giant company's activities are almost so unimaginably complex and far-reaching that the thought of tracing out its "total social impact" seems absolutely boggling.

Against this background, I am inclined to agree with the suggestion of Bauer and Fenn that, at least while we are seeing what, if anything, corporate social audits may develop into, management ought to be encouraged to make them up for their own internal use only.[10] I myself have doubts as to how successfully and far the social audit can evolve even in such a private and nurtured atmosphere. But to my mind, the key point is that even if these experiments never do produce anything terribly useful informationally, along the lines of a true audit,

---

* "Even if the CEO [chief executive officer] wants a social audit, he is likely to encounter foot dragging, if not outright opposition, within his own family. In conglomerates in particular, division managers resent what they perceive as an intrusion into 'their' personal files." Raymond A. Bauer and Dan H. Fenn, "What *Is* a Corporate Social Audit?," *Harvard Business Review* 51 (January-February 1973): 42.

there is still a chance of success from our present viewpoint: from the point of developing a new internal vocabulary of motive that might compete with "profitability" and the profit constellation (sales, costs, etc.). What new constellations of motive would evolve, one cannot say. I would rather suspect that, in contrast with the true audit, different companies would design incommensurable categories and structures, each appropriate to its own fields of operation, capital intensivity, and so forth. Then these categories, in turn, could be worked into the internal evaluation process, so that those divisions and persons who performed in the appropriate way would stand a chance of reward.

### Interchanges

There is no more primitive way to alter intergroup attitudes (hopefully, for the better) than to bring the groups together. On an intracorporate scale, there have been a number of experiments in "sensitivity" confrontations among executives and, to a lesser extent I believe, among management and workers.

But insofar as the boundary between the corporation and the outside world is concerned, the exchanges could barely be worse. The government, for its part, relies largely on lawsuits and the threat of suits—certainly a less than ideal way to communicate values. The public at large—or, at least, the activist groups that purport to speak for it—maintain a shrill criticism that is just overstated enough that managers (even otherwise sympathetic managers) can find grounds to dismiss it in their own minds. The corporate response to the public is either a cynical PR bluff, or a defensiveness no less shrill and hysterical than the criticisms it receives. In a recent interview, Union Oil Company's president dismissed the environmental movement as "a question of people being irrational." Then, thinking a little further he added darkly, "It's more than that, actually. I don't know who's behind the Sierra Club, but it obviously isn't people of good will."[11] Consider, in the same context, the reaction to whistle blowers of former GM chairman, James M. Roche, quoted earlier.

What is called for, obviously, is some improved modes of

communication and understanding—in both directions. Public criticism of corporate behavior certainly should be maintained. But it should be informed enough, and even sympathetic enough, that it does not induce so extreme and inflexible a defensiveness.

One approach to a better understanding is simply to plead for it (which I hereby do). But, we should also try to set various stages for bringing the groups together. This has been done, in a limited way and after its own fashion, by the Executive Interchange Program.[12] The program, established by President Johnson, sends middle- to upper-level government employees for a brief swing in business posts, and brings private-sector managers to Washington. To judge from the brochures the Commission on Personnel Interchange puts out, a certain amount of the businessmen's time involves being photographed at the White House and (in an older one they sent me) listening to Herb Klein and John Ehrlichman.

What effect all this has it is hard to measure. But the evaluations of those who have participated in the program are quite favorable.

Important, to me, is the quite different attitude that I've developed towards Government. . . . More than once I've experienced their frustration. . . . My respect for these people has increased substantially.

I have found that it is perhaps a tougher job to run the Government than a business because there are far more dimensions involved. . . .

I was surprised at the many similarities in problems of managing . . . .

This experience . . . has sensitized me to the necessity for greater industry cooperation with regulatory agencies in providing information and maintaining a strong dialogue.[13]

Granted, a certain number of these comments reflect the skill of middle management to adopt the "line" appropriate to the environment in which they find themselves. Still, no one who has lunched with businessmen cannot but be a little impressed: Even getting them to mouth sentiments like these is no easy task. If they can bring even half of these feelings back with them when they return to industry, the program may be the germ of an idea worth expanding.

## Public Education

Part of the problem corporate reformers face in changing the corporate culture has been mentioned: that the shriller their criticisms, the more the corporate community inclines to discount them as "one-sided" and ill-informed. The reform movement has some particularly sensitive problems, too, in taking its case to the public. How the issues are handled is important, not only because of the obvious implications for garnering legislative support, but because the reactions of the outside world are themselves one of the more significant determinants of the corporation's internal culture. There is an interesting demonstration of this in a study of law violations among shoe manufacturers located in various New England communities. Though the companies studied were operating in the same industry, subject to the same laws, the variations in law obedience were dramatic. In Haverhill, Massachusetts, for example, 7 percent of the companies were law violaters, while in Auburn, Maine, 44 percent were. The author concluded that "one of the reasons is the difference in attitude toward the law, the government, and the morality of illegality" that prevailed in the companies' various home communities.[14]

The point is, altering corporate behavior may involve reexamining the views that prevail in the outside world. And in this regard, one has to be struck by the fact that while the public may be periodically exercised over corporations, corporate wrongdoing simply doesn't command the same dread and fascination as crimes committed by tangible human beings. To an extent, this difference in public reaction toward corporate as opposed to human wrongs probably owes to the different nature of the offenses that are typically involved, rather than to a difference in who the actor is. That is, the Boston Strangler commands headlines because strangulation (and rape) are embedded in the human psyche as particularly fearful acts, whereas price-fixing, stock frauds, and the range of most offenses associated with corporations seem more "technical."

On the other hand, I think we have to consider another factor that is at work, too—one that involves the nature of the corporation, as much as what the corporation is doing. I strongly suspect—although I cannot prove—that where a corporation rather than an identifiable person is the wrongdoer, the hostility that is aroused is less even where the offense is more or less the same. For example, if we are subjected to the noise of a motorcyclist driving up and down our street at night, I think a deeper and more complex level of anger is tapped in us than if we are subjected to the same disturbance (decibelically measured) from an airline's operations overhead. It is not just that the one seems "uncalled for" while the other seems incidental to commerce and progress. It is also that where a tangible person is involved, we can picture him (even if that means only to fantasize him); whereas when the nuisances we are subjected to are corporate, there is no tangible target to fix our anger upon. And it all seems so hopeless anyway. The consequence, if I am right, is that while various small groups are turning increased publicity onto corporate wrongdoing, they are still a long way from bringing about effective changes in corporate laws and corporate performance. A reform movement, to be effective, needs both widespread indignation and widespread hope to sustain itself. Neither by itself will do. So long as the public continues to perceive the wrongs corporations do as impersonal, market-dictated, and somehow inevitable, the reformers will have as little success forcing a change in corporate consciousness as they will in marshaling a public opposition that can seriously challenge the corporation's legislative clout. In all events, those of us who aim to change things have a job to sort out and deal with the various reasons why corporate reform movements have not been more successful after so many decades of agitation. One principal reason, I am sure, is that the public little cares to be reminded, over and over, that it is being victimized by impersonal forces, without being told what it can do about it. I like to think that some of the ideas in this book, expanded upon by others, will suggest the steps we might now begin to consider.

# Notes

### 1: The Corporation as Actor

1. Frederic W. Maitland, Introduction to Otto Gierke, *Political Theories of the Middle Age* (Cambridge: Cambridge University Press, 1927), p. xxi.

### 2: "Corporate" and Individual Responsibility in Early Law

1. Sir Frederick Pollock and Frederic W. Maitland, *The History of English Law*, 2 vols. (Cambridge: Cambridge University Press, 1923), 2: 449–462, 495–497.

2. Jeremy Bentham, *An Introduction to the Principles of Morals and Legislation*, 2 vols. (1789; rpt. London: E. Wilson, 1823), 1: 1.

3. Ibid., 245.

4. Ibid., 2: 16. Bentham is here quoting from Beccaria's *Dei Diletti E. Delle Pene* (1764).

### 3: Corporations and the Law: The First Skirmishes

1. John P. Davis, *Corporations*, 2 vols. (1904; rpt. New York: Capricorn, 1961), 2: 118.

2. This is, indeed, exactly what happened. In the late seventeenth century a man named Sands, deciding to test the monopoly privileges of the East India Company, fitted out a ship, to sail into territory within the company's limits. Child, governor of the East India Company, and Leach, its solicitor, petitioned the Admiralty for a stay of Sands's ship. They won, but technically they were wrong to have brought suit in Admiralty (as opposed to the civil courts) for a matter done on the land. Sands thus found himself with a good cause of action. Instead of tackling the corporation, and facing the doctrinal defenses it could raise, he proceeded directly against Child and Leach. It is interesting that it was not a plaintiff, but two officers, Child and

Leach, who sought to destroy the doctrinal compunctions regarding suits against corporations. Both at trial and on appeal they claimed that "this whole affair being transacted on behalf of the company, the action ought to have been brought against the company, and not against the defendants, their servants." They knew that if the suit could be turned against the corporation, they would have suffered a fractional, rather indirect loss at most. *Sands* v. *Child*, 3 Levinz 351 (1693).

3. Harry G. Henn, *Handbook of the Law of Corporations*, 2d ed. (St. Paul: West Publishing, 1970), p. 16.

4. (1776; rpt. Chicago: Encyclopaedia Britannica, 1952), p. 330.

5. (1765–69; rpt. New York: W. E. Dean, 1836), 1: 397.

### 4: The Industrial Revolution—The Die Is Cast

1. Adolf A. Berle, Jr., "Historical Inheritance of American Corporations," *Social Meaning of Legal Concepts* 3 (1950): 196.

2. J. Brandeis, dissent in *Liggett Co.* v. *Lee*, 288 U.S. 517, 551 (1933).

3. *Jacksonville M. P. Ry. & Nav. Co.* v. *Hooper*, 160 U.S. 514 (1896).

4. Alfred D. Chandler, Jr., *Strategy and Structure* (Cambridge, Mass.: MIT Press, 1962), p. 19.

5. Ibid.

6. Ibid., pp. 21–22.

7. Ibid., pp. 22, 38–39.

8. *Yarborough* v. *Governor and Company of the Bank of England*, 104 Eng. Rep. 991 (K. B. 1812).

9. *Mound* v. *Monmouthshire Canal Co.*, 134 Eng. Rep. 186 (C.P. 1842).

10. *Limpos* v. *London General Omnibus Co.*, 158 Eng. Rep. 993, 995 (Ex. 1862).

11. *Citizens Life Assurance Co.* v. *Brown*, (1904) A.C. 426.

12. *Queen* v. *The Great North of England Ry. Co.*, 115 Eng. Rep. 1294, 1298 (Q.B. 1846).

13. Ibid.

14. *New York Cent. & H. RR. Co.* v. *United States*, 212 U.S. 481, 494–495 (1909).

15. *People* v. *Rochester RR. & Light Co.*, 195 N.Y. 102 (1909).

16. See The Sinking Fund Cases, 99 U.S. 700 (1878).

## Part II. Introduction

1. *Bank of the United States* v. *Deveaux*, 9 U.S. (5 Cranch), 61, 86 (1809).

2. *United States* v. *Kane*, 23 F. 748, 749 (C.C.D. Col. 1885).

3. The idea that the turn-of-the-century "antibusiness" legislation was a victory of the populists over giant enterprise, rather than the other way around, has been strongly debunked. See Gabriel Kolko, *The Triumph of Conservatism* (Riverside, N.J.: Free Press, 1963) and Christopher D. Stone, "The I.C.C.: Some Reminiscences on the Future of American Transportation," *New Individualist Review* 2, 4 (1963): 3–23.

## 6: Measures Aimed at the Organization Itself

1. One of the pending congressional bills to revise the Federal Criminal Code, S. 1, 93rd Cong., 1st Sess., provides that if the offender is an organization its right to engage in interstate or foreign commerce can be suspended for the term to which it might have been imprisoned if an individual. §1–4A1 (c) (1). I doubt that courts will ever be persuaded to shut down a giant corporation's operations throughout the country because a few anonymous individuals at some plant violated the law—or even because some executives did. Too many innocent people are involved. Ralph Nader has recommended that the bill should be amended "to protect innocent employees so that their pay or employment may be continued or compensated during the period of suspension. So, too, contracts and obligations of the corporation should be provided for in such a way as to mitigate the effects of suspension on innocent customers and lenders." Statement by Ralph Nader on Federal Criminal Code Reform (S. 1 and S. 1400), Senate Judiciary Committee, Subcommitte on Criminal Laws and Procedures, July 19, 1974, p. 14.

2. Crane Brinton, *The Shaping of the Modern Mind* (1950; rpt. New York: Mentor, 1953), p. 131.

3. Richard Austin Smith, "How a Great Corporation Got Out of Control: The Story of General Dynamics," *Fortune* 65, 1 (January 1962): 64.

4. Cf. 1974 *Moody's Industrials*, 10025–26.

5. Raymond C. Baumhart, "How Ethical Are Businessmen?," *Harvard Business Review* 39, 4 (July–August 1961).

6. *Hearings Pursuant to S. Res. 52 before Senate Judiciary Committee, Subcommittee on Antitrust and Monopoly*, 87th Cong., 1st Sess. (1961), 16684, 16737.

7. "Executive Compensation: Who Got Most in '72," *Business Week*, May 5, 1973, p. 42.

8. "Executive Compensation: Getting Richer in '73," *Business Week*, May 4, 1974, p. 61.

9. *State* v. *Pacific Powder Co.*, 226 Org. 502 (1961).

10. *Commonwealth* v. *People's Natural Gas Co.*, 102 Pittsb. Leg. J. 348 (Allegheny Co., 1954).

11. See, for example, the opinion of Learned Hand in *U.S.* v. *Nearing*, 252 F. 223 (S.D.N.Y. 1918).

12. The doctrine of "strict liability" for ultrahazardous activities is the way a modern court might attach liability to the hypothetical nuclear station. But on this and other problems of obtaining legal redress for nuclear generator safety failures, see Anthony Z. Roisman, "Suing for Safety," *Trial* 10, 1 (January–February 1974): 13–14, 16, 25, and Harold Green, "The Insurance Umbrella," ibid., pp. 29, 395.

13. N.Y. Penal Law § 20.20 (McKinney, 1967).

14. *Lake Shore & Michigan So. R. Co.* v. *Prentice*, 147 U.S. 101 (1893) and Charles McCormick, *Handbook on the Law of Damages* (St. Paul: West Publishing, 1935), pp. 282–285.

15. *Roginsky* v. *Richardson-Merrell, Inc.*, 378 F.2d 832 (2d. Cir. 1967).

16. The facts that follow in the text are taken largely from *Toole* v. *Richardson-Merrell, Inc.*, 251 C.A. 2d. 689, 60 Cal. Rptr. 398 (1967). See also Sanford J. Ungar, "Get Away with What You Can," in Robert Heilbroner, *In the Name of Profit* (New York: Doubleday, 1972), pp. 106–127.

17. *Roginsky* v. *Richardson-Merrell, Inc.*, 378 F.2d 832, 841 (2d. Cir. 1967).

18. *United States* v. *Richardson-Merrell, Inc.*, Crim. No. 1211–63 (D.D.C. June 4, 1964).

19. Fines paid by a corporation were ruled nondeductible in *Tank Truck Rentals, Inc.* v. *Commissioner*, 356 U.S. 30 (1958), a position that was subsequently codified in the tax code at § 162 (f). At the same time, § 162 (g) was added, which provides that an antitrust violator who suffers a treble-damage judgment can deduct one–third of the judgment (the actual damages) but cannot deduct any greater sum, that is, the punitive damages.

## 7: Measures Aimed at "Key" Individuals

1. "The Lawyer and the Community," Addresses to the 33rd Annual Meeting of the American Bar Association, *Reports of American Bar Association* 35 (1910): 427.

2. *Graham* v. *Allis-Chalmers Mfg. Co.*, 188 A.2d 125, 130 (Del. 1963) (emphasis added).

3. "Voice of Experience: Lamar Hill, Embezzler, Says Stealing Is Easy," *Wall Street Journal*, January 26, 1973, p. 1, col. 4.

4. General Motors Corp., By-Laws No. 31, "Indemnification of Directors and Officers."

5. Del. Corp. Law § 145 (9). See Joseph W. Bishop, Jr., "New Problems in Indemnifying and Insuring Directors," *Duke Law Journal* (1972): 1153–1156.

6. Alan M. Dershowitz, "Increasing Community Control over Corporate Crime—A Problem in the Law of Sanctions," *Yale Law Journal* 71 (1961): 304.

7. See, for example, Gilbert Geis, "White Collar Crime: The Heavy Electrical Equipment Antitrust Cases of 1961," in Marshall B. Clinard and Richard Quinney, eds., *Criminal Behavior Systems* (New York: Holt, Rinehart and Winston, 1967), pp. 139–151.

8. *Sin and Society* (Boston: Houghton Mifflin, 1907), pp. 9–12.

9. "Some Assets Missing, Insurance Called Bogus at Equity Funding Life," *Wall Street Journal*, April 2, 1973, p. 1, col. 6.

10. Ibid., p. 14, col. 6.

## 8: What Exactly Are the "Antis" Against?

1. Barbara Ehrenreich and John Ehrenreich, "Conscience of a Steel Worker," *The Nation*, 213, September 27, 1971, pp. 268–271.

2. (Chicago: University of Chicago Press, 1962), p. 133.

3. Milton Friedman, "The Social Responsibility of Business Is to Increase Its Profits," *New York Times*, September 12, 1962, sect. 6, p. 126, col. 2.

4. "Playboy Interview: Milton Friedman," *Playboy*, February 1973, p. 59.

5. *New York Times*, September 12, 1962, sect. 6, p. 33, col. 2 (emphasis added).

6. Ibid., p. 33, col. 4 (emphasis added).

7. F. A. Hayek, "The Corporation in a Democratic Society: In

Whose Interest Ought It and Will It Be Run?," in H. I. Ansoff, ed., *Business Strategy* (Middlesex: Penguin, 1969), p. 225.

8. "Corporations and Conscience: The Issues," *Sloan Management Review* 13, 1 (Fall 1971): 11.

9. Philip Sporn, "Memoranda of Comment, Reservation or Dissent," in *Social Responsibilities of Business Corporations* (New York: Committee for Economic Development, 1971), p. 63.

10. "Profits, Not People," *Barron's*, November 27, 1972, p. 7, col. 4. According to Peggy Holter, reporting on the same conference, "Bradshaw chose not to mention that Atlantic Richfield spent $60,000,000 to change its name to ARCO during the same period." "Corporate Responsibility Means Never Having to Say You're Sorry," *Los Angeles Free Press*, November 24, 1972, pt. 1, p. 10, col. 1.

11. "New Santa Barbara Oil Slick Blamed on Natural Seepage," *Los Angeles Times*, June 6, 1973, pt. 1, p. 3, col. 2. "A spokesman for Atlantic Richfield said today the oil did not appear to be connected with the company's operation." Ibid., col. 3.

### 9: Why Shouldn't Corporations Be Socially Responsible?

1. *New York Times*, September 12, 1962, sect. 6, p. 33, col. 2.

2. See, for example, *Automatic Self-Cleansing Filter Syndicate Co. Ltd.* v. *Cunninghame* (1906) 2 Ch. 34.

3. "Dow Shalt Not Kill," in S. Prakash Sethi, *Up Against the Corporate Wall* (Englewood Cliffs, N.J.: Prentice-Hall, 1971), pp. 236–266, and the opinion of Judge Tamm in *Medical Committee for Human Rights* v. *S.E.C.*, 432 F.2d 659 (D.C. Cir. 1970), and the dissent of Mr. Justice Douglas in the same case in the U.S. Supreme Court, 404 U.S. 403, 407–411 (1972).

4. Theodore J. Jacobs, "Pollution, Consumerism, Accountability," *Center Magazine* 5, 1 (January–February 1971): 47.

5. Walter Goodman, "Stocks Without Sin," *Harper's*, August 1971, p. 66.

6. *New York Times*, September 12, 1962, sect. 6, p. 122, col. 3.

7. Ibid., p. 122, cols. 3–4.

### 10: Why the Market Can't Do It

1. "Little Puddings in Dangerous Cans," *Consumer Reports*, July 1971, p. 406–407.

2. James D. Thompson, *Organizations in Action* (New York: Mc-Graw-Hill, 1967), pp. 20–23.

### 11: Why the Law Can't Do It

1. Cal. Water Code §13201.

2. Cal. Agricultural Code §§62115, 62121, 62152.

3. See the four-page American Gas Association advertisement, "The Energy Shortage: What It Means to You," *Forbes*, June 1, 1973, pp. 41–44, esp. p. 43.

4. See *Eastern R.R. Presidents Conference* v. *Noerr*, 365 U.S. 127 (1961).

5. See "Change of Heart: Some Leftists Now Hit the Ecology Movement as Unfair to the Poor," *Wall Street Journal*, June 23, 1972, p. 1, col. 1.

6. "Environmental Protection Agency Looks for Way to Measure Bad Smells from Industrial Plants," *Wall Street Journal*, October 18, 1972, p. 34, cols. 1–3.

7. Bruce Ackerman and James Sawyer, "The Uncertain Search for Environmental Policy: Scientific Factfinding and Rational Decision-making Along the Delaware River," *University of Pennsylvania Law Review* 120 (1972): 419–503.

8. See Lon L. Fuller, *The Morality of Law*, rev. ed. (New Haven: Yale University Press, 1969).

9. *Budget of the United States Government, Fiscal Year 1975* (Washington: Government Printing Office, 1974), p. 195.

10. Sam Peltzman, "The Benefits and Costs of New Drug Regulation," in Richard Landau, ed., *Regulating New Drugs* (Chicago: University of Chicago Center for Policy Studies, 1973), pp. 113–211.

11. "State Won't Prosecute in Collapse of Bridge," *Los Angeles Times*, April 7, 1973, pt. 2, p. 1, col. 5.

12. Barry B. Boyer, "Alternatives to Administrative Trial-Hearings for Resolving Complex Scientific, Economic, and Social Issues," *Michigan Law Review* 71 (1972): 111–170.

13. Maurice Rosenberg, "Let's Everybody Litigate," *Texas Law Review* 50 (1972): 1349–1368.

14. Ackerman and Sawyer, op. cit., pp. 428–429.

15. Christopher D. Stone, "The I.C.C.: Some Reminiscences on the Future of American Transportation," *New Individualist Review* 2, 4 (1963): 3–23.

16. Steven Breyer and Paul W. MacAvoy, "The Natural Gas Shortage and the Regulation of Natural Gas Producers," *Harvard Law Review* 86 (1973): 941–987.

17. Simon Lazarus and Leonard Ross, "Rating Nader," *New York Review of Books*, June 28, 1973, pp. 50–55.

18. 48 Stat. (pt. 1) 1070 (1934).

19. 54 Stat. 899 (1940).

20. See Louis J. Hector, "Problems of the C.A.B. and the Independent Regulatory Commissions," *Yale Law Journal* 69 (1960): 933–934.

## 12: What "Corporate Responsibility" Might Really Mean

1. Stephenson, *The New Yorker*, November 7, 1970, p. 47.

2. "Crime in America—Why 8 Billion Amphetamines?," *Hearings Before the House Select Committee on Crime*, 91st Cong., 1st Sess. (November 18, 1969), p. 12 (testimony of Dr. Sidney Cohen). See also "Amphetamines," *Fourth Report by the Select Committee on Crime*, H. Rept. No. 91–1807, 91st Cong., 2d Sess. (1971).

3. *Hearings*, pp. 8–9; *Fourth Report*, pp. 22–23.

4. *Fourth Report*, p. 37.

## 13: Structural Variables: The Room at the Top

1. 83 Stat. 852, 43 U.S.C. §§4321–4347.

2. Cal. Corp. Code §800.

3. Del. Corp. Law §141(a).

4. The most recent survey on the proportion of outside to inside directors appears in Jeremy Bacon, *Corporate Directorship Practices: Membership and Committees of the Board* (New York: Conference Board and the American Society of Corporate Secretaries, 1973). Over half of the 505 manufacturing companies surveyed had a preponderance of inside directors, a situation that was even more exacerbated among the 29 wholesale and retail trade corporations surveyed. Commercial banks, holding companies, and other financial companies, on the other hand, still lean toward a preponderance of outsiders. See Chart 3, p. 3. The survey reports a slight shift in the direction of outsiders since its previous (1967) survey, pp. 2–4.

5. One Goldman, Sachs partner spreads his time over twenty-three

boards. "The Board: It's Obsolete Unless Overhauled," *Business Week*, May 22, 1971, p. 56.

6. Stanley C. Vance, *The Corporate Director: A Critical Evaluation* (Homewood: Dow Jones-Irwin, 1968), p. 4.

7. Myles L. Mace, "The President and the Board of Directors," *Harvard Business Review* (March–April 1972), p. 42.

8. Ibid., pp. 42–43.

9. Some of the literature that the Penn Central collapse has spawned includes Joseph R. Daughen and Peter Binzen, *The Wreck of the Penn Central* (Boston: Little, Brown, 1971); Michael Gartner, ed., *Riding the Pennsy to Ruin* (New York: Dow Jones, 1971).

10. See "The Penn Central Failure and the Role of Financial Institutions," *Staff Report of the House Committee on Banking and Currency*, 92nd Cong., 1st Sess. (1972), pp. 58–66.

11. Ibid., pp. 59, 66; Daughen and Binzen, op. cit., pp. 181–182.

12. The House Banking and Currency Committee report (supra, n. 10), p. 172, reflects the following figures for Penn Central dividends as a function of net income:

TABLE 11. —Dividends compared to reported net income—1963–69.
[Figures in millions]

| Year | Reported net income | Dividends paid | Dividend payments as a percentage of net income |
|------|--------------------|----------------|------------------------------------------------|
| 1963 | $9.1 | $6.8 | 74.7 |
| 1964 | 29.1 | 17.2 | 58.7 |
| 1965 | 33.8 | 27.6 | 89.9 |
| 1966 | 45.0 | 31.9 | 70.9 |
| 1967 | 14.0 | 33.5 | 232.0 |
| 1968 | (−41.9) | 55.4 | —— |
| 1969 | (−91.6) | 43.3 | —— |
| Total | (−2.5) | 215.7 | —— |

13. Ibid., p. iv.

14. See Arthur J. Goldberg, "Debate on Outside Directors," *New York Times*, October 29, 1972, sect. 3, pp. 1–3.

15. Chapter 14, infra.

16. "How Big Shippers Fight to Keep Trains Running on the Troubled Pennsy," *Wall Street Journal*, November 8, 1973, p. 1, col. 8.

17. Cal. Corp. Code §800; Del. Corp. Law §141(a).

18. In Delaware no such committee is allowed the power of the full

board in reference to amending the certificate of incorporation, adopting an agreement of merger, recommending sale or lease of the property to the shareholders, or amending the company's bylaws. Del. Corp. Law §141(c). California excepts from the powers of such committees the declaration of dividends and the adoption, amendment, or repeal of bylaws. Cal. Corp. Code §822.

## 14: Reforming the Board

1. Myles L. Mace, "The President and the Board of Directors," *Harvard Business Review* (March–April 1972), p. 42.

2. Indeed, after the Penn Central troubles became public, several suits were brought against Goldman, Sachs & Co., one of whose partners had been sitting on the Penn Central's board. The suits alleged that through this connection Goldman, Sachs learned of the imminent collapse, and quietly and fraudulently began selling off $20 million of Penn Central commercial paper that it was holding. Goldman, Sachs settled one of the suits for $5.3 million in September 1974. "Goldman, Sachs Settles Fund Suit Over Penn Central," *Wall Street Journal*, September 5, 1974, p. 6, col. 4

3. Mace, op. cit., p. 46.

4. *Lanza* v. *Drexel*, 479 F.2d 1277 (2d Cir. 1973).

5. Joseph W. Bishop, Jr., "New Problems in Indemnifying and Insuring Directors: Protection against Liability Under the Federal Securities Laws," *Duke Law Journal* (1972), 1153–1166.

6. 15 U.S.C. §77(4) (a) 1 *Escott* v. *BarChris Construction Corp.*, 283 F.Supp. 643 (S.D. N.Y. 1968), held that outside directors no less than insiders had to exercise "due diligence" under this provision. And see *Lanza* v. *Drexel*, 479 F.2d 1277, 1282–83 (2d. Cir. 1973).

7. See Del. Corp. Law §174(a) making the directors jointly and severally liable for "any willful or negligent" wrongful dividend. Under California Law a director who concurs in a wrongful dividend is guilty of a misdemeanor "punishable by a fine of not more than one thousand dollars ($1,000) or imprisonment for not more than one year, or both." Cal. Corp. Code §1511.

8. Some stabs have been made in this direction. General Foods Corp. has reportedly established an assistant secretary position with the sole responsibility of preparing objective reports for outside directors. Texas Instruments Corp. has designated an "officer of the board," with the same functions. *Proceedings*, A.B.A. National Institute

on Officers' and Directors' Responsibilities and Liabilities, *Business Lawyer* 27 (February 1972), p. 44.

9. "Southland A-Plant Damaged, Closed: Neither AEC Nor Edison Reported Oct. 21 Problem at San Onofre," *Los Angeles Times*, November 22, 1973, p. 1, col. 5.

10. Cal. Insur. Code §735.5.


## 15: General Public Directorships

1. 12 Stat. 489 (1862).

2. 13 Stat. 361 (1864). See *Report of the Government Directors of the Union Pacific Railroad for the Year Ending June 30, 1877*, complaining that "the law requires certain reports to be made by the company to the Government, but has provided no means for the utilization of the reports when made, and the same defect exists as to the reports of the Government directors." Reprinted in S. Exec. Doc. No. 69, 49th Cong., 1st Sess. (1886), p. 136.

3. Herman Schwartz, "Governmentally Appointed Directors in a Private Corporation—The Communications Satellite Act of 1962," *Harvard Law Review* 79 (1965): 359.

4. Ibid.

5. *Congressional Record* 17 (Pt. 1), 49th Cong., 1st Sess. (January 5, 1886), 408–412. Senator Wilson himself served as one of the public directors.

6. *Report of the Government Directors of the Union Pacific Railroad for 1882*, reprinted in S. Exec. Doc. No. 69, 49th Cong., 1st Sess. (1886), p. 186.

7. Ibid., p. 135.

8. Nor, as the directors complained, had any provision been made for the utilization of the reports when made. Ibid., p. 136.

9. 1 *Testimony Taken by the United States Pacific Railway Commission*, S. Exec. Doc. No. 51 (Pt. 2), 50th Cong., 1st Sess. (1887), p. 329 (testimony of Nathaniel Niles).

10. See *Report of the Government Directors*, 1884, S. Exec. Doc. No. 69, p. 220.

11. Ibid., pp. 220–221.

12. *Report of the Government Directors, 1882*, S. Exec. Doc. No. 69, pp. 184–186.

13. This factor is referred to often. See., e.g., *Report of the Govern-*

*ment Directors, 1884,* S. Exec. Doc. No. 69, p. 221. One director testified of one of his colleagues that he had been offered the choice of serving as postmaster at New London or a government director of the Union Pacific; he "always told me about it, that he had made a mistake, for he did not make so much money out of it." 1 *Testimony Taken by the United States Pacific Railway Commission,* S. Exec. Doc. No. 51 (Pt. 2), 50th Cong., 1st Sess., p. 710 (testimony of F. Gordon Dexter).

14. See Joan Robinson, *The Economics of Imperfect Competition* (London: Macmillan, 1961).

15. *Hearings on Communications Satellite Act of 1962 Before the Senate Committee on Foreign Relations,* 87th Cong., 2d Sess. (1962), p. 70 (testimony of former FCC chairman Newton N. Minow).

16. Schwartz, op. cit., p. 361.

17. See letter of Attorney General Robert F. Kennedy, in "Communications Satellite Incorporators," *Hearings Before the Senate Committee on Commerce,* 88th Cong., 1st Sess. (1963), p. 90.

18. On the matter of "legal audits," see Richard A. Whiting, "Antitrust and the Corporate Executive II," *Virginia Law Review* 48 (1962): 1–57; Louis M. Brown, "Legal Audit," *Southern California Law Review* 38 (1965): 431–445.

19. See Kermit Vandivier, "Why Should My Conscience Bother Me?," in Robert Heilbroner, *In the Name of Profit* (New York: Doubleday, 1972), pp. 3–31; "Air Force A-7D Brake Problem," *Hearings Before the Subcommittee on Economy in Government of the Joint Economic Committee,* 91st Cong., 1st Sess. (1969).

20. "Air Force A-7D Brake Problem," *Hearings,* pp. 245–246.

## 16: Special Public Directorships

1. The facts that follow in the text are taken from *In re Holland Furnace Co.,* 55 F.T.C. 55 (1958), *Holland Furnace Co.* v. *F.T.C.,* 269 F.2d 203 (7th Cir. 1959); *Holland Furnace Co.* v. *F.T.C.,* 295 F.2d 302 (7th Cir. 1961), *In re Holland Furnace Company,* 341 F.2d 548 (7th Cir. 1965), affirmed sub nom *Cheff* v. *Schnackenberg,* 384 U.S. 373 (1966).

2. *Holland Furnace Co.* v. *U.S.,* 158 F.2d 2 (1946).

3. This and the facts that follow in the text are drawn from Paul Bradeur's excellent five-part study, "Annals of Industry," *The New Yorker,* October 29, November 5, 12, 19, and 26, 1973.

4. "More Cases of Liver Cancer Are Reported among Workers at

Vinyl Chloride Plant," Jonathan Spivak, *Wall Street Journal*, February 19, 1974, p. 7, cols. 1–3; see also "U.S. Molds Rules for Handling of Chemicals that Can Lead to Cancer in Plant Workers," *Wall Street Journal*, April 11, 1973, p. 36, col. 1.

5. For example, California Corp. Code §819, provides "if a corporation has an even number of directors who are equally divided . . . as to the management of its affairs, so that its business cannot longer be conducted to advantage . . . the superior court . . . may . . . appoint a provisional director. . . ."

6. "Mattel Must Name 2 SEC Backed Directors," *Los Angeles Times*, August 6, 1974, pt. 3, pp. 6, 11. In July 1973, a "court-appointed public representative" was placed on the board of another corporation, financially troubled Westgate-California Corp., as the result of negotiations between SEC, Westgate, and U.S. District Judge Leland Nielson in San Diego. "Westgate Director Named to Report to Judge in SEC Case," *Los Angeles Times*, July 26, 1973, pt. 3, p. 1, col. 4.

7. Ralph Adam Fine, *The Great Drug Deception: The Shocking Story of MER/29 and the Folks Who Gave You Thalidomide* (New York: Stein and Day, 1972), pp. 193–194.

## 17: Managing with Management

1. *U.S.* v. *Atlantic Richfield Co.*, 465 F.2d 58 (7th Cir. 1972).

2. Brief for the United States, *U.S.* v. *Atlantic Richfield Co.*, p. 2.

3. Ibid., p. 11.

4. 465 F.2d 58, p. 61.

5. "Lavanthol Agrees to Allow Review by Fellow CPAs," *Wall Street Journal*, May 24, 1973, p. 6, col. 1.

6. Ibid. Touche Ross & Co. has more recently agreed to a similar review in accepting SEC censure of its audits of U.S. Financial Inc. "Peat Marwick Is the First Big C.P.A. Firm to Submit to 'Quality Review' by Peers," *Wall Street Journal*, June 17, 1974, p. 10, cols. 2–3. Peat Marwick, subject of several SEC antifraud complaints, including the Penn Central case, has agreed to a "voluntary" review procedure. Ibid.

7. *S.E.C.* v. *Koenig*, 71 Civ. 5016 (S.D.N.Y., June 19, 1972); affirmed, 469 F.2d 198 (2d Cir. 1972).

8. "Mattel Must Name 2 SEC Backed Directors," *Los Angeles Times*, August 6, 1974, pt. 3, p. 6, col. 8; 1974 C.C.H. *Federal Securities Law Reports*, No. 546 (August 7, 1974), p. 3. A stockholder's suit

against Northrop, arising out of that company's illegal campaign contributions, was settled in January 1975 upon terms that included adding several independent outside directors to the board. *Springer* v. *Jones*, Civ. No. 74-1455-F (D.C.C.D. Cal.).

9. *In re Holland Furnace Co.*, 341 F.2d 548, 552 (7th Cir. 1965).

10. Code of Federal Regulations §130.3(13)4c. See also, for example, C.F.R. §130.3(13)4b: "The investigator is required to maintain adequate records of the disposition of all receipts of the drug, including dates, quantity, and use by subjects. . . . Adequate precautions must be taken, including storage of the investigational drug in a securely locked . . . enclosure. . . ."

11. See "Deliberate Suppression," *Trial* 6, 7 (October–November 1970): 7, and "Corvair Defects Known from Start, Ex-GM Technician Says," *Los Angeles Times*, May 28, 1971, p. 3, col. 6.

12. See In the Matter of Atlantic Industries, Inc., F.T.C. Dkt. 8941, 83 F.T.C. (1973); In the Matter of Hearst Corporation, F.T.C. Dkt. 8832, 82 F.T.C. 218 (1973).

13. Ralph Adam Fine, *The Great Drug Deception: The Shocking Story of MER/29 and the Folks Who Gave You Thalidomide* (New York: Stein and Day, 1972), p. 25.

14. Reporting and Disclosure Act of 1959, 73 Stat. 536, 29 U.S.C. §504.

15. There is an exception in banking laws that disqualify persons convicted of certain offenses from holding positions in banks where deposits are insured by the FDIC, 12 U.S.C. §1829.

16. Judgment and Sentence, *State of California* v. *Lockheed Shipbuilding and Construction Co.*, Dkt. No. 413019 (Munic. Court, L. A. Jud. Dist., L. A. Cnty.), December 17, 1973, p. 1. The facts that follow in the text are all drawn from Judge Trammell's opinion.

17. Ibid., pp. 1, 7, 3.

18. There has been, I am pleased to say, some concern over this anomaly. The National Commission on Reform of Federal Criminal Laws, in its officially authorized study draft toward a new federal criminal code, recommended at §406(2) that

When an executive officer or other manager of an organization is convicted of an offense committed in furtherance of the affairs of the organization, the court may include in the sentence an order disqualifying him from exercising similar functions in the same or other organizations for a period not exceeding five years, if it finds the scope or willfulness of his illegal actions make it dangerous or inadvisable for such functions to be entrusted to him.

See the proposed revision of the federal criminal code, S1, 93rd Cong., 1st Sess. (1973), which would adopt the sense of this recommendation at §1–4A3(b). The so-called Nixon Administration proposed revision, S1400, 93rd Cong., 1st Sess. (1973) is much too vague on this score. See §2001(d).

19. Joseph R. Daughen and Peter Binzen, *The Wreck of the Penn Central* (Boston: Little, Brown, 1971), pp. 90–91.

20. "Emergency Loan Guarantee Legislation," *Hearings Before the Senate Committee on Banking, Housing and Urban Affairs*, 92nd Cong., 1st Sess. (pt. 1, June 7–16, 1971), p. 254.

21. Emergency Loan Guarantee Act, §6(b), 85 Stat. 178 (1971).

## 18: Mending the Information Net

1. "Dita Beard of I.T. & T. Touches off Rush to Find Bigger and Better Shredders," *Los Angeles Times*, January 21, 1973, pt. 4, p. 1, col. 2.

2. Ibid., p. 3, col. 1.

3. Robert D. Verhalen, "Keying Product-Related Accidents," *Trial* 8, 1 (January–February 1972): 32–33.

4. "Adverse Reaction: Richardson-Merrell Is Facing the Aftereffects of MER/29," *Wall Street Journal*, June 15, 1964, p. 12, cols. 3–4.

5. Consent Decree, January 18, 1973, Civ. No. 73–149 (E.D.Pa.), C.C.H. *Employment Practices Guide* pp. 1533-3 through 1534. (Includes Model Affirmative Action Program for the Bell System.)

6. One Richardson-Merrell memo that went out to the detail men advised them:

> When a doctor says your drug causes a side-effect, the immediate reply is "Doctor, what other drug is the patient taking?" Even if you know your drug can cause the side-effect mentioned, chances are equally good the same side-effect is being caused by a second drug! You let your drug take the blame when you counter with a defensive answer.

Robert Heilbroner, *In the Name of Profit* (New York: Doubleday, 1972), p. 112.

7. Cal. Insurance Code §735.5.

8. Hearst Corp. F.T.C. Dkt. 8832, 82 F.T.C. 218 (1973).

9. C.C.H. *Employment Practices Guide*, 1533–21.

10. See Atlantic Industries, F.T.C. Dkt. 8941, 83 F.T.C. (1973).

11. See Daniel Katz and Robert L. Kahn, *The Social Psychology of Organizations* (New York: John Wiley, 1966), pp. 236–242.

12. Ralph Adam Fine, *The Great Drug Deception: The Shocking Story of MER/29 and the Folks Who Gave You Thalidomide* (New York: Stein and Day, 1972), p. 81.

13. R. A. McLaughlin, "Equity Funding: Everyone Is Pointing at the Computer," *Datamation*, June 1973, p. 91.

14. See 21 C.F.R. §130.3.

15. In New York City, corruption of police in connection with the enforcement of construction-site laws (a related, but not identical, procedure) had gotten so out of hand that the police department, on the advice of the Knapp Commission, decided to bar patrolmen from enforcing most such laws "in an effort to reduce the opportunities for corruption among its men." "Key Housing Aid Suspended Here," *New York Times*, August 24, 1972, p. 27, col. 1.

16. "Federal Insepctor Was in Plant During Packing of Tainted Soup," *Los Angeles Times*, August 24, 1971, p. 1, col. 2.

17. Department of Defense, Military Specification, "Inspection System Requirements," Mil-I-45208A, December 16, 1963, §3.1 "Contractor Responsibilities."

18. "The Whistle Blowers," *Time*, April 17, 1972, p. 85.

19. Timothy H. Ingram and Jerry W. Finefrock, "General Telephone's Fickle Finger," *The Progressive*, September 1969, pp. 37–40.

20. "The Whistle Blowers."

21. Ralph Nader, Peter Petkas, and Kate Blackwell, *Whistle Blowing* (New York: Grossman, 1972), p. 208.

22. Arthur S. Miller, "Whistle Blowing and the Law," in ibid., p. 31.

## 19: Redesigning the Decision Process

1. "Licensee Responsibility to Review Records Before Their Broadcast," Public Notice of March 5, 1971, 28 F.C.C. 2d 409.

2. Some of the more considered objections to the commission's actions appear in the dissenting opinion of Commissioner Nicholas Johnson, "Licensee Responsibility to Review Records Before Their Broadcast," Memorandum Opinion and Order, August 18, 1971, 31 F.C.C.2d 385, 386–388.

3. "Licensee Responsibility to Review Records Before Their Broadcast," Memorandum Opinion and Order of April 16, 1971, 21 Radio Reg. 2d 1698, 1699; see 31 F.C.C.2d 377, 379–80. The ruling survived a court review in *Yale Broadcasting Co.* v. *F.C.C.*, 478 F.2d 594 (D.C. Cir. 1973).

4. 284 F.Supp 809 (E.D.Pa. 1969).

5. 359 F.2d 994 (D.C. Cir. 1966).

6. *Friends of Mammoth* v. *Board of Supervisors*, 104 Cal. Rptr. 761.

7. Anthony D'Amato and James H. Baxter, "The Impact of Impact Statements upon Agency Responsibility: A Prescriptive Analysis," *Iowa Law Review* 59 (1973): 199–200.

8. "Nature Study: Required Statements on Environmental Impact Are Stirring Criticism," *Wall Street Journal,* September 27, 1973, p. 1, col. 1.

9. Ibid.

10. Technology Assessment Act of 1972, 86 Stat. 797 (1972).

11. U.S. Code Congressional and Admin. News, 92nd Cong., 2d Sess., pt. 2, p. 3577.

12. Ibid., p. 3579. Lead poisoning from paint is no more serious than the poisoning children who live in the vicinity of lead mills have been discovered to be suffering. See editorial, "For Millions, No Place of Refuge," *Los Angeles Times*, September 29, 1974, pt. 5, p. 2, cols. 1–2.

13. "Human Exposure to Chemicals Suspected in 80% of Cancers," *Los Angeles Times*, March 31, 1974, p. 1, col. 1. (Other scientists thought this estimate too high.) Ibid.

14. Ibid.

15. "Vinyl-Chloride Risks Were Known by Many Before First Deaths," *Wall Street Journal*, October 2, 1974, p. 1, col. 1; p. 17, cols. 1–4.

16. "Increase in U.S. Skin Cancer Cases Seen," *Los Angeles Times*, October 4, 1974, p. 3, col. 1.

17. *Los Angeles Times*, pt. 2, p. 1, col. 5.

## 20: The Culture of the Corporation

1. Sanford H. Kadish, "Some Observations on the Use of Criminal Sanctions in Enforcing Economic Regulations," *University of Chicago Law Review* 30 (1964): 436.

2. Ibid.

3. Eugene V. Rostow, "To Whom and for What Ends Is Corporate Management Responsible," in Edward Mason, ed., *The Corporation in Modern Society* (Cambridge, Mass.: Harvard University Press, 1959), p. 65.

4. Daniel Katz and Robert L. Kahn, *The Social Psychology of Organizations* (New York: John Wiley, 1966), p. 407.

5. "Coal-Mines Study Shows Record Can Be Improved When Firms Really Try," *Wall Street Journal*, January 18, 1973, p. 1, col. 6.

6. Ibid., p. 7.

7. Richard Austin Smith, *Corporations in Crisis* (New York: Doubleday, 1964), p. 165.

8. A Report from the Board of Advice to Westinghouse Electric Corporation (1962), p. 10.

9. "Enter the Social Auditors," *London Sunday Times*, June 21, 1973, p. 72, col. 5.

10. Raymond A. Bauer and Dan H. Fenn, "What *Is* a Corporate Social Audit?," *Harvard Business Review* 51 (January–February 1973): 43–44.

11. Digby Diehl, "Q & A: Fred L. Hartley," *West Magazine* (*Los Angeles Sunday Times*), February 20, 1972, p. 30.

12. See Executive Order 11451 "Establishing the President's Commission on Personnel Interchange," January 19, 1969, Federal Register, 34, p. 921 (January 22, 1969).

13. All quotations from President's Commission on Personnel Interchange, "Executive Interchange Program 1973." All the quotes in this particular brochure appear to be from the businessmen in government, rather than from their civil service counterparts on leave to industry.

14. Robert E. Lane, "Why Business Men Violate the Law," *Journal of Criminal Law and Criminology* 44 (1953): 159.

# Index